1079

THE OVERWHELMING FORCE
OF DYATLOV PASS

IGOR PAVLOV
TEODORA HADJIYSKA

Copyright © 2021 Igor Pavlov and Teodora Hadjiyska

ALL RIGHTS RESERVED.
This book contains material protected under International and Federal
Copyright Laws and Treaties. Any unauthorized reprint or use of this
material is prohibited. No part of this book, including the cover, and photos,
may be reproduced or transmitted in any form or by any means, electronic
or mechanical, including photocopying, recording, or by any information
storage and retrieval system without express written permission from the
author / publisher. All rights reserved.

ISBN 9780578845913

In memory of Igor "π" Pavlov
(1964 – 2021)

CONTENTS

In the winter of 1959, a group of hikers from Sverdlovsk died in the Ural Mountains under mysterious circumstances. This is a new and shocking version of the tragedy, meticulously based on documentary evidence.

In this book have been used the reminiscences of the following individuals:

M.A. Akselrod, V.G. Aleksandrovskiy, V.M. Askinadzi, E.F. Bachurin, P.I. Bartolomey, G.K. Batalova, V.N. Bienko, Y.A. Blinov, V.F. Bogomolov, Y.A. Bondarev, V.D. Brusnitsyn, B.M. Bychkov, F.T. Ermash, I.V. Fomenko, E.V. Grigoriev, O.T. Gubanova, L.N. Ivanov, V.G. Karelin, G.A. Karpushin, V.N. Klimenko, Y.E. Koptelov, V.I. Korotaev, V.S. Krylov, N.I. Kuzminov, V.A. Lebedev, V.A. Lyubimov, A.G. Mohov, E.S. Nevolin, E.F. Okishev, E.V. Pavlov, V.V. Plotnikov, E.I. Postonogov, V.V. Potyazhenko, V.I. Prudkova, V.D. Pudov, Y.A. Sahnin, Z.N. Savina, R.V. Sedov, M.P. Sharavin, V.V. Shlyapin, V.A. Shulyatiev, A.S. Shumkov, B.E. Slobtsov, S.N. Sogrin, G.S. Solovyev, P.I. Solter, B.L. Suvorov, H.F. Syunikaev, A.P. Taranova, S.A. Tipikin, N.V. Tokarev, M.K. Vladimirov, V.G. Yakimenko, Y.E. Yudin, and E.G. Zinovyev;

documents from the archive of the Dyatlov Group Memory Fund (Yekaterinburg, Russia);

materials from the publications by "Komsomolskaya Pravda", as well as:
Aleksander Alekseenkov, Oleg Arhipov, Taisiya Belousova, Stanislav Bogomolov, Olga Boguslavskaya, Vladimir Borzenkov, Ildar Garifullin, Aleksander Guschin, Aleksey Koskin, Denis Milkov, Maya Piskareva, Galina Sazonova, Olga Solyar, Raphael Torosyan, Olga Vedeneeva, and Yuri Yarovoy

CRASH COURSE

The Dyatlov Pass incident is a tale of bizarre, seemingly inexplicable events which has captivated the collective imagination for over sixty years. It is the well-documented story of nine seasoned hikers who went missing in the Northern Ural Mountains, and whose bodies were found in a gruesome state for which, so far, there has been no plausible explanation. Amateur and professional investigators alike have been scrutinizing the same facts and timelines for decades, and have been unable to reach an agreement on any of their conclusions. Facts that do not fit into their diverse hypotheses have mostly been conveniently dismissed. So far, not a single theory proposed can account for the date on the Case files cover February 6, 1959 (Dyatlovpass.com/1079#feb6); the severe physical traumas on three of the bodies; the shoeless footprints and the tent slashed open from the inside; the sighting of both the tent and the bodies in a location different from where they were found; the clothes on the bodies that belonged to other members of the group, or even the actual number of bodies brought to the Ivdel morgue... The more the evidence accumulates, the less any currently existing theory can explain the facts as we know them. Until now, that is.

What follows is a meticulously researched and well-annotated theory that ties all the events and circumstances of the Dyatlov Pass story into a logical sequence of causes and effects.

Intro

Speaking metaphorically, in the anatomy of this book, it is I, Teodora Hadjiyska, who will be putting flesh on the bones provided by the main author, Igor Pavlov, who has finally succeeded in solving the case.

I am all over the map: born in Bulgaria and raised in Cuba, I lived for ten years in the US, am currently based in Austria, and never stay for too long in one place. My lifestyle is that of a traveler, explorer, and mountaineer, with a propensity for finding myself in the center of disasters. I have been caught up in avalanches, volcano eruptions, rockfalls, and permafrost slide. Staying home does not help much – one evening, while I was watching TV, the ceiling collapsed right on top of me. If I am going to die, I prefer to do it somewhere with a view. In 2012, I was evacuated from Karangetang, an active volcano on the island of Siau, Sulawesi, Indonesia. I found myself bedridden with a subdural hematoma, shattered elbow and scapula, flail chest, and six broken ribs after a near-death accident with a runaway truck. If you know anything about the Dyatlov case, you will notice a close similarity between my trauma and that of two of the hikers – a trauma that, in 1959, the pathologist described as hard to explain under the circumstances. It looked as if it had been caused by a fast moving car, and he referred to it as a high velocity trauma, but the nearest road was hundreds of miles. It so happened that, after surviving Karangetang, I read about the incident on Dyatlov Pass, and I have not stopped researching it since. Soon after that, I started working with Igor Pavlov. If I have an emotional and karmic bond with the case, Pavlov has the best sources of all kinds.

Igor Pavlov is a nuclear physicist. He has taken part in decontamination activities in Chernobyl, as well as in various international research programs, and has been investigating the Dyatlov case since 2009, focusing on the analysis of archival documents and witness recollections. Author of the best-known textual transcripts of handwritten documents from 1959 – criminal case files, diary entries, and testimonies of the search group members – he has the complete archive of materials on the topic and collaborates with the leading researchers of the tragedy.

As you can see, Igor Pavlov is the real McCoy, and I am merely the conduit, the missing link between the source and the reader.

The Book

"If there's a book that you want to read, but it hasn't been written yet, then you must write it." — *Toni Morrison*

There are many books on the case, so why write another one? Because we are bringing to light a mountain of information that has never been published before. The case is cold but not frozen in time. The new investigation which began in 2018 ended with a fiasco in 2020, but it did bring out some new information that only the prosecutor's office had access to. The tireless "Komsomolskaya Pravda" ("Komsomol Truth" in English), a Russian tabloid, has two dedicated journalists who have been turning the ground for nine years. They even managed to arrange for the exhumation of one of the hikers, and are tirelessly unearthing documents from the archives to this day. Besides film crews and tourists, researchers also frequently go to Dyatlov Pass and bring back data for analysis.

The existing theories have to be checked against all new evidence that comes to light, as in time the desire to keep fabricating bizarre scenarios seems to prevail over the reality check. I can't blame only the fascination with the mystery, and the tantalizing desire to keep it unsolved. The facts don't have a mold to fill, they can only make a dot or line on the investigation wall, and how to connect the dots is up to the reader. The more dots a theory connects, the stronger it is - but people tend to put dots where they don't exist. Here is an example: some time back, a highly popular site interviewed me. In the article that followed, they had a short paragraph listing some of the strange facts about the case. These included, as usual, the missing tongue and eyes, radioactive clothes, KGB, flying saucers, but there was also something new to me. Somehow a line from the autopsy report – *"On the middle phalanx of the third finger is a defect in the epidermis with the same shape and form as that found in the oral cavity"* – had been transformed into *"One hiker was missing a finger and it was found in his mouth."* This about sums up the media coverage of the case. Even funnier was the answer I received when I strongly objected to having my name present in an article with such a claim: I was told that the whole case is so incomprehensible anyway that no one would find having your finger in your mouth in any way stranger than everything else.

I can see you roll your eyes with impatience, but there is one more proviso. The case is very popular and many of you will be eager to read the theory right away. Theory of what? How they died? Who killed them? Who found them? Who covered up the whole thing? Newsflash: the Who, the How and the Why may not be connected. Never thought of that, did you? So give me credit for this nugget and sit tight for another paragraph so I can explain how this book is organized. I apologize for any exotic metaphors or similes in advance.

We are starting a journey together. The problem is, some of you are very advanced, real experts, and eager to jump ahead. But some people have never heard of the case before. My way of evening the pace is to give newbies a crash course on the case. You cannot, and should not, throw people in the deep end of the pool without teaching them how to swim first. I don't mean disrespect – I only want everyone to enjoy this book. Which will be hard. Reading it will be like opening countless dusty, moldy boxes full of faded dossiers brought up from the basement, with no one knowing what is important and what is not. Maybe we do, but I don't want to filter only the information that is pertinent to the case. In the end, you will see that if we only publish what is important, you may not recognize the case at all. Besides, we have accumulated so much data that this is our chance to make a systematic account of all documents. If you find yourself overwhelmed, skip the indented paragraphs, they are usually about a person whose name is in bold, and whose particular role in the case is in the main narrative. During the writing process, a lot of information remained on the cutting room floor, but instead of discarding it, we are publishing it on Dyatlovpass.com/1079, where you can find extras and updates by chapter. The biographies have been intentionally abbreviated and cut off to the time of the events in 1959. More information can be found in the Who Is Who database.

Dyatlov Pass for Dummies

There was nothing foreboding at the beginning of the trek. They were a group of young, happy campers singing songs and hoping to fall in love, but as we know that they all died five days into the trek, I am going to sound the alarm so we don't have to retrace for signs of trouble. Each alarm is the point where the theories branch out. Before you read on, here is a crash course on the case, the way it is seen at the moment. We don't think this is what happened, but we can't tell you any more at this point, because then you won't get the mystery of the whole case. In other words, as authors of this book, we are giving you a chance to make up your own scenario before you find out what we think actually happened.

"The Owls Are Not What They Seem" — Twin Peaks

A group of ten ski hikers went a trek, ranked as being in the highest – at the time – category of difficulty (3), in the Northern Ural Mountains. They were good for it, they had done it before – not this particular peak, but other difficult winter hikes. They knew each other, as they all studied or had graduated from the Ural Polytechnic Institute in Sverdlovsk (now Yekaterinburg) – all but one, who joined the group at the very last moment, causing a certain sense of unease not only because he was a stranger, but also because he was older, and seemed somewhat different from them. **The first alarm goes off.** On the very last day that they had some means of transportation for their backpacks – a horse-driven sled hired from the last logging settlement – one of the students had to turn back due to aggravated chronic illness (sciatica). His name was Yudin and he was the medic of the group. He is, in my opinion, wrongly called a survivor. To survive something you need to go through it. He turned back before the unsupported hike started. That is the right thing to do if you feel sick. But did he really? **Another alarm goes off.** The others distributed his supplies and gear among themselves, borrowed some clothes (wait, they were going on a sub zero trek without enough clothes?), thus making their own backpacks even heavier, and went off to Mt. Otorten. This was supposed to be the first recorded winter ascent.

You will read that in Mansi, the language of the indigenous local people by the same name, Otorten means "Don't Go There". This is not true. The Mansi call it "The Windy Mountain", and windy it is. People may have told the hikers *"Don't go there"* as a piece of advice, a suggestion, or a warning. **An alarm sounds.** Forewarned or not, nine of them continued on their journey. On the first and second day of their trek, they circled summit Hoy Ekva, Mansi Хой Эква (хой - stop, эква- woman). The name says it all – women are not allowed. There were two girls in the group – Lyuda, the treasurer, and Zina, responsible for providing a personal diary for each hiker, and a separate one for the group. There is a photograph taken the day before the group split up, of the alleged (Dyatlovpass.com/1079#sanctuary) Lozvinskaya, or Sheytan pit, a Mansi sanctuary. With time, this photo has given rise to considerable controversy, some even claim to see ominous petro- glyphs on the rock face, supposedly a warning sign for the tragic fate the group was to meet. **Another alarm is tripped.** The next four days of camping in the woods are well documented, with diary entries and photos to match, showing the presence of Mansi everywhere in the woods. The last diary entry was written by the leader, Igor Dyatlov, on January 31:

"Weather today is a bit worse – wind (west), snowing (probably from the pines), since the sky is perfectly clear.

Started relatively early (around 10 am). Got back on the Mansi trail. (Up to now we are following a Mansi trail on which not so long passed a hunter with deer.)

Yesterday it seems we stumbled upon his resting stop. Deer didn't go any further. The hunter took the beaten trail by himself, we are following in his steps.

Had a surprisingly good overnight, air is warm and dry, though it's -18°C to -24°C. Walking is especially hard today. We can't see the trail, have to grope our way through at times. Can't do more than 1.5-2 km (1 mile) per hour.

Trying out new ways to clear the path. The first in line drops his backpack, skis forward for five minutes, comes back for a 10-15 minute break, then catches up with the group. That's one way to keep laying ski tracks non-stop. Hard on the second hiker though, who has to follow the new trail with full gear on his back. We gradually leave the Auspiya valley, it's upwards all the way but goes rather smoothly. Thin birch grove replaces firs. The end of the forest is getting closer. Wind is western, warm, piercing, with speed like the draft from airplanes at takeoff. Firn, open spaces. I can't even think of setting up storage here. It's nearly 4. Have to start looking for a place to pitch the tent. We go south in the Auspiya valley. Seems this place has the deepest snow. Wind not strong, snow 1.2-2 m deep. We're exhausted, but start setting up for the night. Firewood is scarce, mostly damp firs. We build the campfire on the logs, too tired to dig a fire pit. Dinner's in the tent. Nice and warm. Can't imagine such comfort on the ridge, with howling wind outside, hundreds of kilometers away from human settlements."

With hindsight, knowing now that they were all going to die on the next day, we can find several foreboding signs in the above entry:

– 10 am is a late start for a day in the mountains, so why is Dyatlov considering it relatively early, compared to other days?

– They follow a Mansi hunter, and hunting almost certainly means firearms.

– The winds are likened to the jets of a departing airplane. I cannot but think of the scene with Cusack and Thornton in the Pushing Tin movie.

– The hikers are off track, could it be that they are lost?

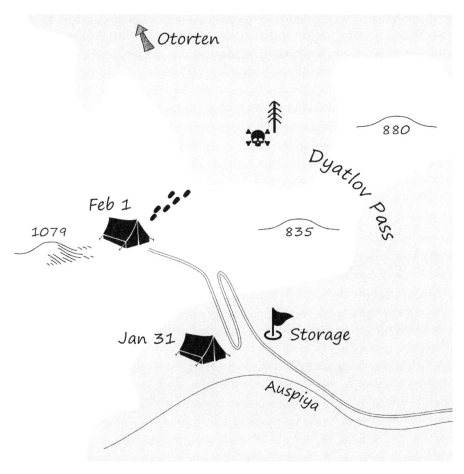

Otorten

880

Dyatlov Pass

Feb 1

1079

835

Jan 31

Storage

Auspiya

The group lightened their backpacks, leaving behind supplies for five days, spare boots, a mandolin, a set of batteries, and a lamp. The cache site is called "labaz", after the Mansi wooden structures raised above ground to leave game for later – and sometimes used for burials, too. But the Dyatlov group labaz didn't look anything like that: the hikers dug a hole and marked it with ski propped in the snow and a torn gaiter slipped onto it. Researchers familiar with mountain trek rations claim there are 40 kg missing from the provisions – so, there is something fishy about this labaz. **An alarm sounds again.**

This is believed to be their last photo. There are, in fact, two very similar photos from this point in the hike and we don't know which of them was taken last, but we have chosen to show the one in which Krivonschenko is looking at the camera. The other one is almost the same, but he is looking down.

How come we don't know in what order they were taken? We don't have the negative. We don't even know who developed the film. The photos taken during the Dyatlov group trek have created a universe of conspiracy on their own. The inventory shows four cameras, but based on known films and photographs, there were at least five. We have the negatives of six films: four of them were still inside the cameras, and two more rolls were found in the tent. There are also loose photographs that do not belong to any of these six films. Some of them were developed by the student who did not go with the group and was replaced by Zolotaryov. The chain of custody is non-existent in this case, and the same applies to the diaries and the last document found in the tent, dated February 1, 1959.

31

TRANSCRIPT OF DYATLOV GROUP COMBAT PAMPHLET

" EVENING OTORTEN " № 1

February 1, 1959   Publication of the trade union
committee of the "Khibina" group

Editorial

GREETING THE 21th PARTY
CONGRESS WITH INCREASED
BIRTHRATE AMONG HIKERS!

SCIENCE

In recent years, there has
been a heated debate around the
existence of Yeti. According to
the most recent reports, the Yeti
live in the Northern Ural, near
Mount Otorten.

PHILOSOPHIC SEMINAR

on the topic of "Love and hiking",
taking place daily on the tent
premises (main building).
Lectures are given by Dr. Thibeaux
and Dubinina, PhD (Love Sciences)

An Armenian Quiz.

TECHNOLOGY NEWS

Hiking drag sled

Good while riding by train, car
or horseback. Not recommended
for freight transportation on
snow. For further information
contact chief constructor
com. Kolevatov.

SPORT

Team of radio technicians
including com. Doroshenko and
Kolmogorova has set a new world
record in portable stove assembly
– 1 hour 02 min. 27.4 sec.

Can nine hikers get warm
with a single stove and
blanket?

As you can see, this is a satirical pamphlet. The diaries that were arbitrarily chosen to be included in the case files were typed. The public was never shown the originals, which were not scanned or photographed, so all we have to this day are typed copies. I can now hear a siren. There is mention of Yeti. The Discovery Channel makes a movie, Russian Yeti: The Killer Lives.

Fast-forward. When the Dyatlov group did not report back on time, initially no one seemed to find this a cause for worry. The parents of the students, however, had the gut feeling that something was wrong. They voiced their concerns and even sent a telegram to Nikita Khrushchev, urging him to have a search organized for their children. I wouldn't highlight this moment, but conspirators are highly suspicious. There is a three-volume book, "The Half-Life of the Khibina Group" (the Dyatlov group called themselves Khibina group – see the pamphlet), based on the fact that the time elapsed between the date of expected return and the discovery of the tent was exactly fourteen days, which coincides with the half-life of radioactive isotope phosphorus-32; the book posits the theory that the Dyatlov team were on a scientific expedition and that Zolotaryov was, in fact, a kamikaze.

"Common sense is not so common." — Voltaire

Back to common sense. The tent was found on a slope where the group had no place to be. **Flashing red light.** The best practice for spending the night on a hiking trip is to do so in the woods. The team's tent, which was old and made by stitching two tents together to accommodate ten people, was designed to hang on trees. It could be pitched on skis in emergencies, such as weather closing in. The weather reports from the nearby meteorological station for these dates do not mention storm conditions, but they do show extremely low temperatures and winds stronger than the average for the area. From there on, there is no need to bring your attention to the suspicious moments because it is all a free fall into the rabbit hole.

The tent was slashed from inside. The hikers' belongings, including food supplies, personal effects, and equipment, were haphazardly heaped together in an ice and snow covered mount. Money, alcohol, coveted food such as cocoa and smoked pork, valuable cameras, and a flashlight, were all there. Outside the tent, their footsteps, frozen rigid and raised above snow level due to the rapid drop in temperature and strong winds, showed that the hikers had moved in an orderly way, without stumbling, panicking, straying, limping, or dragging. The photos taken of their footprints in 1959 indicate that they did not turn around, either, to face the danger that had scared them away from the tent in the first place. They walked for about a mile in the dark, the temperature presumably being -30°C (-22°F). They lit a fire, dug up a den in the snow, laid down branches and clothes, but all to no avail. The pathologist concluded that the traumas on three of the bodies were the result of a forceful impact, as one might expect from being struck by a fast-moving vehicle. However, there was nothing on the scene to support such a scenario. These three victims were found in a ravine where there were no fallen rocks or trees, hundreds of miles away from the nearest road.

Most theories that attempt to explain what scared the group into cutting the tent open and fleeing (infrasound, microburst, gravity tunnel, wolverines, hallucinogens, UFOs) conclude their scenarios with a twenty-plus feet drop which would explain the injuries sustained. The terrain has been carefully examined, however, and there is no drop or crevice on the path from the tent to where the bodies were discovered. The most widely spread and commonly filmed scenario is that the major chest fractures and caved-in skull were caused by an avalanche or a snow slab which did not fully cover or destroy the tent, but was enough to mortally injure three of the hikers, who were then carried down the slope by their comrades and left on the branches in the den. The fact that they were found not in the den but twenty feet downstream is apparently of little or no importance. Kuryakov in his capacity of Head of the Department of the Prosecutor's Office of the Sverdlovsk Region, tried to push a scenario of the "overwhelming force" which we were left with in 1959, but all he could come up with was that being afraid of a snow slab the group cut their tent to get out faster, went down to the forest to spend the night without outerwear and shoes, and while hiding into a snow bivouac a snow cornice or a snow slab tore from the bank of the stream and crushed them to death. In other words, the group had the bad luck to be hit by two improbable avalanches, one forcing them to flee the tent and then another one to finish off those determined to survive the night. This theory is violently disputed as, according to scientific evidence, the region is not avalanche-prone, and in fact there is no record of avalanches ever occurring there. The tent was still standing after a month, and the footprints and traces of urination were still visible when it was found. One can not ace the testimony of the pathologist: *"Dubinina died 10-20 minutes after the trauma."* Apparently one can't walk, with or without support, with a hemorrhaging heart. Period.

There has been no satisfactory explanation of the cause of the high velocity traumas. We provide one, and that is the easy part. The difficult part is to prove why no one has ever thought of something hidden in plain sight.

I know the experts are getting impatient. I am teaching them how to tie shoelaces when they know all the climbing knots. I can't cover all the bases here, but let at least me mention the clothes.

The hikers who were still alive apparently took clothing from the dead, thus leaving us a ghastly timeline of the order in which they died. On a hunch, the lead investigator ordered a test for radioactive contamination of the clothes. Three pieces of clothing showed levels of beta particle contamination relatively higher than normal for people working with radioactive substances, which would suggest the clothes had been contaminated via direct contact with something radioactive. The misinterpretation that the hikers were radioactive head to toe is countered by the fact that only three of the nine clothing items tested showed higher readings. It is known that one of the hikers (Dyatlovpass.com/yuri-krivonischenko) worked in Mayak, where on September 29, 1957, the Soviets nuked themselves (Dyatlovpass.com/kyshtym-disaster), and that one of the girls (Dyatlovpass.com/zinaida-kolmogorova) came from a village in the contaminated zone. Other theories propose tests in Novaya Zemlya (Dyatlovpass.com/stanislav-bogomolov-1#novayazemlya) as an explanation, and then there is the exoticism of Rakitin's version (Dyatlovpass.com/theories#kgb-agents) that someone in the group was carrying a pure beta isotope. But the basic question remains: why would Ivanov order a radioactive test for people who died in the mountains with no apparent signs of foul play, only to close the case the day after the results came out?

Traceologists were not asked to examine the tracks for the presence of strangers in the area, so there were only the subjective opinions of the searchers, who said there were none – just the ski tracks of the group in the forest and their shoeless footprints going from the tent down to the place where the bodies were found.

The searchers saw the footprints going down the slope for half a mile, and somehow it did not occur to them that something ominous had taken place. They missed the hints that this was no longer a rescue operation. The problem we now face is that we are trying to solve a crime committed sixty years ago in the remote mountains, and the evidence we are left with would never stand up in any court.

Lights were seen in the sky by many witnesses. The lead investigator Lev Ivanov believed in flying saucers. The official case files are ridden with inconsistencies, but it seems this is not unheard of for the time. There are recollections of the tent and bodies seen before the official discovery. A sheath turns into a knife in the official protocols describing the scene. For two months the case became cold even before it was closed. The decision on the cause of death was made before the last four bodies were found. Thirty years later Lev Ivanov apologized to the families of the deceased for not being just in his investigation in 1959, without giving any further details.

I will now conclude the crash course on the Dyatlov Pass incident with the date on the cover – February 6, 1959. This is the date of the earliest testimony in the case files. Who was asking questions, and why a week before the group was due back? There is more than one document bearing a suspiciously early date, giving rise to numerous cover-up theories. No one has so far ever attempted to explain the date February 6, 1959, on the cover. In this book, we offer an explanation that fits the facts like a glove.

Remember – as you read on, you may skip through the indented paragraphs like the one below.

> I am a designer. I had this idea of creating a mosaic of the photos from the 165 photos taken from the films found in the Dyatlov group tent. In the process, I realized the following – the grand image doesn't emerge from the tiles, but rather the other way round. One needs to choose the theory in advance, and then piece together the evidence to match the theory. How does one solve a jigsaw without knowing the final image? Staring at the evidence. That is what Igor Pavlov did for ten years. And when he found a theory that seemed to explain all the facts, he sat on it and waited to see how the new discoveries would fit. They all confirmed his theory.

> There is more to it, though. My Master's degree in Civil Engineering can be blamed for the next three references. In the Dyatlov group case, there are more strange episodes than potential culprits can account for. One cannot fit into the same theory suspicious Mansi testimonies, bad weather, elemental forces, radioactive clothes, the KGB, a tent cut open from the inside, violent death, UFOs, the strange behavior of the investigator, an orderly walk by the victims to their death without clothes and shoes, all the activity around the cedar, digging up a den but not taking shelter in it, dying from hypothermia but not making use

of all clothing available, while at the same time wearing other people's clothes, at least two bodies found in positions suggesting they had been moved postmortem... That amounts to seventy-five theories filed with the Prosecutor's office. What could be the facts that suggest so many different scenarios?

In mathematics, a system is considered **overdetermined** if there are more equations than unknowns. An overdetermined system is almost always inconsistent, it has no solution. This is my first reference. Secondly – in statically definable structures all sheer (overwhelming) forces can be determined only by equations. If the stiffness of the parts of the structure needs to be taken into account, the system becomes **indeterminate**. The theories, in general, are built on photos, diary entries, and witness testimonies. If you have to take into account how reliable they are, the system becomes indeterminate. There are claims that the photos cannot be trusted and the diaries are doctored. Igor Pavlov not only analyzed all the information but also took into consideration how and if it can be verified and/or trusted. He researched and compiled the Who Is Who database related to the case.

And now for my third and final mathematical reference. My Statics professor taught us that, before we lose any hope (actually, his exact words were *"lose our mind"*), we should check if the system is not **instantaneously changeable**. Instantaneously changeable systems may occur if two rigid discs of a structure join inappropriately. Like the fact, the hikers died a violent death and the conjecture that someone moved their bodies. The inappropriate connection is that these must be related. Then the system allows for very few relative displacements before reaching a dead end. This means it can only support a very limited subset of evidence and must leave the rest out. Here is an example: if the Mansi are at fault, you can't attribute to this theory any of the inconsistencies in the case files. The Mansi had no access to the investigation. But if one breaks the connection between who, how and why, then the system may have a solution. For example, if the theory doesn't depend on how and when the tent was cut, or who left the footprints, or how the dead were dressed. Imagine not having to account for this. Our theory gives you this freedom. We were robbed of the chance to have any plausible explanation when some of the bodies were moved. Who, why, why some and not all? It is in the book.

You have just received a snapshot of the case. On the site Dyatlovpass.com you can read the case files, the autopsies, the diaries, see the photos the hikers took during the trek. The book includes the most accurate and descriptive maps and diagrams on the case. The pages that follow will feel like deep diving. Some of the creatures have never seen the light. You will move in unknown and uncharted obscure territories. You will have panic attacks. You will feel lost. But remember your lifeline is Dyatlovpass.com/1079. We will try to answer all your questions and keep publishing new information as it comes in. We have taps everywhere.

To thank you for your patience, here is a hint from me. Something to bring all of you together, under the same common numerator of bewilderment.

Six of the Dyatlov group died twice.

"Sell your cleverness and buy bewilderment." —*Jalaluddin Rumi*

MAPS

We have paid special attention to maps. The location of the bodies and tent has never been properly marked in relation to landmarks. The Dyatlov group case researchers have heatedly discussed and gone to the pass year after year to measure distances and places of trees seen in the background of the photos taken during the 1959 search operation. Witnesses and members of the search have testified, their recollections have been compared, and the items found analyzed. Behind the nice icons, you will see on the maps in this book is the colossal work of the entire community invested in the case. We used data as of 2021.

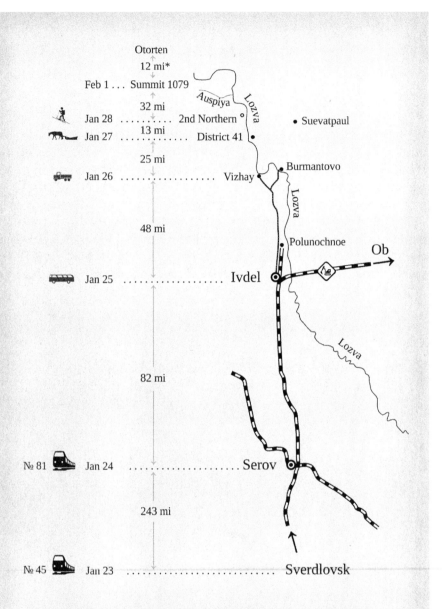

Otorten
↑
12 mi*
↓
Feb 1 . . . Summit 1079

32 mi

Jan 28 . . . . 2nd Northern

Jan 27 . . . . 13 mi District 41

25 mi

Jan 26 . . . . Vizhay

48 mi

Polunochnoe
Ob

Jan 25 . . . . Ivdel

82 mi

№ 81   Jan 24 . . . . Serov

243 mi

№ 45   Jan 23 . . . . Sverdlovsk

Auspiya

Lozva

Suevatpaul

Burmantovo

Lozva

Lozva

* The actual distance the hikers would have had to travel, taking into account the terrain.

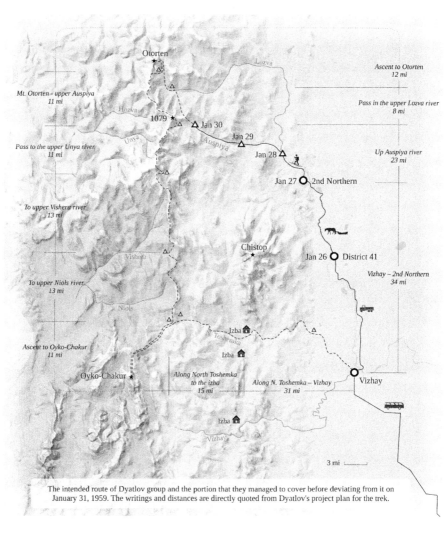

The intended route of Dyatlov group and the portion that they managed to cover before deviating from it on January 31, 1959. The writings and distances are directly quoted from Dyatlov's project plan for the trek.

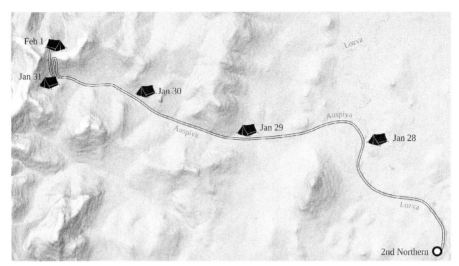

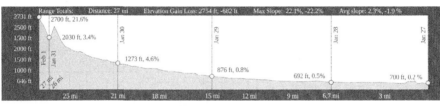

N

1 mile scale

❶ Feb 26

❸ Feb 27 KOLMOGOROVA

❹ Mar 5 SLOBODIN

❸ Feb 27 DYATLOV

KOLMOGOROVA ½ mi
500 ft
SLOBODIN
600 ft
DYATLOV
1000 ft

1st creek

Den

KOLEVATOV
ZOLOTARYOV
THIBEAUX
❺ May 5
DUBININA

Left creek

20 ft 164 ft
4 bodies
2 bodies 2 ft
3 ft

Cedar
❷ Feb 27 KRIVONISCHENKO
DOROSHENKO

2nd creek

Photo Maxim Popov | Distances are given on the basis of data from the protocols of the criminal case.
Dark circles mark the order of discovery; the skull icons indicate if the body was found face up and its orientation.

PROLOGUE. FEBRUARY 1959.
POLUNOCHNOE

The railway to the north of the Sverdlovsk Region of the RSFSR ends in the small village of Polunochnoe. The settlement clings to the easternmost slope of the Ural Mountains. To the left is the blue stone belt of the ridge, to the right the West Siberian Plain, going beyond the horizon. The village is called Midnight (Polunochnoe), the very name evoking something dark and dreary. The first settlers were surveyors and geologists. Then the convicts resettled during the Second World War. The Germans from the Volga region were not happy to explore this deserted mountain-taiga region, but the Russians had to, as the country desperately needed manganese to make super-strong steel for tanks and firearms.

Polunochnoe is 21 km (13 miles) north of Ivdel. In February 1959, the streets were covered with a blanket of snow, the rustic houses looking like something straight out of a fairy tale. Then the militia station in the village received some disturbing news: strange objects had been spotted from a flight over the Main Ural Ridge south of Mount Otorten. They looked like human bodies.

Death in the taiga is not uncommon, but this time the news was taken personally - the Shumkov group that had started their trek from here just a few days before included Zhora Klein, the son of a local well-respected family. His father was the chief engineer of the local manganese mine, his mother was a teacher in the primary school. The hikers had been welcomed for the night into the home of the Klein family, visited the manganese mine, and left on their trip in the taiga, deep into the mountains, into uninhabited territories not so long ago.

Leonid Mihaylovich Chudinov, head of the Polunochnoe militia station, took the disturbing news close to heart. Chudinov was not yet 40, but he had seen many deaths.

Leonid Mihaylovich Chudinov (38) was born in 1921 in the village of Harenki, Visimskiy district, Sverdlovsk Region. Together with other relatives, he worked on the "Red Plowman" collective farm. In 1940, he left his native village to attend the school for medical orderly in Ryazan. In October 1941, Chudinov was drafted into the army. He fought on the Western, Bryansk, and Byelorussian Fronts, rising from a medical orderly to Sr. Lieutenant. He was awarded the "Order of the Red Star" and the "Order of the Patriotic War", 2nd degree, and the medal "For Courage". At the front, he joined the Komsomol, and in 1942 he became a member of the Soviet communist party VCP(b). After the end of the war, he continued to serve in the Volga Military District as Komsomol organizer of the regiment and then as secretary of the party bureau of an artillery battalion. After being demobilized in 1947, he started working for the Ministry of Internal Affairs (MVD). After demobilization in 1947, Chudinov entered into the service of the MVD forces. In 1951, he completed secondary education at an evening school for working class youth in the city of Nizhny Tagil. In 1955 Chudinov became a case officer at the Ivdel group of the MVD Office of the Sverdlovsk Region. Since 1957 Chudinov had been head of the Burmantovo, and later the Polunochnoe Militia station in Ivdel.

His wife, Nina Vasiyevna, died early, leaving Leonid Mihaylovich with four children. Chudinov knew very well how the Klein family would feel if rumors of their son's death spread. It would be better not to disturb them ahead of time before the information had been thoroughly checked.

Getting to the site of the alleged accident is difficult, especially in the winter. Nevertheless, they managed to come to an agreement with local geologists. A search party will be sent for verification.

But how had the hikers ended up in that area? The local population was questioned. Post offices were the best source of information because the hiking groups had to report their location and travel plans to the Sports Clubs. There was a communications center in Polunochnoe, in the same building that housed the Militia station, the reception of the chairman of the village council, the registry office, and the passport office. Soon it was established that the hikers had spent the night at the Northern logging site, 12 km (7 miles) north of Polunochnoe. Their next stop was Burmantovo, 60 km (37 miles) from Polunochnoe, then the Mansi yurts of Lyamyapaul and Suevatpaul. From there they went west into the taiga, towards Mt. Chistop, and their tracks were lost.

Meanwhile, the dreadful suspicions were confirmed. The search party found several frozen bodies and a tent. But Captain Chudinov experienced a sense of relief: the documents discovered at the scene confirmed that the deceased were not from Zhora Klein's group. True, the dead hikers were also from Sverdlovsk, but from the Ural Polytechnic Institute (UPI). Apparently, they did not have enough experience to survive in the winter taiga. There had always been and would be, cases like this one.

Residents had seen many such deaths. Death is always a tragedy, but at least Leonid Mihaylovich would not need to avert his eyes and tell his close friends that their son was dead. It was already confirmed that Zhora Klein's group had all reached the barracks of the District 41 logging site. The hikers suffered from the freezing temperatures, some fell through the ice – but everyone was alive, and they had already hitched a ride from District 41 to Ivdel. They would soon be home in Sverdlovsk.

All the materials collected during the short time the Polunochnoe village militia department were overseeing the case were then transferred to Ivdel. It was in Ivdel that the multiple threads of fatal coincidences, incorrect assessments of events, and erroneous decisions would soon be interwoven into the web that would come to be called the secret of Dyatlov Pass. It was in Ivdel that the legend was born.

PART 1

HIKING TO THE DEAD MOUNTAIN

CHAPTER 1. JANUARY 1959.
DYATLOV THIRTEEN.

A group of hikers from the Ural Polytechnic Institute saw the New Year in – and, with it, the winter vacation of 1959 - on the bank of the Chusovaya River not far from the "Boitsy" station of the Perm railway. Winter vacations were the time of the long-awaited hikes that would take students away from the city for many days. The hikers, under the supervision of Igor Dyatlov, UPI fifth-year student, were now testing checking out their tent and personal equipment in anticipation of the ski trip in the Northern Ural Mountains.

 **Igor (Gosya) Alekseevich Dyatlov (23)** was born on January 13, 1936, in a common working-class family in the city of Pervouralsk of the Sverdlovsk Region. His father, Aleksey Aleksandrovich, worked as a mechanic at the "Hrompik" factory. His mother, Klavdiya Ivanovna, worked as a cashier at a factory club. Igor had an offer to stay at the UPI specialized chair of radio engineering after he would graduate from the UPI, where from January 1959 he was employed as a part-time research assistant. Igor was involved in hiking thanks to his elder brother Mstislav, who in 1954 graduated from the UPI radio engineering department and was at the time working as an engineer-in-chief at the Pervouralsk New Pipe Works. Igor went on his first hike as early as 1951, together with his brother as part of a UPI hike group. Since then he went through ten hikes, including as part of a combined team of the city of Sverdlovsk. On six occasions Dyatlov was the group leader. His authority among the UPI hikers was very high. Igor Dyatlov was repeatedly elected a member of the bureau of the UPI hiking club, as chairman of the UPI qualification board and hiking club.

Igor had come up with the idea of a winter hike to the Subpolar Urals in the fall of 1958. At that same time, a few other hikers were getting ready for hikes of their own to various areas of the Ural

Ridge. Sergey Sogrin (22), a 4-year student of the UPI Metallurgical Department and one of the Institute's most experienced hikers, was also preparing for a hike in the Subpolar Urals. By 1959, Sergey had fulfilled the standards of Master of Sports in hiking, achieved 2nd grade in mountaineering with the rank of instructor, and was now chairman of the mountaineering section of the Sverdlovsk regional council of the "Burevestnik" ("Petrel") sports association. On consulting with Sogrin, Igor Dyatlov realized that a hike through that area would take a really long time, so he then changed his route for the Northern Urals, where two other experienced UPI hikers, Yuri Blinov and Zinaida Kolmogorova, were also planning a hike.

Zinaida (Zina) Alekseevna Kolmogorova (22) was born on January 12, 1937, in the village of Cheremkhovo of the Kamensky district of the Sverdlovsk Region. Her father, Aleksey Ivanovich, had been disabled at the front; he worked at Kamensk-Uralsky non-ferrous metal works. Her mother, Varvara Vasilievna, was a disabled person of group III. From childhood, Zina was a responsible and diligent girl, used to help her parents and sisters. After graduating from a vocational school at the Kamensk-Uralsky radio factory and then an evening secondary school for working youth, Zina was admitted to the UPI. In 1959 she was a 5th year student of its radio-engineering department. She had an experience of eight hikes, in the two of which she was the group leader. As a member of the bureau of the UPI hiking club, she had earlier been elected as a member and chairwoman of the Qualifying Commission of the UPI hiking club.

Yuri Blinov (22) was a 4th year student of the UPI School of Physics and Engineering, and administrative manager of the bureau of the hiking club. A year earlier he had served as head of the UPI hiking club.

During the organizational stage, Blinov and Kolmogorova invited Georgiy Krivonischenko, Aleksander Kolevatov, and Yuri Yudin to join their group, and they all confirmed their participation. All the more or less experienced hikers, such as Krivonischenko, for instance, had already graduated from the UPI, but had not broken their ties with the Institute's hiking club.

Georgiy (Yuri) Alekseevich Krivonischenko (23) was born on February 7, 1935, in the settlement of ZuGRES in Ukraine. Due to

his father's frequent change of jobs and WWII time evacuation, the family often changed its residence. In 1957, Georgiy graduated from the UPI Construction department and was given a job at the PO Box 404, Construction site №247 of the Ministry of Middle Machinery Manufacturing in Chelyabinsk-40, now known as the city of Ozersk. From September 1957, Georgiy was working as a foreman of an industrial site of district 1 in the territory of Works №817, which was a radiochemical plant engaged in plutonium extraction and procession for nuclear warheads, known as Production Facility "Mayak" ("Lighthouse"). In 1957 Georgiy took an active part in the liquidation of the consequences of an accident at "Mayak". In May 1958, he was shifted to the position of a foreman of the 3rd section of the 10th district. He was supervising the prisoners, who were working at the "Ozero" ("Lake") site – the sites of the northern technological chain of the so-called 'alternate B', which would later be known as plants №35 and №235. In August 1958, Georgiy tried to resign for personal reasons in view of his *"complete unwillingness to work in the given system"*, but his application was refused. In 1959, an order was signed to detail him to PO Box 73 in Krasnoyarsk, where a chemical plant was being constructed. Yuri, as his friends commonly called him, was to arrive at Krasnoyarsk on February 21. Meanwhile, to go on a hike, he took his regular leave and the unused additional days due to him for health hazardous production. From 1954, Yuri had been on six treks, three of which he led. He proudly wore his lapel badges "Tourist of the USSR" and "Ready for Labor and Defense" of the 1st and 2nd degrees. In 1955-56, he was elected member of the UPI hiking club and as chairman of its agitation committee. In 1957, he was awarded the 2nd degree in hiking and the qualification of a junior instructor in hiking.

Aleksander (Sasha) Sergeevich Kolevatov (24) was born in Sverdlovsk on November 16, 1934. In 1953 he graduated from the Sverdlovsk I.I. Polzunov mining and smelting junior college with qualification of heavy nonferrous metals technician, and was detailed to the NII (Research Institute) of the Main City Construction (Glavgorstroy) PO Box 3394, where he worked as a senior research technician. The Institute's name was changed several times (The Institute of Special Metals, NII-9) and was involved in the development and testing of technologies of extraction of metallic plutonium from nitric-acid

solutions for industrial production. By 1955, Sasha had mastered a second skill – that of a glass-blower. From 1955, he was a correspondence student at the All-Union Correspondence Polytechnic Institute, majoring in the metallurgy of non-ferrous metal. In September 1956 he transferred to the UPI as its 2nd year student and moved back to Sverdlovsk. Most probably it had something to do with his plans to return to the NII Glavgorstroy as a specialist in the most prospective and needed field. At the time one could get the qualification of 'metallurgy of radioactive metals' only at the UPI Department of Physics and Technology, with the UPI featuring in the list of the institutions of higher learning, which, under the Resolution of the Council of Ministers of the USSR from 1951, were detailed for training professionals with college degrees for the Glavgorstroy of the USSR. In 1959 Sasha was a 4th year student of the UPI Department of Physics and Technology and was representative of his group. He had an experience of six hikes behind, two of which he led.

Yuri Yudin was a 4th year student at the UPI Engineering-Economical Department. Since his second year at the Institute, he had been a member of the UPI hiking club, with six hikes behind him. For a few years, he also frequented the UPI figure skating club.

Everything was going according to plan until, in December, Blinov was invited to head a simultaneous hike in the Northern Urals. The change in Dyatlov's plans came in handy: he was offered to take charge of the group instead of Blinov. In late December 1958, Dyatlov submitted his first report to the UPI hiking club, stating that his preparations for a trek to the North Urals were underway.

The organization of the group did not proceed as smoothly as Igor would have liked it to. Evgeniy Chubarev refused to take part in the hike; like Blinov, he went as a group leader on another route. For Pyotr Bartolomey, Nikolay Tregubov, Vladimir Shunin, Nataliya Sharnina, and Maria Pliusnina the timing of the trek coincided either with the deadlines for their diploma project development or with practical training in various cities. For various reasons, Vyacheslav Halizov, Pavel Tarzin, Vladimir Pudov, Valentina Baldova, and Tamara Vedyakina could not go, either. For some time Zinaida Kolmogorova contemplated going on a trek to the Subpolar Urals together with Sogrin, but eventually decided to stay on with Dyatlov. The group was also joined by Vladislav Bienko, Yuri Vishnevskiy, and Lyudmila Dubinina, who had failed in the organization of their own treks to the Subpolar Urals.

Lyudmila (Lyuda) Aleksandrovna Dubinina (20) was born on May 12, 1938, in the township of Kegostrov in the Archangel Region. Her father, Aleksander Nikolaevich, served as director of a number of timber works of the Ministry of Timber Industry of the USSR, which meant frequent changes of residence. From 1953, the Dubinin family had settled in Sverdlovsk. In 1959 Lyuda was a 4th year student of the UPI Department of Construction. She had taken part in four hikes and on one occasion she led the group herself.

Nikolay Popov, a graduate of the UPI who worked in the city of Bugulma as an engineer at the Tatar Research Institute of Oil Machine Building (TATNII), wanted to go with Dyatlov, but he was not sure if he could get a leave from work. Nikolay Thibeaux-Brignolle, Rustem Slobodin, and Yuri Doroshenko had agreed to take part in the hike.

Nikolay (Kolya, Tibo) Vladimirovich Thibeaux-Brignolle (23) was born on June 5, 1935, in Osinniki, where his father, Vladimir Iosifovich, served his term, to die in 1943. At the time Osinniki was the site of a branch of Gulag Siblag (Siberal Camp), where his father was serving his 10-year term. His mother, elder brother and sister were likely banished to the same place as "the family of the enemy of the people". His father, Vladimir Iosifovich Thibeaux-Brignolle, was born on May 13, 1886, in Yekaterinburg in the family of a mining engineer. After graduation from the Freiberg Mining Academy in 1912 or 1913, he worked in the Urals from 1913. As of October 1917, he was the manager of the mines of the Revda Mining Region. After 1924 he took part in drafting a plan on the development of the Urals mining industry, including the Magnitogorsk metallurgical works, the largest such enterprise in Europe in that period. However, in January 1931, he was arrested on falsified charges of participation in a non-existing Urals Industrial Party. Sentenced to 10 years in the Gulag, from 1932 he served his time at the camp, working at the Osinnikovskiy mine works. In 1933, he was permitted meetings with his family, resulting in the birth of his younger son, Nikolay. It is not clear if Nikolay was born in the camp or in the settlement.) However, in 1937 the restrictions were back, with the father sent to a camp in Eastern Siberia to work at the Kuznetskiy coal-mining works, where he died in September 1943. Nikolay's elder brother, Vladimir, died in the Battle of Kursk in the summer of the same year. Nikolay started school in Osinniki in 1943. In 1946 the family moved to Kemerovo, where he graduated from school in 1953. In the same year, thanks to Stalin's death in March 1953, he was admitted to the Department of Construction of the UPI, from which he graduated in 1958 and then worked in a construction trust in Sverdlovsk. In 1955-56 Nikolay was a member of the qualifying commission of the UPI hiking club. He had taken part in five hikes, one of which he led.

Rustem (Rustik) Vladimirovich Slobodin (23) was born in Moscow on January 11, 1936, in the family of instructors at the Timiryazev Agricultural Academy. His father was the son of an officer in the Russian Imperial Army. He joined the Red Army in the summer of 1941, with the mother staying in Moscow with two sons throughout the war. In 1947 the family was banished from Moscow to Sverdlovsk, where it lived in the hostel for the students of the agricultural institute – along with other scientists banished from Moscow in the post-war wave of repressions against intellectuals. In 1953 Rustem graduated from school with a silver medal. He also finished a music school, violin class. In 1958 he graduated from the UPI Mechanical Department, majoring in the technology of machine building. He was offered to stay at the chair as a graduate student but decided to take some time to work. In September 1958, he became a designer at PO Box 10, which was the Sverdlovsk Research Institute of Chemical Machine Building, developing original equipment for radio-chemical production. After four months, he asked for leave on his own account, to go on a trek with the Dyatlov group. Rustem had an experience of six hikes behind him.

Yuri Nikolaevich Doroshenko (21) was born on January 29, 1938, in the village of Dvoretskaya Polyana, Streletsky District of the Kursk

Region in the family of an engineer. After the Nazi attack of June 22, 1941, the family was evacuated with the father's plant to the town of Rezh of the Sverdlovsk Region. In spite of the death of his father, Nikolay Danilovich, in 1954, next year Yuri graduated from school with a medal and was admitted to the UPI without exams. In 1959 he was a 4th year student of the Department of Radio Engineering. He had an experience of four treks, one of which he led. In 1958 he became a 3rd class sportsman in hiking. Yuri was involved in the organization of sports and hiking as the board member of the UPI sports club. His mother, Nadezhda Artemovna, moved with the other children to Aktyubinsk in Kazakhstan after Yuri was admitted to UPI.

On January 8, 1959, the route commission of the Sverdlovsk city committee for physical culture and sports, chaired by Vasiliy Korolyov, an engineer of the UPI Department of Physics and Technology, approved the project of a trek for a group of hikers led by Igor Dyatlov along the route of the 3rd category of difficulty: Vizhay village, Sverdlovsk Region – 2nd Northern settlement – Otorten – Oyko Chakur - Toshemka River - Vizhay village.

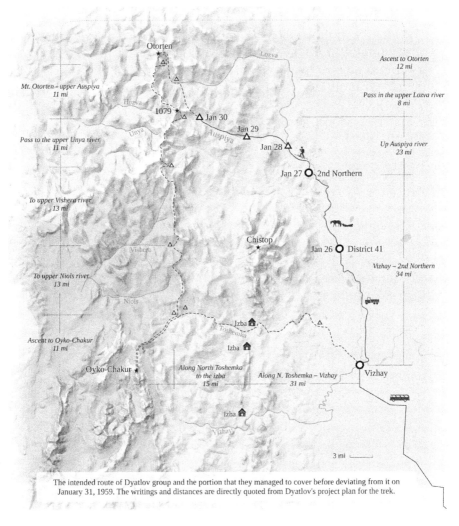

The intended route of Dyatlov group and the portion that they managed to cover before deviating from it on January 31, 1959. The writings and distances are directly quoted from Dyatlov's project plan for the trek.

Members of the Commission were experienced mountaineers Evgeniy Maslennikov and Victor Bogomolov.

Evgeniy Polikarpovich Maslennikov (35) graduated from the Mechanical Department of UPI in 1948. Received the title of Master of Sports in Tourism in 1955. In 1959 he was the chairman of the Regional Federation of Tourism and worked as deputy lead mechanic at the Verh-Isetskiy metallurgical works.

Victor Fyodorovich Bogomolov (26) was a 1955 graduate of the UPI Mechanical Department. In 1959 he was the chairman of the Sverdlovsk hiking club and worked as a design engineer at the PO Box 320, currently Scientific and Production Association of

Automatics named after academician N.A. Semihatov.

They had no doubts about the qualifications of the Dyatlov group. As of the date of approval of the expedition project, the team included fifth-year students Igor Dyatlov and Zina Kolmogorova; fourth-year students Lyudmila Dubinina, Aleksander Kolevatov, Yuri Doroshenko, Yuri Yudin, Vladislav Bienko and Yuri Vishnevskiy; and UPI graduates Rustem Slobodin, Georgiy Krivonischenko, Nikolay Thibeaux-Brignolle, Nikolay Popov and Yuri Verhoturov. Thirteen people in all.

CHAPTER 2. JANUARY 1959.
DYATLOV ELEVEN.

On January 20, Dyatlov received three copies of the route book from Valerian Ufimtsev, the instructor of the city committee for physical culture and sports. Two copies of the protocol of the route commission from January 8 were left in the files of the route commission and the city committee. Dyatlov was supposed to deliver the third copy to the UPI sports club on receipt of the equipment, but he had apparently forgotten to do so. There is a conjecture that this was not accidental, as the revised return dates affected the beginning of the term. On the suggestion of Maslennikov, the initial target dates of January 26 - February 9, 1959, were changed to January 28 - February 12, 1959. This resulted in two simultaneous violations of the process of issuing the equipment: one by Dyatlov as the group's leader, and another by Blinov, who as manager of the bureau of the UPI tourist club was responsible for issuing the inventory at the UPI Sports Club.

Dyatlov made one more blunder. The leader of the group should have kept only one copy of the route book out of three. Although the copies of the route books were to serve for reporting purposes and not for monitoring the group's movement, which was done on the basis of the protocol of the Routing Commission, the second copy was to be retained in the files of the Routing Commission, along with a copy of the protocol, while the third copy was to be held by the controlling organization, in this case, the UPI Sports Club. Dyatlov, however, kept all the three copies of the route book.

Meanwhile, the members of the group were banding together in Sverdlovsk. By January 15, Georgiy Krivonischenko had come on leave lasting until February 20. On January 22, Zina Kolmogorova arrived from Kamensk-Uralskiy after she was granted a leave of absence from her pre-graduation practical training at the Radio factory, PO Box 33. Aleksander Kolevatov had managed to discuss the forthcoming trek with Ignatiy Fokich Ryagin, a family friend and deputy head of the Uralgipromed Trust, who was familiar with the area and supplied Kolevatov with a map of the region.

But there were also unforeseen circumstances. Popov was not released from work. Vishnevskiy failed one of the exams in the winter session and was denied leave by the dean's office. As it later emerged, Verhoturov, who worked as an engineer at the Lysva turbine generator plant, had no idea that his name was on the group's preliminary list and only learned about this in 2000. Most likely Dyatlov included him to simplify the trek application procedure since Verhoturov was the most experienced among the listed hikers.

Slobodin and Bienko were running into certain difficulties. Slobodin was released from work for the duration of the trek only on short notice thanks to the letters from the UPI sports club and the city committee for physical culture and sports. From the draft of that letter:

"To Comrade M. F. Matveev, Head of the PO Box 10:

The Sverdlovsk tourist section at the city committee for physical culture and sports requests permission to grant leave from work to Comrade R.V. Slobodin from January 20 to February 10, 1959, to participate in a hiking trip in the Northern Ural of the highest degree of complexity, dedicated to the 21st Party Congress.

V. Bogomolov, Section chairman."

In the final version of the letters there was no mention of the 21st Congress of the CPSU, which would be held from January 27 to February 5, 1959:

"The sports club and the hiking section of the S.M. Kirov Ural Polytechnic Institute earnestly request permission to grant a leave from work from January 21 to February 13, 1959 to the Institute's graduate, comrade R.V. Slobodin, to participate in a hiking trip of the highest degree of complexity as part of the Institute's combined group.

L.S. Gordo, Chairman of the board of the sports club."

"The Sverdlovsk tour club is organizing a trek of the highest degree of complexity in the Northern Urals from January 21 to February 14. The group includes comrade R.V. Slobodin, an employee of your enterprise. We are asking to grant comrade R.V. Slobodin a leave of absence without pay for the specified time for going on the trek.

V. Kurochkin, the Chairman of the city committee for physical culture and sports"

Nevertheless, the myth that the trek was dedicated to the party congress is still alive, although Yuri Yudin explained it back in 2012:

"Some people say that the trek was dedicated to the party congress. That is not so. The treks had never been dedicated to party congresses. But this was only on paper so that the members of the trek could be granted leave from work."

Bienko had not received a leave of absence from the UPI Dean's office. He was instead replaced by Semyon Zolotaryov, an instructor at the Kourovskaya tour base, who had earlier been approved as a member of the Sogrin group by the city routing commission.

Semyon (Sasha) Alekseevich Zolotaryov (38) was born on February 2, 1921, in the Cossack village of Udobnaya in the Northern Caucasus (Otradnensky District of the Krasnodar Region) in the family of a paramedic. In 1941 he was drafted into the Red Army – immediately after he had graduated from a secondary school. Simultaneously with attending school, he managed to teach first graders at the Udobnenskoe secondary school and as a foreman at the winery works of the Udobnenskoe Food Processing Factory. After graduating from a Noncommissioned Officer school, he fought in the sapper forces at the South-West, Don, Stalingrad, Central, and Belorussian fronts. He fought in the Battle of Stalingrad, took part in the liberation of the western regions of Belorussia, East Prussia, and Pomerania. He was awarded the "Red Star" order, the medals "For the Defense of Stalingrad", "For the Capture of Konigsberg" and "For the victory over Germany in the Great Patriotic War". In 1945 he was detailed to the Moscow Red Banner Military Engineering School, from where he was transferred to the Zhdanov Leningrad Military Engineering School. After demobilization in 1946, he went to Minsk, where he studied at the State Institute of Physical Culture of the BSSR, from which he graduated in 1950 with qualification as an instructor in physical training. Zolotaryov was to be assigned to the city of Grodno, to its regional committee for physical culture and sports as head of the regional "Spartak" sports association. However, for reasons unknown in August 1950 the Ministry of Education of the RSFSR sent him to the Pyatigorsk Pedagogic Institute, where from September 1950 he worked as a physical education instructor. From 1951, Semyon taught physical education at the Pharmaceutical Institute in Pyatigorsk. Simultaneously he studied at night classes of the University of Marxism-Leninism under the Pyatigorsk city committee of the CPSU, from which he graduated in 1953. By order of the Minister of Higher Education of the USSR №1177 from August 18, 1947, the diploma of two-year party schools was to be recognized as an equivalent of the diploma of teachers' institutes. Even though by 1953 Zolotaryov already had two

degrees from institutes of higher learning, in 1954 he was fired for no-
show due to his part-time job. Semyon then got a job as a school
teacher of physical education and military training. However, in 1955
he was relieved of his duties as the secretary of the school's party organization, and in 1958 he quit that job, which coincided with his final
breakup with his common-law wife. Most likely, Semyon's problems
had something to do with his brother - Nikolay Alekseevich Zolotaryov. In 1942-43, Nikolay served with an auxiliary police unit under a
local Nazi occupation administration, and in 1943 he was sentenced
to death by the court-martial of the Armavir garrison. The brother of
a high traitor could not work as a teacher. At that point, Semyon got
professionally engaged in hiking. From 1951, he was working as a
freelance hiking instructor at hiking camps in the North Caucasus, the
Carpathians, and the Altai. In 1953, he graduated from a two-month
instructor course at the "Iskra" ("Spark") Voluntary Sports Society in
the city of Pyatigorsk with the qualification of a junior instructor of
mountaineering and hiking. In 1957 he went through a merit rating at
the Pyatigorsk Tourism and Excursions Administration with the
qualification of an instructor. In the same year, he received the badge,
"Mountaineer of the USSR". In 1958 he qualified as a Junior Water
Trekking Instructor. In October 1958, Zolotaryov found a job as a senior instructor at the Kourovskaya tour base in the Sverdlovsk Region,
which had started an All-Union route along the Chusovaya River. By
1959, Semyon had taken part in 14 hikes of the 1st and 2nd degree of
complexity, including four winter ski treks, and was granted athletic
titles in trek and field sports, mountaineering, shooting, and skiing.

A man who had faced numerous hardships and challenges in his
life, Zolotaryov was at that time interested in participating in a ski trek
of the highest degree of difficulty, to fulfill the standard for obtaining
the title of the Master of Sports in Tourism, which could improve his
career prospects. As a pragmatic individual, instead of going to the
Subpolar Urals, he preferred a shorter and easier route with the Dyatlov group, none of whose members knew him. As Dubinina wrote, *"At
first, nobody wanted to take on this Zolotaryov, because he was a stranger,
but later we thought, what the hell – and took him along, for how could we
refuse him?"*

As of January 20, the group list still comprised 11 people: Dyatlov,
Dubinina, Kolmogorova, Kolevatov, Slobodin, Bienko, Krivonischenko,
Thibeaux-Brignolle, Doroshenko, Yudin, and Zolotaryov. But the matter of Bienko would soon be settled. On January 22, as part of the first
shift of the UPI group of virgin land developers, Bienko left for the Un

station 180 km (112 miles) from Sverdlovsk, where the UPI student timber industry enterprise would start work. Now they were ten.

CHAPTER 3. JANUARY 23-28, 1959. DYATLOV TEN.

On January 23, with the end of the winter examination period, several UPI hiking groups set out on the routes they had long been preparing for. Fourth-year students named Skoreva, Andreeva, Pechenkin, Zubareva, Kotova, Radosteva, Barusevich, Churakov, Strelnikova, Kosnarev, and Suhova set off on a hike of the 2nd degree of complexity in the South Urals. Shortly after midnight, the Sogrin group left for the Subpolar Urals, including Martyushev, Malyutin, Zinovyev, Kuzminyh, Plyshevskiy, Pasynkov, and Sedov. Kolmogorova and Zolotaryov could have gone along, as well, but life had other plans for them. Four hours earlier, at 9:05 pm, UPI students Eroshev, Devyatov, Sinitsyn, Krotov, Avdeev, Strelnikov, Svechnikova, Obodova, and Tomilova, led by Yuri Blinov, boarded train №45 Sverdlovsk-Bogoslovsk to go to the North of the Sverdlovsk Region, as did the Dyatlov group. They were to travel together on the first legs of their routes to the Northern Ural Mountains.

At 7:39 am on January 24, the groups arrived in the city of Serov, from where the train to Ivdel, the northernmost city of the Sverdlovsk Region, would depart that same evening. Until mid-1939, Serov's name was Nadezhdinsk, but the name of the city's railway station had not yet been changed. The station would be renamed from "Nadezhdinsk" to "Serov" only in 1964. Before their departure, the hikers had time to meet with the students of railway school №41 and give them a talk on the intricacies of hiking, including tips on how to prepare and pack their equipment. It was from Serov that Zina Kolmogorova wrote her last letter to her friend, Valentina Baldova:

"My dear Valka! Here we are on our way to the mountains. And guess what, Yuri Doroshenko is coming with us. I don't know how I'll feel around him. So far, I have been treating him like the rest, but it's really hard because we are together and yet we're not together. At the moment, everyone's asleep. Yudin, Krivonischenko, and Kolevatov are sitting next to me, and they send you their best regards. Rustem Slobodin sends his, too. The train is moving, in 3 hours we'll be in Serov. The Ural taiga is behind the windows. My darling, it's still great to be alive! You know this state of mind

when you feel sad and happy at the same time?! Somewhere there is the city of Kamensk, waiting for me to take the job. For now, I am going to stop writing, as we have just departed and the ticket inspector will probably be coming along soon – and we, as usual, do not have enough tickets for all of us.

Live, Valyushka, and rejoice in the good things of life! There is nothing to be done when you sometimes feel sad. After all, we should go on with our life, shouldn't we? One should see only the sunny part of life, and try and make it more joyous. I pray that all will be well. Today I feel very sad because he is walking hand in hand with one of the girls. I am jealous."

Shortly before the start of the trek, Doroshenko and Kolmogorova had broken up after a long relationship. In December 1958, Zina wrote to her friend, Lidiya Grigoryeva:

"Lida, we are no longer friends with Yuri. Surprising, isn't it? Everyone is surprised. We're not even talking, not saying hello to each other. He's already going everywhere with another girl. At first, I was heartbroken, I lost weight, I was exhausted, but now I've somehow calmed down. It's two months now that we haven't been together. Last summer, he would come to see me in Kamensk every Saturday. When I came back here after practical training, everything was still fine, but then I began to notice that he had changed. You see, he wrote to his mother about me, she replied that he would be a fool and fall for me, that I was older than him, and he was still young. His friends were saying the same. Then he started telling me that he wanted freedom (as if I was holding him down!), that I was standing in his way. Well, that's how we parted company, without quarreling: we simply began to ignore each other. He has changed a lot. He's going to dances all the time; at first, he wouldn't show up at the club at all, as that was where I was trying to find comfort, but now it's all over. We sometimes go hiking together, but we take care to avoid each other. One thing I regret, Lida, is that he visited our place so many times. You know, in the village they all thought that if we weren't married yet, we would soon be. And now I'm ashamed to go home. After him I can't be with anyone else, I can't even look at anyone, and he and I won't ever be together again, I know that for sure. That's is the current state of my private affairs, Lida"

On the eve of the trek, Zina wrote:

"I'm going with Dyatlov to the Northern Ural. And you know what, Lida, Yurka is coming with us again. I didn't want him to - can you imagine reopening the old wounds? In Kamensk, I'd managed to put it all out of mind, though not a single day passed when I wouldn't think of him, I was finally able to do so with no pain in my heart, only sadness.

Lidushka, how can I trust anyone after this all? And now here we are again, on the same trek. He has invited himself along. They had agreed to take him on, but wouldn't tell me to the very end. Lidushka, I'll have a very hard time on this trek, you can see that, can't you? I intend to treat him just like everyone else, or at least I will try. After all, he could go with the same group as me, which means I should pull myself together. I'll try, but it is going to be hard, because I love him after all, Lida!"

Igor Dyatlov was trying to take the place of Doroshenko, but Zina would not even notice his wooing.

The group had another potential source of conflict. Yuri Blinov's profile of Aleksander Kolevatov was far from complimentary: *"Sashka Kolevatov was my fellow student: we were in the same group №457. stubborn and self-confident, not averse at times to bragging of his merits or qualities. True, he was always careful with his words, but at times it was unpleasant to listen to him... The girls couldn't stand him."* This was in tune with Kolmogorova's letter to Lydia Grigorieva from January 22, written only a day before the start of the trek: *"The group is not bad, though I'm not sure how we will feel on the trek – or if there will be squabbles, considering Kolevatov's presence."*

The hikers left for Ivdel at 6:15 pm by train №81, en route from Nadezhdinsk to Polunochnoe, where they arrived around midnight. By that time, they had already had to face the authorities twice. The first encounter took place at the train station in Serov, where Krivonischenko decided to earn money for candy by singing, and then had to be rescued from the militia station. Then on the train, a half-drunk man tried to accuse the hikers of stealing his bottle of vodka. They spent the night at the Ivdel-1 train station, taking turns on duty throughout the night. At around 6:00 am on January 25, they took a bus from the railway station to the city of Ivdel. They dropped at the post office to stamp their route books and at around 7:00 am the bus took them on a 90 km (56 miles) trip to the village of Vizhay, where they arrived at around 2 pm.

The ride was not uneventful. The bus was to ride to the village of Shipichnoe, which was a digression from its route and then come back. It was suggested that the hikers should get off and take a walk until the bus returned. While part of the group was helping to pull out a logging truck that had got trapped in the snow, four of them, led by Kolevatov, managed to reach the village of Talitsa and went sightseeing around the local power plant. Suddenly, someone shouted, "The bus!" The hikers rushed to the door, but it was too late: the bus would not slow down and they could not catch up with it. Fortunately, a local woman hailed it down on the road, and it stopped – great luck indeed, as it might otherwise have just driven by. It was not uncommon for the local drivers not to wait even for schoolchildren on special rides taking them back home from school. Or to come out with responses such as, "My way, or the highway."

The group stamped the route books for the second time at the Post Office at Vizhay.

Vizhay was one of the many campsites which by 1959 had survived the infamous Gulag system. It so happened that on that day there was a general meeting of Komsomol members from all campsites. After the meeting, Blinov had arranged with one of the departing trucks to take his group to District 105, about 15 km (9 miles) west of Vizhay. From that point the Blinov group hikers were planning to start their ski trek of about 220 km (137 miles), so they took a warm farewell of the Dyatlov group. No one could know that they would never see each other again.

The first prisoners appeared in this area in the late 1920s when the Ural regional committee and the regional executive committee decided to involve the camp inmates in the logging works at the Ivdel timber industry enterprise of the Ural Forest trust. The latter was based on the Kama Ural Paper Trust forest plot. The camp division of the village of Samskiy with the mine of the Urallag prison camp had become a transit camp for convicts sent for logging at the Ivdel timber industry enterprise. In 1930, the families of dispossessed kulaks were brought within the boundaries of the Ivdel forestry. In 1935, they were joined by those exiled in the aftermath of S.M. Kirov's assassination in Leningrad.

In 1937, the Ivdel timber industry enterprise was liquidated, with the Ivdel corrective labor camp (Ivdellag, known at the time as enterprise N-240) established on its base on August 16, 1937. Since then, all economic activity in the Ivdel region, except for gold mining and exploration, had been concentrated at the Ivdellag. As of January 1, 1938, the average number of inmates at the Ivdellag was 13,500. In 1941, the Ivdellag was assigned to fulfill the construction and maintenance requirements of the Polunochnoe Manganese Mine. On October 27, 1941, an agreement was signed between the Ivdellag of the People's Commissariat of Interior (NKVD) and the Polunochnoe Mining Administration, under which the Ivdellag was to provide up to 2,000 workers for the construction of the Ivdel-Polunochnoe railway line.

On January 12, 1942, the first unit from among the mobilized Soviet citizens of German origin was organized at the Ivdellag. By July 1942, the number of such units had increased to seven. In the period from July 1941 to January 1945, the mortality rate among the Ivdellag inmates varied for the different units from 0.2 to 27.9%. As of January 1, 1945, the Ivdel inmates numbered 16,529. In April 1946, the penal labor army was eliminated, with the Germans transferred to a special settlement under the administrative oversight of the regional offices of the MVD. Hundreds of former members of the Labor Army remained in service at the camps, where they had previously served time during their labor mobilization. This included Paramilitary security services. Work record books for these people were opened only after 1947.

In 1949, the construction of a hydrolysis factory began in the vicinity of the Pershino Power Plant for the production of industrial alcohol from sawmill waste. Its construction was carried out by teams of inmates from the Ivdel and Pershino labor camps. The power plant started using lignin as fuel. Lignin was a waste from the Ivdel Hydrolysis Plant, which produced weapons-grade cellulose, in addition to alcohol and food-feed yeast. As of January 1, 1950, the Ivdellag had 21,642 inmates.

In 1955, the Ivdel logging operations were reconstituted with production sites in the villages of Lyavdinka and Ous. The enterprise had nothing to do with the Ivdellag and was an independent logging division of the Ministry of Timber Industry.

On December 1, 1957, after the last of the regular reorganizations, authority over all the logging works corrective labor camps, including the Ivdellag, was transferred to the Ministry of Internal Affairs of the RSFSR (MVD). In February 1958, the Main Special Directorate of Timber Industry (Glavspetslesprom) was established within the MVD to manage the timber industry camps.

As of 1959, the structure of the Ivdellag included five branches and four separate colonies. The branches were: N-240/2 in the village of Lesozavod, N-240/6 in the village of Shipichnoe, N-240/7 in the village of Horpiya, N-240/8 in the village of Vizhay, and N-240/9 in the village of Ponil. The colonies were: N-240/4 at Ivdel, N-240/12 in the village of Kombinat, N-240/13 in the village of Losiniy, and N-240/25 in the village of Nadymovka. As of January 1, 1959, the inmates of the Ivdellag numbered 15,148.

The Dyatlov group was staying at Vizhay, but they were not wasting time. They consulted with Ivan D. Rempel, a forest officer of the Vizhay forestry, who helped them reconfirm their route, copy the layout of the forest plot along their route, and mark up the boundaries of the planted forest.

Ivan Dmitrievich Rempel (53) was convicted in 1937, and since then had lived in Vizhay. At first, he served his time at the labor camp and after the end of his term stayed back at the local forestry.

Rempel warned the group of the perils of the route, particularly the heavy winds at the Ural Ridge, but the hikers did not take his warnings seriously. They were looking forward to the evening entertainment – the famous Symphonie in Gold (1956) movie at the local club, followed by a night at the Vizhay hotel.

At about 10 am on January 26, they sent their last messages to their relatives and friends. Dyatlov wrote to Pervouralsk, Slobodin to Sverdlovsk, and Kolmogorova to the village of Cheremkhovo.

"Hi everyone! Today, January 26, we are starting the trek. The trip was fine. Between February 12 and 15 I should be in Sverdlovsk, but I probably won't be stopping at home, so let Rufa bring under-linen to our room for my trip to Penza. I will be coming back from Penza between March 5 and 7. Greetings, Igor"

Rufa, Igor Dyatlov's sister, was at the time a student at the UPI radio department. From all appearances, after the trek, Igor was going to Penza for his pre-graduation practical training, where radio production was organized in 1959 on the Frunze plant base.

"January 26, 1959, 10 am: Hello to the sedentary residents of Sverdlovsk! Yesterday we safely reached the village of Vizhay. Now we are riding in a special truck to our point of departure –the 2nd Northern. The weather is nice and warm (~10 -15°). Everything is fine. I am sorry I didn't say goodbye – I had to run. All the best, R. Slobodin."

"Hello, my dear mom, dad, Toma, Galya, and Lusya! Greetings from Zina! Well, I'm away from you once more, we are now in the city of Serov, where we have a transfer, so I can write while waiting. How are you all? What's the news? We are going on a trek – there are ten of us, the group is good. I managed to arrange leave from the plant, and I have all the clothes I need, so don't worry about me. How are you getting on? Write to me in Vizhay, I will be looking forward to it. Has the cow calved or not? I am longing for some milk! How is mom's work? How is dad's and mom's health? How are Galya and Lusya doing at school? Lusya, make sure you don't get any Bs this term. Galya, try to upgrade your Cs in sports to Bs. Spend more time skiing, and running, too. See you soon and goodbye. Big kisses to you all, Your Zina. Write to me, I'll be looking forward to hearing from you. January 26, 1959."

Dyatlov was also supposed to send telegrams with mandatory checkpoint notification of their coming on the trek to the UPI Sports Club and the Routing Commission CC for PCS, but there is no evidence that he did. Perhaps he forgot to do that, as well.

After lunch, at 1:30 pm, the Dyatlov group hitched a ride to the District 41 settlement 40 km (25 miles) north of Vizhay, on a Vizhay logging camp truck with ineffective brakes and broken springs. The departure from Vizhay is confirmed by the stamp of the Ivdel MVD corrective labor camp's office from January 26 in the group's route book. Riding along with the hikers was one Aleksey Hatanzeev, head of the "Red Chum" division in the village of Sosva, who was in charge of cultural and propaganda work with the local population; he was traveling to District 41 to organize a film screening.

Aleksey Vladimirovich Hatanzeev (46) was born in 1913. After completing 5 grades at school, he worked as a shepherd and a handyman with mining parties from Saranpaul to Ivdel. In 1938, he got a job as a translator from his native Nenets language at a community center in the village of Sosva. In 1940, he was drafted into the Red Army, took part in the battles at the Karelian-Finnish, the 2nd Baltic fronts, and was wounded three times. He was a commander of a gun group and an artillery section in the rank of a sergeant of Guards. In 1945, he served as a gun aimer of an artillery squadron at the battlefield junior lieutenant's school at the Leningrad front. In that same year, he was recommended for decoration with the 2nd degree of the "Order of the Patriotic War". After the end of the war, Aleksey joined the party. He worked as a propagandist, conducting talks with and giving lectures for the local population.

Around 4:30 pm they arrived at District 41, where they were warmly greeted by civilian workers. In the evening they were treated to one more cultural program, including two Soviet movies, On His Own (1939), Est takoy paren (1956), and once again the Symphonie in Gold (1956). Then they spent the night at the District 41 dormitory.

The morning of January 27 was clouded by Yudin's sudden sickness, an inflammation of the sciatic nerve. Yudin said he had experienced such bouts earlier – during the 1958 Altai expedition, when Dyatlov was leading the group, and in 1955 when Yuri was hospitalized with rheumatic heart disease. On the current trip, he had caught a chill while traveling in an open-back truck to District 41. Nevertheless, Yudin decided to continue with the group to the abandoned 2nd Northern settlement, 22 km (13 miles) north of District 41. They got lucky that Georgiy IvanovichRyazhnev, head of the 1st forest plot of the Energolesokombinat (Energy ForestWorks), who lived in District 41, let the group load their backpacks on a horse-driven sleigh, that was going to the 2nd Northern to bring some pipes back.

While they were waiting for the sleigh, the group's common equipment, which Yudin had been carrying, was divided among the remaining hikers to carry in their backpacks. They also bought some food at a local store. One of the local workers made a lasting impression on the group's members. As Dubinina wrote in her diary: *"I particularly remembered Ognev with his ginger beard and his Beard nickname. Generally, you don't often meet people like him in such a hole. He is a true romantic, a geologist, and above all, intelligent."*

Nikolay Grigorievich Ognev (28), although not yet 30, had a considerable life experience behind him. After graduating from the Ufa Mining College, for several years he worked with the Tolinsk party of the Ural Geological Office. In 1957, the Tolinsk party was transferred under the Tyumen Geological Office, the works were terminated with all the workers fired. Ognev joined a coop, where he was driving limestone for burning on reindeer sleds along winter roads from a quarry at the Yatriya River. Later he got a job as an assistant tractor driver with a Northern Expedition, based at Ivdel. Nikolai told Dyatlov how to find a log cabin in the 2nd Northern for an overnight stay.

At 4 pm the group started on skis along the Lozva River towards the 2nd Northern. Their backpacks were put on a sleigh by one Stanislav Valyukyavichus, a carter of the 2nd Northern logging site.

Stanislav Aleksandrovich Valyukyavichus (56) was sentenced in 1974 to 10 years in labor camps for profiteering. In 1953, his criminal record was cleared, but he stayed back at Ivdel to work as a civilian. At first, he worked as a groom of the horse pool during the construction of the Hydrolysis Plant, later he was shifted to the logging plot of the 8th camp branch at Vizhay.

Late in the evening, at around 11 pm, they arrived at the 2nd Northern, where they spent the night in an abandoned log house.

From Yudin's diary: *"We spent the night in a hut at the 2nd Northern settlement. There are lots of houses, warehouses, old vehicles, and machine tools. Everything was abandoned in 1952. A geological expedition worked there, who then took away whatever they could, drew up an official record for the rest, and left it all behind. All the houses have been ruined, there is a single one left with a stove and glass in the windows. The place is nice and picturesque. The Lozva River is wide. There are many limestone cliffs. Grandpa Slava insists that in summer you can cross the river by ford. There are many hot springs. There are frequent ice-free open water spots and places with ice-free water under a thin layer of snow; after passing which we need to break the ice off our skis."*

After breakfast on January 28, Yudin, Thibeaux-Brignolle, and Doroshenko inspected a core logging facility, which was an open warehouse of geological samples kept under a shed. Yudin took several cores with him since he was in the habit of bringing samples of rocks and minerals for the museum of the UPI Geology Department from all his trips. That was the reason for his trip to the 2nd Northern.

It was time to part with Yudin. Around 10 am, Valyukyavichus departed from the 2nd Northern, taking along the pipes and Yudin's backpack. The sleigh would arrive at District 41 at around 3 pm. Yudin bid his final farewell to his comrades. At the last moment, Dyatlov asked Yudin to warn the Institute of the group's possible two or three-day delay, given the heavy ice built up on their skis during the passage to the 2nd Northern along the Lozva River, with the route planned along the rivers. However, Yudin would forget to send a telegram to the UPI sports club with that warning.

Around noon Yudin skied light-handed along the trail of the sleigh riding to District 41, where he would pick up his backpack and spend the night at the same hostel as the day before. On the morning of January 29, Yudin would leave by truck to the village of Vizhay, together with Ryazhnev. There he would try to find the medications he needed at a local drugstore, managed by one Teodor Gerzen. Teodor Abramov-ich Gerzen was fond of drawing and making Christmas nativity scenes inside glass bottles. He had a sort of a museum inside the drugstore.

From Yudin's diary: *"The pharmacist is an artist, he is German. The family is idyllic. The walls are decorated with bas-relief paintings, intricately carved and made with amazing artistic finesse. There is a box with a view of the Lozva River in summer and another one in winter. All around you can see other boxes and paintings. There are red wax roses with fluorescent ingredients all around the drugstore. There is a replica of the Kremlin made of test tubes with fluorescent ingredients, which is glowing. There is a built-in Pobeda wristwatch, which is going fine. The pharmacist is an amazingly gentle and kind person. His wife is German, a very sweet and hospitable woman. They care deeply about the medications. He is saving the best ones for kids. He begged with me to get penicillin pills at Ivdel since he had very few available. It's hard for them to get good medications."*

From Vizhay, Yuri would go home, to the village of Emelyashevka of the Taborinskiy District of the Sverdlovsk Region. He would return to Sverdlovsk only on February 19.

CHAPTER 4. JANUARY 28-31, 1959. DYATLOV NINE.

After parting with Yuri Yudin, at 11:45 am on January 28, the nine hikers took the route up the Lozva River. The weather was good, with a temperature of -8°C (18°F). Going on skis on the first day with the entire load on is never easy, and the group had to make frequent stops to scrape off wet snow from their skis to continue.

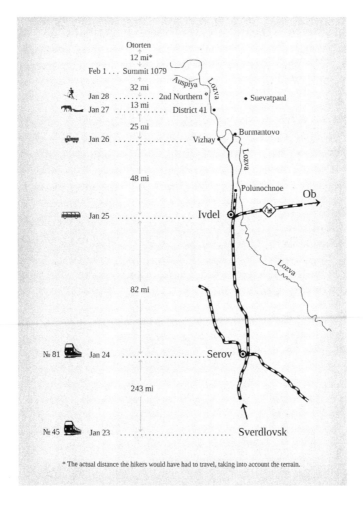

Otorten
↑
12 mi*
↓
Feb 1 . . . Summit 1079
↑
32 mi

Jan 28 . . . . 2nd Northern °
13 mi
Jan 27 . . . . District 41 •

25 mi

Jan 26 . . . . Vizhay •

48 mi

Jan 25 . . . . Ivdel ⊙

82 mi

№ 81   Jan 24 . . . . Serov ⊙

243 mi

№ 45   Jan 23 . . . . Sverdlovsk

• Suevatpaul

• Burmantovo

• Polunochnoe   Ob

* The actual distance the hikers would have had to travel, taking into account the terrain.

"We have done the first 30 minutes. Sure, the backpack is heavy, but it is manageable. The first day is always hard... Yesterday it was much easier to go without backpacks", Zina wrote in her diary. Aleksander tried to use drags made from a spare pair of skis to pull his backpack, but they were not much help, so in the end the backpack went back onto his shoulders. Yuri K. was walking behind the group, making a sketch map. That was unusual. Previously, if Nikolay Thibeaux-Brignolle was part of the trek team, it was he who made maps along the route. He was so good at it that his maps would be used by other groups going on that same route. Perhaps Yuri K. believed that he could do even better.

Around 4 pm the group had lunch, then covered one more passage and, at about 5:30 pm, arrived at an encampment on the bank of the Lozva River.

That was their first night in the tent. They got busy setting up the stove and sewing a makeshift curtain from a bed-sheet. Zina set about mending holes in the tent. Soon they all sat down to dinner, lengthy conversations, mostly about love, and song-singing to Yuri K.'s mandolin. All that time, a conflict was building up between Igor and Zina.

"We settled down to sleep. Throughout the whole evening Igor was so rude, I couldn't recognize him. I had to sleep by the stove on top of the firewood", wrote Zina in her diary.

On the next day, January 29, the group continued skiing up the Lozva River. They had good weather, with a temperature of -13°C (8°F) and a light breeze, but experienced continuous ice-built on their skis. The plan was that they reach the mouth of the Auspiya River – the right tributary of the Lozva River – and then proceed westward towards the Ural Ridge, this time along the Auspiya River.

"We first went along the Lozva, then turned onto the Auspiya. Beautiful places", Zina wrote. The group was following a Mansi trail which began at the Auspiya River's confluence into the Lozva River, and then went towards the ridge along the Auspiya River. They spent the night not far from the ski track. Kolevatov and Tibo were on duty. Kolmogorova and Doroshenko were reminiscing about their past relationship. *"Yurka and I were chopping firewood, talking about the past. What a playboy!"*, Zina wrote in her diary.

Dubinina had a clash with Tibo: *"...they were arguing for a long time about who was to mend the tent. Finally, Kolya gave up and took up the needle. Lyuda remained sitting while we were all mending the holes. There were so many of them that there was enough work to keep everyone busy, except for the two on duty and Lyuda. This made the guys very angry."*

They then had to celebrate Doroshenko's birthday without Lyuda, who retired into the tent after dinner and wouldn't come out throughout the night. The birthday present, a tangerine, was divided only into eight pieces.

The next morning, on January 30, the temperature fell to -17°C (1°F). Nobody wanted to get up from bed. To quote from one of the diaries, *"The guys on duty (Sasha Kolevatov and Kolya Tibo again, as punishment for slowing down the group the day before) took their time starting the campfire. Last night we decided to get up and vacate the tent within eight minutes of the wakeup call. So we all woke up long ago, waiting for the signal. But there was none. At around 9:30 am, we slowly began to rise."* After breakfast, the group resumed their trek up the Auspiya River, their pace once again impeded by ice-built on the skis. They continued to move up the river bank, skiing along the Mansi trail and stopping to examine the Mansi signs on the trees and a recent encampment site.

At around 2 pm, the group paused for a modest lunch of smoked pork loin, a handful of croutons, sugar, garlic and coffee, all stocked up in the morning. There was a strong southwest wind accompanied by snow-fall. Then the trail came to an end: it was hard to move cross-country in snow up to 120 cm (4 feet) deep. After two more stretches, at around 5 pm the group decided to stop for the night. In the evening, the temperature fell to -26°C (-15°F), with a heavy west wind knocking snow down the cedar and the pines. Luckily, thanks to the deadwood and high fir-trees, they had everything necessary for an overnight stay: a blazing campfire and a tent on fir twigs.

On the morning of January 31, a new conflict erupted as Nikolay refused to stay on duty and Zina and Rustem, who had to take over, accidentally burnt Krivonischenko's mittens and sweatshirt. He went into a fit and started screaming and swearing at them, but the group still managed to start relatively early, at about 10 am. They were moving along the Mansi ski trail, which would frequently disappear, forcing them to feel their way forward.

Dyatlov wrote in the group's diary: *"Walking is especially hard today. We can't see the trail, have to grope our way through at times. Can't do more than 1.52 km (1 mile) per hour.*

Trying out new ways to clear the path. The first in line drops his backpack, skis forward for five minutes, comes back for a 10-15 minute break, then catches up with the group. That's one way to keep laying ski tracks non-stop. Hard on the second hiker though, who has to follow the new trail with full gear on his back."

Gradually, the group was moving away from the Auspiya River: *"We gradually leave the Auspiya valley, it's upwards all the way but goes rather smoothly. Thin birch grove replaces firs. The end of the forest is getting closer."* Judging by Zina's wording in her diary *"Today, we'll probably be building a storage"*, the group had discussed laying down a cache site before the radial ascent towards Mt. Otorten. That was not a spontaneous decision. During the planning stage of the route, Dyatlov had realized that a cache site in the upper reaches of the Auspiya River should make going to Otorten with lighter backpacks easier, and had discussed the idea with Sergey Sogrin. The site was intended to be above the forest line but, as it turned out, that was not to be: *"Wind is western, warm, piercing, with speed like the draft from airplanes at takeoff. Firn, open spaces. I can't even think of setting up storage here."*

By that time, it was already around 4 pm, and the group had no choice but to return to the valley of the Auspiya River. Dyatlov wrote down: *"We're exhausted, but start setting up for the night. Firewood is scarce, mostly damp firs. We build the campfire on the logs, too tired to dig a fire pit. Dinner's in the tent."*

We can only speculate about what happened next. By the evening of January 31, the group was slightly behind schedule: they were supposed to cross over into the valley of the Lozva River that day, but the elements forced them to stay in the valley of the Auspiya. Did they intend to make up for that lag and make changes to the trek route? Could it be they didn't see the situation as critical? Were they planning to get into higher gear or to continue at their usual pace?

The only thing we know is that on February 1, the group set off from the valley of the Auspiya River towards a pass which at that time had no name, but would later come to bear that of their group. They were not to write down anything further in their diaries, nor would they ever be heard from again.

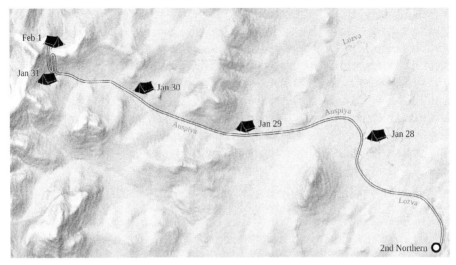

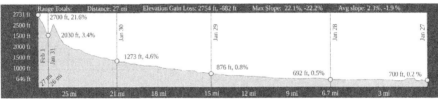

The diagram illustrates the traveled section of the route.

CHAPTER 5. FEBRUARY 11-26
1959. SVERDLOVSK.

On February 11, some of the UPI courses and departments have already started classes. The UPI hikers were returning from their treks. Yuri Blinov's group had returned with a two-day delay after the deadline. They had covered more than 200 km (124 miles), conquering the peaks of Molebniy Kamen (Prayer Stone), Martay, Beliy Kamen (White Stone), and Denezhkin Kamen (Money Stone). They had met with the Mansi in the headwaters of the Vizhay River and with a group of Moscovites traversing from the Perm Region towards the Denezhkin Kamen. The temperatures had dropped to -50°C (-58°F), but the hikers had overcome all hardships.

The next day, February 12, saw the return of the group of Boris Slobtsov, a third-year student of the UPI Department of Power Engineering. They had been to the South Urals, to the Taganay peaks 200 km (124 miles) from Sverdlovsk. February 12 was as well the deadline for the return of the Dyatlov group. Igor had not sent a telegram from Vizhay with a notification of the end of their trek, however, that didn't ring any alarm bells at the UPI sports club, nor at the city committee for physical culture and sports. Blinov assumed that given the actual situation along the route, a realistic date for the return of the Dyatlov group to Sverdlovsk might be February 15-16.

For some part of the UPI students, the winter vacations were only beginning. On February 13, a UPI group led by Evgeniy Chubarev set off by a night train from Sverdlovsk on a ski hike along the route of the city of Pokrovsk-Uralskiy – Mt. Olvinskiy Kamen – Mt. Konzhakovskiy Kamen – Kytlym settlement – the city of Karpinsk. They would return to Sverdlovsk only on February 27.

A few more days passed. Worried by the absence of his son, Vladimir Mihaylovich Slobodin, the father of Rustem Slobodin, Doctor of Agricultural Sciences, head of the department of the Ural Research Institute of Agriculture, telephoned the UPI sports club. He was told that the return of the Dyatlov group might be delayed until February 16. Most likely, such an answer was based on Blinov's assumptions.

On February 15, the UPI students Galina Radosteva, who was a member of the routing commission of the UPI sports club, and Igor Krivonischenko, the brother of Georgiy Krivonischenko, requested that the UPI labor union committee should send an official inquiry to the Vizhay settlement – the final destination of the Dyatlov group.

On February 16, alarmed by the lack of information about the Dyatlov group, Yuri Blinov and Lev Gordo, board chairman of the UPI sports club, initiated an inquiry. Blinov telephoned Valerian Ufimtsev, inspector of the city committee.

Valerian Mihaylovich Ufimtsev (44) was born in 1915 in the city of Krasnoturyinsk. In 1939 he graduated from the Perm physical culture training college. When he was drafted into the Red Army, he volunteered into the recently organized airborne forces and was sent to Khabarovsk, where he graduated from a Noncommissioned Officer school. After the Nazi attack on the Soviet Union, Ufimtsev was sent to a short-term officer school and was commissioned as a junior lieutenant. In 1942, his airborne brigade was shifted from Khabarovsk to the western front. He later fought in the formation of the 2nd Ukrainian Front in the rank of junior lieutenant. He was awarded the order of the Red Star and the 2nd degree order of the Patriotic War. At the end of 1943, he was seriously wounded and had both legs amputated. In 1946 Ufimtsev moved to Sverdlovsk, where he worked at the city committee for physical culture and sports (city committee).

It was ascertained that no telegram confirming the completion of the route had been received from the Dyatlov group. The UPI sports club requested a long-distance call with Vizhay. Late in the evening, they were put in touch with Zakiy Hakimov, the head of the Vizhay corrective labor camp branch, who reported that the Dyatlov group had not returned to Vizhay and that they had not planned to return before February 15.

On February 17 at Sverdlovsk, there was a mounting concern. Blinov telephoned Ufimtsev for the second time. Rimma Kolevatova, the sister of Aleksander Kolevatov, also called the City sports committee. There had not yet been any telegram from the group, however, Ufimtsev felt certain that there was nothing to worry about. Kolevatova was trying to reach Lev Gordo, but the latter was absent from his office. Later, Gordo would explain that at the time he was trying to arrange for the allocation of an aircraft for the group's search.

Lev Semyonovich Gordo (47) was born in 1912 in the Grodnenskoy Oblast, in 1938 he graduated from a 7-year secondary school in Sverdlovsk. Before the war of 1941-45 he managed to change several jobs in Sverdlovsk - as secretary of his factory's and later trust's Komsomol committee, then as head of the pioneer division at the Komsomol district committee; further as a commandant of an NKVD transit camp, as deputy director of the "Dynamo" society sports complex, as a senior inspector of the Ural Coal Works (Uralugol). In 1938 he was briefly imprisoned while under investigation. In 1941 Gordo was drafted into the Red Army, serving as a quartermaster in the engineering forces in the formations of the Leningrad, Volkhov, Bryansk, and the Baltic Fronts. He was awarded the "Red Star" order and the medals "For the Defense of Leningrad" and "For the Victory over Germany". After the war, he served as a senior inspector of the MVD Office of the military construction battalions in the city of Riga. In 1946 Gordo returned to Sverdlovsk, where for some time he worked as chief supply management officer at a vodka distillery. In 1947 he shifted to the position of senior laboratory assistant at the UPI, later worked as a technician mechanic, and from 1955 he served as board chairman of the UPI sports club.

Lev Gordo was very well connected, however, he had not managed to secure assistance from the "Burevestnik" sports association, which included student sports organizations. Next, Gordo tried to come to terms in person with the leadership of the 123rd flight detachment of the Ural Civil Aviation Office, which was based at the Uktus airport not far from Sverdlovsk.

On February 18, Gordo informed the UPI party committee of the situation with the missing group and asked to file a request for an air search with the 123rd flight detachment. Dyatlov's sister came to the party committee meeting with a request to begin the search. For some reason, the information was not brought to the attention of Nikolay Siunov, the Rector of the Institute. As a result, the application was most likely issued on behalf of the UPI sports club. The city committee telegraphed an official request to Vizhay. At the same time, Gordo was calling Vizhay again. He was informed that a group of locals was preparing for the search and that recently someone had seen a group of hikers. Probably that was the Dyatlov group and everything was OK with them. This gave Ufimtsev a reason to tell the parents of Dubinina, who by that time had managed to put through a call to the city committee, that there was no reason to fret.

The desperate relatives of the missing hikers had nothing left but to turn to the authorities for help. Aleksander Dubinin appealed to the Sverdlovsk regional committee of the CPSU to bring the situation to the attention of Afanasiy Eshtokin, the Secretary of the regional committee of the CPSU. Rimma Kolevatova called the city committee of the CPSU. Appeals to party authorities had provoked counter-moves by the authorities. It is possible that the professional standing of some of the parents of the missing hikers had something to do with it. Aleksander Dubinin was a senior engineer at the Office of the Timber Industry Sovnarhoz. His wife was the secretary of Nikolay Semihatov, the director of the Sverdlovsk Research Institute of Automatics, which was developing missile control systems. It appears that an appeal from Georgiy's (Yuri) father– Aleksey Krivonischenko – could have been the most efficient. He had the rank of Major General of the Engineering Corps, serving as the head of the Urals Power Construction Mechanization which was building the Beloyarsk Nuclear Power Plant. However, his career was not all roses: soon after the death of his son he would be laid off for mishandling his job, and in the spring of that same 1959 he would be transferred to the city of Pavlodar, Kazakh SSR, to serve as head of construction management office of the Yermakovskaya State Hydroelectric Power Plant. According to the reminiscences of the relatives, after his appeal, Krivonischenko was summoned to the Sverdlovsk regional or city party committee. After that, there were no more complaints or appeals.

Local party authorities opened an internal investigation, which was followed by telephone calls to the city committee and the UPI. Ufimtsev had to inform Boris Zhuravlyov, then an instructor of the Sverdlovsk regional committee of the CPSU, about the missing group. Ufimtsev would later say that he informed the regional committee on his initiative. NikolaySiunov, the UPI rector, was forced to give an account to E.P. Fedchenko, a representative of the Investigating Committee. Later, the bureaucratic machine transformed this into the following message: *"On February 19, the Institute turned to the local party and Soviet authorities with a request for assistance in the search for the missing students."*

Due to the attention to the situation on the part of the city and regional CPSU committees, the UPI was forced to start the search. Aleksander Kondratyev and Georgiy Ortyukov, the professors at the UPI reserve-officer training department, were called in to assist with the organization.

Aleksander Vasilyevich Kondratyev (58) was born in St. Petersburg in 1901. He was a career soldier from early 1918 when he volunteered into the Red Army. In 1919 and 1921, Aleksander graduated from the Petrograd cavalry school and the Frunze Military Academy in 1938. He took part in the Russian Civil War, the Great Patriotic War (1941-45), and the Soviet-Japanese War of August 9 – September 3, 1945. His combat record included deputy commander, commander of armored and mechanized forces in the formation of the Far Eastern Front. From 1946, he served in the Kubansky, North Caucasian, and later in the Baltic Military Districts. Kondratyev was awarded the orders of Lenin (1945), the Red Banner (1944, 1948), the Red Star (1944), and the Patriotic War (1945), 1st degree. In 1951, Kondratyev was promoted to Major General and appointed the head of the UPI reserve-officer training department.

Georgiy Semyonovich Ortyukov (45) was born in 1914 in the village of Maminskoye of the Pokrovskiy district of the Sverdlovsk Region. In 1936 he volunteered into the Red Army as a cadet at the Sverdlovsk infantry school, from which he graduated in 1939. Later that same year he volunteered for the Soviet-Finnish war, where he served as a commander of a ski battalion in the formation of the Karelian Front. After the Nazi attack on the Soviet Union, in October 1941 in the battle at Elnya (aka Yelnya Offensive), he was wounded in the heel with a dumdum (expanding) bullet. In 1942 he returned from the hospital to Sverdlovsk as a non-combatant officer and taught at a military infantry school. He was awarded two Orders of the Red Star (1944; 1951); the medals "For the Victory over Germany in the Great Patriotic War 1941-1945" (1945) and "For Military Merit" (1946). In 1948 Ortyukov was transferred to the staff of the Ural Military District. From 1950, he served as secretary of the Military Council of the Ural Military District. After his demobilization in 1956, in the fall of 1957, in the rank of a colonel, he was appointed head of the training unit of the UPI reserve officer training department, teaching tactics.

An agreement was reached with the 123rd flight detachment on detailing an aircraft and a helicopter for the search right at the Ivdel district. We cannot disregard the possibility of preliminary negotiations with Dmitriy Lelyushenko, a four-star General of the Army, then the commander of the Ural Military District, on assistance in conducting the search. The UPI Department of Radio Engineering collaborated with the Ural Military District in 1957-58 by taking part in the development of the new radio reconnaissance systems ("Eye" scientific research project), as well as the systems for creating aimed jamming systems ("Smoke" scientific research project).

Vladimir Aleksandrovich Pervago, the head of the Ural Geological Office, had given assurances of assistance in the search for the group from the Northern Geological Expedition based at Ivdel. Probably that was facilitated by the fact that the children of Pervago studied at the school where Rimma Kolevatova worked. Vladimir Pervago was transferred to Sverdlovsk in 1958, and before that, he had worked in the Far East and South Yakutia.

It was decided that the first search group would fly to Ivdel. The UPI sports club was in charge of the logistics. Gordo was responsible for the material support. Blinov, who had taken part in the preparation of the Dyatlov group trek, was to organize the ground search. Suddenly it turned out that the UPI sports club did not have the Dyatlov group route plan. Lev Milman, an instructor at the UPI and deputy board chairman of the sports club, turned to Nina Anisimova, Aleksander Kolevatov's sister, who worked as a radiologist at the UPI hospital. Nina and Rimma had no map, Aleksander had taken it along with him on the trek. At the sisters' request, Ryagin reconstructed the route from memory and mapped it out. Rimma Kolevatova handed the map in person to Colonel Ortyukov.

Meanwhile, Yudin returned to Sverdlovsk from his native village. He was welcomed and quickly barraged with questions, *"At last! Is everything OK with the group?" "Were you delayed along the route?"* At first, Yuri didn't understand the reason for all the questions. When it dawned on him that his comrades were missing, he fell into a state of shock. For the rest of his life, Yuri Yudin would treasure a small souvenir teddy bear, which Lyuda Dubinina had given him when they bid farewell at the 2nd Northern. Until his death in 2013, Yuri Yudin would be unable to give a coherent account of what happened with him in the first days upon his return to Sverdlovsk, except for a vague memory of his meeting with Andrey Kirilenko, the first secretary of the Sverdlovsk regional committee of the CPSU. *"Kirilenko had summoned me and Siunov, the Institute's Rector. The latter was all a-tremble while walking into his office ahead of me. Kirilenko came in and hugged me. He wanted to take a look at me. Why would he want to take a look at an obscure student?"*

On February 20, Vladimir Slobodin made another call to the UPI sports club, where he was told that a plane had been sent on a search for the missing group. Gordo and Blinov flew to Ivdel from Uktus in a Yak-12 of the 123rd flight detachment. Following the interference of the party authorities, the pilots could no longer question the mission. The aircraft was personally flown by Ivan Spitsyn and Georgiy Karpushin, the commander and senior navigator of the 123rd flight detachment.

At around 3 pm, there was a telephone call between Ufimtsev and Maslennikov, the chairman of the Region's Federation for Tourism and a member of the Routing Commission. They decided that the search should be organized by the UPI. It did not take much time for the sports officials to obtain approval from the authorities. The executive committee of the regional soviet was to be responsible for the general oversight. A telegraph notification of the disappearance of the group was sent to all the chairmen of the city, settlement, and village Soviets in the name of Vasiliy Alekseevich Pavlov, the deputy chairman of the Sverdlovsk regional executive committee. The UPI was officially made responsible for the search. Its Rectorate, party, labor union organizations, and sports club were involved. The search headquarters was organized. The UPI tourist section was urgently convening a meeting under the slogan "Dyatlov group emergency". Its participants included Boris Martyushev, the chairman of the tourist section, V.E. Slobodin, the chairman of the union committee, and Andrey Vishnevskiy, head of the Department of Physical Education.

> **Andrey Mihaylovich Vishnevskiy (52)** was born in 1907 in the village of Sychevskoe, Kurgan district of the Perm Governorate of the Russian Empire. After graduation in 1929 from the State Central Institute of Physical Culture, he was sent to Sverdlovsk as an instructor in physical culture at the regional committee of the Union of Soviet Commercial Employees. In 1932 he shifted to work at the Ural Specialized Construction Institute, which in 1934 was integrated into the Ural Industrial Institute, and in 1948 changed its name to the S.M. Kirov Ural Polytechnic Institute (UPI). From 1934 he served as head of its Department of Physical Education. During the war of 1941-45, he was appointed assistant to the chief for physical training of the Ural Military District. In 1945 he returned to the UPI department of physical education.

Soon they managed to organize around-the-clock telephone communication with Ivdel. They learned that Gordo and Blinov had landed safely, that the flight had taken three hours. Then Spitsyn and Karpushin got to studying the maps of the area, weather conditions, and information on the movement of the Dyatlov group. According to the most recent information, the group had taken a logging truck to the village of Burmantovo and then left, moving along the winter trail.

Local geologists promised to help with recruiting for the search local Mansi hunters, who were familiar with the terrain.

The organization of the first UPI search group began under the supervision of Andrey Vishnevskiy. The selection procedure was not quite clear. On the one hand, the senior students' winter recess had begun a month earlier than the one of the junior students: the former, starting in late January, ended in late February, when junior students were to go on vacation. From the materials of the UPI small newspaper, For Industrial Personnel, we know that the winter term exams for 5th year students had been over by mid-January, with the work on final papers to begin. 4th year students were to complete their examination term by late January. For the 1st, 2nd, and 3rd year students, the winter term examination period lasted from early to late February, with the winter recess of only a single week. The day before, on February 19, 3rd year students of the UPI Department of Radio Engineering had their last exam. Hence it was logical to expect volunteers from among junior students in the search group; however, that was not the case: there was a sufficient number of senior students in the search group, including some who had recently returned from the Blinov group trek. We cannot rule out that participation in the search brought some benefits, such as being granted academic leaves, leniency during pass-fail tests, exams, and final papers.

According to the recollections of Vladimir Lebedev, a participant in the search, he was supposed to lead a 2nd category of difficulty trek to Konzhakovskiy and Denezhkin Kamen. All equipment was ready, except for the skis and the tent, which he had to get from the Dyatlov group. As soon as it became known that Dyatlov group went missing, the inexperienced rookies were removed from the Lebedev group, and the rest became part of the first search group.

Vadim Brusnitsyn, who had taken part in the search, recalled that the labor union committee had to organize the first search group on short notice. Hence, the participants were recruited at random, and they virtually did not know each other. Boris Slobtsov was appointed the group's leader since he was the first to enlist into the search group. Brusnitsyn was the second to sign up. This partly explains why it was Slobtsov who was appointed the leader of the search group even though the group included more experienced hikers, for instance, Brusnitsyn, who had earlier led the groups, of which Slobtsov was a rank-and-file member. However, the most realistic explanation is different: Boris was the son of Efim Timofeevich Slobtsov, the head of the Non-Ferrous Metals Directorate under the Middle Urals Council of

People's Economy (Sovnarhoz). He was the kind of man to be entrusted with an assignment, which should be carried under the aegis of party authorities.

At the very last moment, the composition of the group changed somewhat. Yuri Koptelov replaced Valentin Yakimenko, a sophomore student, who was supposed to lead a group of 2nd and 3rd year students in a ski trek of the 1st category of difficulty along the Chusovaya River. It was decided not to cancel the trek, with Yakimenko removed from the Slobtsov search group. The Yakimenko group would start on February 23 to return to Sverdlovsk only on March 3.

From among the search group, Koptelov was acquainted only with Slobtsov and Brusnitsyn. He did not know the members of the Dyatlov group either.

The UPI amateur film studio "BOKS-film" suggested sending a two or three member film crew along with the search group, but they were denied.

At 11 am on February 21, the regional council of labor unions began to discuss the situation involved with the Dyatlov group. The meeting was chaired by Chevtaev, the secretary of the Sverdlovsk regional labor union council. Evgeniy Maslennikov was summoned to the meeting with the approval of Boris Chernavin, the director of the Verkh Isetskiy Metallurgical Plant, the being meeting continued until the evening.

Slobtsov's group was finally organized at the UPI, including the following: third-year students Boris Slobtsov from the Department of Power Engineering, Vadim Brusnitsyn from the Department of Metallurgy and Vladimir Lebedev, student of the Department of Physics and Technology, as well as 4th year students Mihail Sharavin from the Department of Metallurgy, Yuri Koptelov from the Department of Mechanical Engineering and Yaroslav Krotov from the Department of Radio Engineering. Less than a month ago, 5th year students Stanislav Devyatov, Vyacheslav Halizov from the Department of Radio Engineering, and Vladimir Strelnikov from the Department of Physics and Technology said goodbye to the Dyatlov group at Vizhay, with nothing foreshadowing a disaster.

Food was being bought and equipment was being assembled. The Sverdlovsk Military School received signal flare pistols for the search group. Ivdel reported that the air search on that day had not been productive, due to heavy winds and low visibility. Gordo, who was ill, did not take part in the air search. Yak-12 turned out to be inconvenient for the air search that is why an An-2 had already been called from

Sverdlovsk. In its turn, the UPI notified Ivdel that tomorrow, February 22, a search group led by Slobtsov would fly to Ivdel.

On February 22, around-the-clock search headquarters was launched under the UPI labor union committee. 3rd year students Galina Batalova and Galina Hamova, 4th year students Galina Radosteva and Kseniya Svechnikova were taking turns on phone duty. Their task included recording all conversations and telephone messages related to the search.

By the evening, news from Ivdel had arrived. The subsequent Yak-12 air search, when Blinov took over the place of the navigator, who had fallen sick, and the questioning of the Mansi people in the villages on the North Toshemka and in the upstream of the Vizhay River, where Gordo went by helicopter, had not produced any result.

The Slobtsov group, which took off from Uktus by An-2 at around 9 am, had safely landed at Ivdel. They had already been instructed to avoid contact with strangers; they would spend the night at the airport hotel.

On the morning of February 23, Maslennikov reported to Ufimtsev over the phone, but except for the information on the Slobtsov group's departure by plane, there was no further news. At 9:00 am a conference began at the UPI with Siunov, Vishnevskiy, Slobodin, and Fedor Zaostrovskiy, the Secretary of the UPI party committee, taking part.

> **Fyodor Petrovich Zaostrovskiy (39)** was born in 1920 in the Chelyabinsk region and completed his 4th year of the UPI Department of Chemistry at the time of the Nazi attack on the USSR. In June 1941, he was drafted into the Red Army and was sent to the Irbit Artillery School. After graduation, he was sent to the front as commander of an anti-tank field battery. He took part in the Battle of Kursk and reached Berlin in the rank of chief of staff of a mortar battalion. After the V-Day, he was left in service in Hungary. In 1946 he resumed his studies at the UPI, from which he graduated in 1947 as a chemical engineer. After graduation, Fyodor Petrovich briefly worked as a design engineer at the Ural Chemical Machine Building Works (Uralkhimmash) then shifted to the UPI in the same year, where he worked until 1960 as an instructor and then associate professor. In 1953-55, he was repeatedly elected chairman of the labor union local committee, and in 1955 he was elected chairman of the regional committee of the labor union of the Workers of Higher Education. As of 1959, he was the secretary of the UPI party committee.

A message came from Ivdel that Mansi hunters had discovered the hiker's campsite. A search team of geologists from the Northern Expedition moved to follow the track of the Dyatlov group. Three search groups of the Mansi hunters were sent along the Ural Ridge and to the vicinity of Mt. Oyko-Chakur and Mt. Otorten.

Maslennikov was summoned to a conference, which lasted until midnight. Information was received that the Slobtsov search group was dropped off in the vicinity of Mt. Otorten. It was decided to send a second UPI group to Ivdel to search in the vicinity of Mt. Oyko-Chakur. Oleg Grebennik, a 4th year student of the Department of Mechanical Engineering and an experienced mountaineer, was offered to lead that group. In 1958, Oleg traveled to Austria as a member of the Sverdlovsk mountaineering team and had the "USSR Mountaineer" badge received at the "Ullu-Tau" alpine camp in the Elbrus region.

According to the recollection of Grebennik, after his return from an expedition to Kazakhstan, he learned that the Dyatlov group had disappeared, and a search group had already been sent to follow its track. At the UPI sports club, Grebennik was asked to organize a group to track the final part of the Dyatlov group's route, from the Otorten back.

The members of the newly organized search group spent the night at the UPI labor union committee. Flying out was scheduled for the next day. Throughout the night, they were packing their equipment and food supplies. The UPI students helped to prepare food rations; one of those students was Kira Obodova, a 4th year student of the Department of Radio Engineering and the future wife of Oleg Grebennik. She was a member of the Blinov group, that had traveled together with the Dyatlov group to Vizhay.

Ortyukov was in charge of the travel arrangements. There was an orientation session for the members of the search group on the premises of the UPI labor union committee; Maslennikov took part in the orientation session and agreed to leave for Ivdel as a consultant at the request of the Institute.

On February 24, the Sogrin group returned to Sverdlovsk from an expedition in the Subpolar Urals. They had not managed to carry out all of their scheduled tasks. They were supposed to go through a 500 km circular route, including path-breaking winter ascents to the peaks of the Sablya, Neroyka, and Telpoz-Iz Mountains. However, several emergencies caused a change in their plans. In the very first days, their tent was burned down, hence the hikers had to spend the remaining nights in snow bivouacs. The many-day-long blizzard and the sickness of one of the hikers forced the group to go back along their contingency route. Nevertheless, theirs was the world's first winter ascent on both the Sablya and the Neroyka.

Around 11:00 am, the UPI second search group departed for Ivdel. It included Oleg Grebennik, Vladimir Shlyapin, Ivan Tatsienko, Vladimir Skachkov, Vladislav Kirsanov, and Victor Kostrulin. The group included experienced mountaineers and hunters. For instance, in 1957 Tatsienko met the standards for the "Mountaineer of the USSR" badge at the "Varzob" alpine camp, and next year he was elected chairman of the UPI mountaineering section. He was a participant in the first UPI Alpinists' academic competition, went through a training camp for junior mountaineering instructors at the "Dzhan-Tugan" alpine camp. Shlyapin was taught by his father about life in the taiga from early childhood. From the age of 14, he was hunting and going in for hiking and mountaineering.

The search party was joined by the UPI Deputy Rector Nikolay Fyodorovich Pletnev, as well as by Zaostrovskiy, Vishnevskiy, Maslennikov, and Ortyukov, who had already appeared in this story. There were 12 people on the plane in total.

Colonel Ortyukov was entrusted with coordinating the activities of civilian and military searchers and aviators, maintaining contact with the search groups, local and regional authorities, and the UPI administration. In the morning, before the departure from Sverdlovsk, Ortyukov had already met with the Military District's Air Force Commander, Lieutenant General of Aviation David Slobozhan, arranging the allocation of one aircraft and two helicopters for reconnaissance by the Ural Military District.

The transportation of the UPI search party to the Uktus airfield was provided by the Institute. Stanislav Tipikin, at the time a 5th year student of the Department of Physics and Technology, would later recall that, in general, the organization of the departure was not ideal. An experienced hiker, who had previously been elected chairman of the bureau of the UPI mountaineering club, Tipikin was part of the Grebennik search group, but couldn't fly out on that day due to the aircraft overload. His equipment, including his rifle, flew away to Ivdel, loaded along with other luggage. The UPI sports club would return his rifle in a broken condition after a month and a half; they would not be able to find the cartridges and his other belongings altogether. Tipikin would be able to fly away to join the search only the following day.

We cannot rule out that Yuri Yarovoy, a newspaperman, head of the department of the "Na smenu!" ("On duty!") daily, the official publication of the Sverdlovsk regional committee of the Komsomol flew as number twelve together with the UPI representatives. He might have been dispatched to supervise the progress of the search. Likely that was the reason why there was no seat for Tipikin. It was customary for the Komsomol to send an internal informant to observe and document operations like this. According to existing recollections, following his return from the search operation, Yarovoy gave an account of the details of the search to the regional Komsomol and party committees.

> **Yuri Evgenievich Kosobryuhov (27)** was born in 1932 in the Far Eastern Region. In 1937 his family moved to Aktiubinsk to join his paternal grandparents. It was there that Yuri graduated from high school in 1950. By that time, for his age, he had an imposing life experience. In 1946, while still a school student, Yuri graduated from instruction courses of geologists-collectors under the "Gold Exploration" geological office. Next, in 1949, he graduated from flight radio operators training courses. In 1946 he managed to work as a junior geologist at the "Southern Ural Gold Exploration" searching party, and in 1949 to gain experience in the Photostating Design Workshop. In 1953, during his summer vacations, he worked as a senior collector with the Special Geologic Team at the "Kazgosstroyproekt" (Kazakh State Construction Project) Research Institute (city of Aktyubinsk.) In 1950 he was admitted to the Power Engineering Department of the M.I. Kalinin Leningrad Polytechnic Institute, from which he graduated in 1956, and was assigned to work at the Sverdlovsk plant №91 of the Ministry of Transport Engineering. In 1955, he married Zoya Yarovaya, a student of the Moscow S. Ordzhonikidze Aviation Institute, and changed his last name to that of his wife, thus becoming Yarovoy. While still a student, he was elected as a labor organizer, secretary of the Komsomol committee, group elder, member of the department's student council. In Sverdlovsk, he was pretty quickly elected secretary of the factory Komsomol committee. In 1959, Yarovoy held the office of the head of his newspaper's (Na smenu!) department covering Komsomol activities. Soon after the search campaign was completed, his first short novel, "Down the Volga River", would be published in his paper. In that same year of 1959, Yuri Yarovoy would join the communist party.

On the morning of February 25, one Moisey Akselrod showed up at the UPI labor union committee. Akselrod was a 1956 graduate of the Department of Metallurgy, who at the time was working as a senior foreman at the Ural Hydraulic Machine Plant. He had known Igor Dyatlov for a long time; they went together on 3rd category hiking trips –to the Eastern Sayan Mountains in the summer of 1956 and to the Subpolar Urals in the winter of 1958. Back on February 22, Akselrod learned about the disappearance of the group from Georgiy Chigvintsev, who lived in the same UPI dorm as Dyatlov. In the evening the day before, February 24, he talked to Raissa Rubel, an instructor at the Sverdlovsk Pedagogic Institute, who was well known at Sverdlovsk as a mountaineer. She told him about the departure of Maslennikov for Ivdel. Akselrod was eager to join the search. V.E. Slobodin, chairman of the labor union committee of the city party committee, at first refused. Milman had to turn to Pyotr Repyev, the head of the Sverdlovsk regional committee for physical culture and sports.

Pyotr Aleksandrovich Repyev (45) was born in Sverdlovsk in 1914. Before the Nazi attack on the Soviet Union, he was the first secretary of the Komsomol organization at the Uralmash plant. In the war of 1941-45, he fought with the Ural Tank Corps. At the end of the war, Pyotr Aleksandrovich was an assistant to the chief of the division political department. For courage and heroism, he was awarded the Red Star and the Patriotic War orders. After the war's end, he returned to Sverdlovsk, where he was invited to head the Sverdlovsk city committee for physical culture and sports. In 1958 Sverdlovsk lost its "republican city" status to become a regional city. Consequently, Repyev became the head of the committee for physical culture and sports of the Sverdlovsk region.

On obtaining Repyev's approval, Milman arranged with the city committee for physical culture and sports to detail Moisey to join the search and rescue operation. Akselrod flew out to join the search together with the UPI students Sogrin, Tipikin, Chigvintsev, and Boris Yaburov, who was much older than his comrades and had combat experience as a front-line radio operator.

On the way, there was to be an intermediate landing in the city of Artemovskiy to pick up two radio stations. However, it turned out that there was none at the factory warehouse. It had taken time-consuming clearances to obtain two radios weighing together around 200 kg (441 lbs) with fixed frequencies from a local military installation. Unfortunately, the frequencies were different and therefore not compatible.

In the afternoon, a phone rang at the Sverdlovsk regional committee. The caller was one Vladislav Karelin, the UPI 1956 graduate, at the time a junior research associate at the Sverdlovsk All-Russian Research Institute of Metallurgic Heat Engineering and deputy chairman of the Sverdlovsk city tourist club. A hiking group he led had just reached the city of Serov, following the route of Ivdel – Vizhay – inflow of the NorthToshemka River – District 83 –Toshemka River – the city of Chistop – Toshemka River – Vizhay River – Mt. Oyko-Chakur – Peak Molebniy – Vels River – Churola River – Kutim River – Solva settlement – Mt. Denezhkin Kamen – Pokrovsk-Uralskiy.

The group included Georgiy Atmanaki, a workshop foreman at the Pervouralsk New Pipe Plant, Viktor Granin, a resident of the village of Gari in the Sverdlovsk Region, Oleg Goryachko, an employee of the Sverdlovsk Mining Institute, Boris Borisov, a student of the Geological Survey Department of the Siberian State University, as well as the students of the Sverdlovsk Pedagogical Institute Vladimir Skutin, Evgeny Serdityh, and Vladimir Shevkunov.

There were compulsive changes in their route due to the failures in transport communications, and failures in climbing the peaks of Chistop and Denezhkin Kamen due to nasty weather. They met with the Mansi Bahtiyarovs on the North Toshemka River and ascended the peaks of Oyko-Chakur and Molebniy Kamen. On February 17, the hikers observed a strange celestial spectacle.

The groups of Karelin and Dyatlov had a common point in their routes - the top of Oyko-Chakur, however, on February 16, while climbing it, Karelin did not find any traces of the Dyatlov group. True, that on February 18, Igor's note was discovered at the top of the Molebniy Kamen. But that note was left behind by Dyatlov in February of 1957 when he led a group of the UPI students along the route of the 2nd category of difficulty. When on February 13 they had tea at Bahtiyarov's yurts, the Mansi men had some vague conversations about a certain group that was wandering for a long time and had returned to where they came from. What kind of group was it? Had they been lost? Had they died? They couldn't get any sensible response.

Finally, the Karelin group found itself at Serov, where they were to make a transfer to Sverdlovsk. At the canteen, where the hikers had dinner while waiting for the train to Sverdlovsk, they were approached by a man, who introduced himself as a geologist from the Northern Geological Party. He asked if they were the hikers everybody was looking for? He said that a search for a lost group of Sverdlovsk hikers was underway in the north of the region – they were even using aviation. He also said that the search headquarters was at Ivdel.

Vyacheslav, the elder brother of Evgeniy Serdityh, who was also a student of the Sverdlovsk Pedagogical Institute, was expected to return from a trek in that same area around the 10th of February. Was his group the one that was missing? True, on February 9 they heard from some residents at Vizhay that the group of the Pedagogical Institute had returned one of those days. But what if it was a mistake?

At the station, they simultaneously ordered operator-assisted telephone calls to Sverdlovsk and Ivdel. There was no communication with Ivdel. From Sverdlovsk, they heard from Orlova, an instructor at the City committee for physical culture and sports, and the head of its Mountaineering Section, that it was the Dyatlov group that was missing. The deadline for their return had expired nearly two weeks ago. The situation was not yet clear. However, her voice did not betray any particular alarm.

From all appearances, the Sverdlovsk officials were planning to intensify the search operations. One more group, led by Evgeniy Artsis, chairman of the routing commission of the Moscow tourist club, which was returning to Moscow via Sverdlovsk from a trek along the Subpolar Urals, was instructed to prepare for the search for the Dyatlov group. However, the Muscovites went home before long, since they were told that the search operation had been terminated.

In the evening of February 26, the search headquarters at the UPI labor union committee received a radiogram: *"Found the tent. There are no people."* The relatives of the missing hikers did not yet know about that latest development, hence at midnight, a telegram was sent to Moscow, for Nikita Khrushchev, the First Secretary of the Central Committee of the CPSU, in person:

"Dear Nikita Sergeevich,

By the deadline of February 9, a group of hikers from the Sverdlovsk Polytechnic Institute had not returned from their trek in the Northern Urals. The search operations began very late, only after 10 days had passed. The regional organizations have not yet taken any efficient measures. We are earnestly asking for your assistance in the urgent search for our children. Every hour counts now."

The telegram was sent by Nina Sergeevna Anisimova, who had earlier appeared in this account as one of the four sisters of Aleksander Kolevatov. It is possible that the idea to appeal to the supreme authorities was suggested by her husband, Nikolay Anatolievich Anisimov, the UPI 1940 graduate and senior design engineer at the Uralmash plant. He had taken part in the development and organization of mass production of field, tank, and self-propelled guns and was repeatedly awarded by the government.

In the morning of February 27, the telegram would be registered at the executive office of the Central Committee of the CPSU.

CHAPTER 6. FEBRUARY 11-26, 1959. IVDEL.

The Ivdel leadership was always actively supporting the sports life of the city. Its best athletes had just returned from the Sverdlovsk Region individual skiing competition, which took place on February 7-8 in the Uktus Mountains near Sverdlovsk, with over one hundred skiers of the region as participants. Less experienced skiers had their own agenda. On February 14, five Ivdel Komsomol members led by Vladimir Parshakov, who was a functionary of the Komsomol city committee, went on a propaganda ski trek, dedicated to the elections to the Supreme Soviet of the RSFSR and to the local soviets councils of working people's deputies along the route of Yekaterininka – Lyavdinka – Lachi – Mityaevo – Ponil – Arya.

Besides local skiers, hiking groups from different cities were passing daily through the settlements around Ivdel. A couple of days earlier, another hiking group from Sverdlovsk consulted with the Vizhay forestry concerning their route. That latter group looked comprised of more mature people – engineers and professors. The hikers in a group that had passed right before them were quite young. The students from Sverdlovsk and Rostov had gone to the northern part of the area. One hiker had already returned, unable to endure the trek. His comrades were likely two or three days behind the schedule due to the unfavorable weather conditions. Lest them from freezing down. Just a very short while ago, a frost-bitten group of Sverdlovsk students was evacuated to Ivdel from District 41. By the end of the day, it seemed that everything had worked out: at the time they were likely on the way home.

Late at night on February 16, the switchboard of the Vizhay labor correction camp received a telephone call from Sverdlovsk. One of the UPI hiking groups had not returned home. It was led by Dyatlov. They were to return on February 12. Zakiy Hakimov, head of the camp division, replied that the Dyatlov group had not reached Vizhay and had said that they will return no earlier than the 15th.

Zakiy Gasimovich Hakimov (36) was born in 1923 in the village of Aminovo, Chelyabinsk region. He graduated from a 7-year secondary school. In 1942 he was drafted into the Red Army and fought in the formations of the Voronezh, South-Western, and 3rd Ukrainian Fronts in the rank of a private 1st class. In 1944, he was awarded the "For Courage" medal. After demobilization, he returned to the Urals. From 1953 he served as a case officer of the 13th division of the Ivdel corrective labor camp (Ivdellag, known at the time as N-240) in the rank of second lieutenant. In 1956, he was elected member of the Ivdel city committee of the CPSU. From 1957, Hakimov held the office of the chief of the N-240 8th camp division.

The night of February 16-17 was marked by long polar lights in the north-east of Ivdel, which lasted from 11 pm to 5:30 am. Something strange was observed a little later. *"At 6:50 am on February 17 an unusual phenomenon appeared in the sky. A star with a tail was moving across the sky. Its tail had the shape of a dense cirrus cloud. Then the star got rid of its tail, growing brighter than other stars, and took wings. It was gradually expanding visually, turning into a large ball shrouded in smoke. Then a star flamed up inside that ball which first transformed into a crescent moon, then into a smaller ball, which was not as bright as the first one. The big ball was gradually fading, reducing to a blurred spot, which completely vanished at 7:05 am. The star was moving from south to north-east."* according to the report of Valentina Piguzova, head of the Ivdel Meteorological Station, and Natalya Tokareva, a meteorologist. Similar phenomena were observed throughout the Sverdlovsk region: they were seen by the Karelin group at 6:30 am from the Oyko-Chakur region; at 6:40 am by the personnel of the military unit 6602 in the city of Ivdel; from 6:50 am to 7:00 am, in the eastern part of the sky in the city of Turinsk; at 6:55 am from the Vysokogorskiy mine area; in the interval between 6:00 and 7:00 am in the Novolyalinskiy district; around 7:00 am in the village of Verkhoturye; at 7:10 am in the settlement of Polunochnoe; at 8:00 am by the Chubarev group from the area of the Yelovaya Greva ridge to the southeast of the city of Pokrovsk-Uralskiy.

The description of the unusual celestial phenomenon hit the newspapers, *"Yesterday, at 6:55 am local time, a luminous ball with the size of the Moon's visual diameter appeared in the east-southeast at an altitude of 20 degrees from the horizon. The ball was moving in the north-eastern direction. At about 7:00 am there was a flash inside the ball with its core getting very bright. The ball shining was intensifying, with a luminous cloud appearing beside it, extending in the southern direction. The cloud spread into the entire eastern part of the sky. Soon after, there was a second blaze, in the shape of the moon crescent. The moon-like object was gradually growing in size, with a luminous dot remaining in its center (the glow's size varied.) The ball was moving in the direction of the east-north-east. It reached its highest angle of elevation – 30 degrees – at around 7:05 am. While continuing its movement, the unusual phenomenon was getting weaker and was blurring."* The sighting was explained in different ways – as something like a passing satellite or a flying bolide. Many residents of Ivdel would later recall that in early February they saw something similar, to the north of Ivdel, in the sky over the Ural ridge.

On February 18, at Vizhay they received a telephone message from the city committee for physical culture and sports regarding the missing group from Sverdlovsk. That was immediately followed by a call from the UPI sports club. To comfort the people of Sverdlovsk, at Vizhay they promised to organize a group from among the local population to search for the students. It was unlikely that something serious had happened. They had already ascertained that a week earlier a group of hikers spent one night at the Bahtiyarovs at the Northern Toshemka. That must be the group in question. There was nothing unusual in not meeting the deadline: the taiga in winter is a dangerous place even for much more experienced people than the tourists from the city. Just a very short while ago, a group of geologists from the Northern geologic exploration party №7 of the Bazhenovskiy's expedition got lost. They were ultimately discovered by the pilots of the 123rd flight detachment in the vicinity of the settlements of Vershyna and Pelym, near the mouth of the Atymya River – the left tributary of the Pelym River.

In Sverdlovsk, they were reevaluating the seriousness of the situation. On February 20, representatives of the UPI arrived at Ivdel to organize the search. Abram Sulman, the head of the Northern geological exploration expedition, had already received an instruction from Vladimir Pervago to provide all-round support to the people of Sverdlovsk.

> **Abram Markovich Sulman (55)** was born in 1904 in the Vitebsk Governorate of the Russian Empire into a large poor Jewish family. In 1926 he was drafted into the Red Army; after discharge from which he graduated from a one-year course at the Moscow Institute of Applied Mineralogy with the qualification of a drilling foreman. Sulman's geological career began in 1930: he worked as a senior drilling foreman, engineering manager, head of exploration parties, department head, and a manager of a trust. He was awarded two orders of the "Red Banner of Labor", and medals "For Labor Valor" and "For Valiant Labor in the Great

Patriotic War 1941-1945". In 1952, he was awarded the Stalin Prize, 2nd degree, for his participation in the discovery and exploration of the Kushmurunskiy brown coal deposit. In 1958, Abram Markovich was appointed head of the Serovskaya, and a little later – of the Northern geological exploration expedition of the Ural Geological Department.

Sulman even managed to call his son Leonard, a metallurgical engineer who lived in Sverdlovsk, asking him to contact the UPI to clarify the details about the missing group. But Leonard Sulman could not find any reliable information.

By that time, Aleksander Deryagin, the chairman of the executive committee of the Ivdel city council, had received a telegraphic message from the deputy chairman of the Sverdlovsk regional executive committee about the disappearance of the group.

Aleksander Petrovich Deryagin joined the VCP(b) in 1931 and soon became its local functionary. He worked as head of a propaganda room aka "red corner", as agitator aka agitprop and the party promoted him to the head of a goldmine. In early 1940 he was appointed the first secretary of the Ivdel district party committee. In 1944, Deryagin was detailed to Moldavia to restore its war-torn economy. Following his return to the Urals, Deryagin became the chairman of the executive committee of the Ivdel city council.

Deryagin was fully aware that such a telegram could mean only one thing: the search for the group would be conducted under the control of the regional authorities.

As luck would have it, the day before, on February 19, a group of inmates escaped from the 2nd camp outpost of the 6th division of the Ivdel corrective labor camp (Ivdellag) at the Shipichnoe settlement. It would, therefore, be unlikely for the people at Sverdlovsk to obtain approval by Vitaliy Ivanov, the head of the Ivdellag administration, for detailing his soldiers for their search needs.

Vitaliy Alekseevich Ivanov was transferred to Ivdel in 1956, in the rank of the MVD captain. Previously he had served as the head of the Tagil corrective labor camp (Tagillag). In 1958 Ivanov was promoted to lieutenant colonel of the domestic service, and would not risk his career.

The escape was made by dangerous criminals: Sultan Gamzabhanovich Madzhigatov, born in 1938, was sentenced to 12 years; Vasiliy Georgievich Ivanov, born in 1933, serving 25 years, and Yuri

Yakovlevich Nadvornyi, born in 1931, sentenced to 6 years. They had managed to escape through the cordon due to the poor organization of the security service. The camp administration, which was to be on alert, had not received any information on the planned escape from its informers among inmates. The preliminary investigation was poorly organized, with the head of the camp guard taken aback. The pursuit began only with a four-hour delay. At that moment all N-240 resources were mobilized for recapturing the fugitives – with a shortage of manpower to start with. Not only was the security personnel undermanned with a shortage of around a hundred men, but its best-trained guards had gone to Nizhne-Isetsk for the All-Union ski championship, organized by the "Dynamo" sports association. That was an important event, with the combined teams of the main directorates and divisions of the MVD and the KGB taking part - with nine teams totaling 287 athletes. The championship organizing committee was chaired by Major General Mihail Shishkarev, the head of the MVD Department for the Sverdlovsk Region. The chief referee was Major General Vasiliy Abyzov, the head of the Ural District Office of Military Procurement of the MVD of the USSR. The championship would last from February 19 to February 24.

Sulman offered to organize a search group with the participation of the local Mansi hunters. Negotiations with the Mansi hunters began at the Suevatpaul settlement and would drag out until February 23.

Meanwhile, the pilots of the 123rd flying detachment were scrutinizing the maps of the area and weather conditions to prepare themselves for the next day's overflight of the group's route. According to the most recent questioning of residents, the hikers had been taken by a timber truck to the Burmantovo settlement, 70 km (44 miles) north of Ivdel, from where on January 28 they started along a winter trail.

On February 21, Vasiliy Ivanovich Tempalov, the prosecutor of Ivdel, learned from Ivan Prodanov, the 1st secretary of the Ivdel party city committee, about the search for the missing group from the UPI.

Ivan Stepanovich Prodanov (53) was born in 1906 in the Saratov Governorate of the Russian Empire into a peasant family. From the age of 14, he worked as a shepherd for hire. From 1924 he served as chairman of the village committee of peasant mutual assistance, then as secretary of a Komsomol cell. In 1928 he was drafted into the army, where he served with a separate horse-artillery division in the Novgorod district and joined the VCP(b). After demobilization, he moved to Sverdlovsk, where he graduated from the Ural Forestry Institute in 1936. Then he worked as an engineering manager of a logging works outpost, later as head of the production units of various divisions of the Eastern Urals Camp (VostUralLag) of the Gulag NKVD. From 1942 he became a party functionary, working as a secretary for industry and secretary of the district committee of the VCP(b) in the cities of Turinsk and Novaya Lyalya. In 1952 Prodanov became the First Secretary of the Ivdel city committee of the CPSU.

Vasiliy Ivanovich Tempalov (38) was born in 1921 in a factory settlement of Nizhnaya Salda, in the Ural Governorate of the RSFSR in a large family of employees of the Verkhnaya Salda metallurgic plant. He graduated from ten-year secondary school in 1940 and was admitted into a military officer school. Tempalov fought in World War II from 1942, taking part in its key battles at the eastern front, beginning with the Battle of Stalingrad, where he served as commander of a 120-mm mortar battery. In 1943 he fought in the Battle of Kursk as commander of a heavy mortar battery. In 1944 he took part in the forced crossing of the Dnieper River, which was followed by the battles to liberate Polish cities; followed by a forced crossing of the Order River and the Battle of Berlin. He was among the force, which took the Reichstag building in Berlin. Tempalov finished the war in the rank of Sr. Lieutenant of Guards, and was awarded the orders of the Red Banner and the Patriotic War, 2nd degree, the medals "For the liberation of Warsaw", "For the conquest of Berlin", and "For the victory over Germany in the Great Patriotic War of 1941-1945". After the end of WWII, he was appointed a commandant of a small German town, got married, with a daughter born in 1947. After demobilization in 1948, he returned to the Urals and embarked on a law career, working as an assistant prosecutor of Verkhnyaya Salda, Sverdlovsk region. At the same time, he studied as an off-campus student of the Department of Jurisprudence of the Sverdlovsk Law Institute, from which he graduated in 1953. After graduation, he was appointed as the prosecutor of the city of Ivdel. As of 1959, Tempalov had a civil service rank of a Junior Counselor of Justice.

The Yak-12, piloted by Spitsyn and Karpushin, made an overflight along the route of Ivdel – Vizhay – the Lozva River – District 41 – 2nd Northern – up the Auspiya River – 2nd Northern – District 41 – the North Toshemka River – the Ural Ridge – Ivdel. An attempt to fly over to the western slope had failed. The bad-weather air search in high winds and undercast had failed. The participants in the air search included Blinov and Mihail Dryahlyh, the acting engineer of the Power Forest Combine (Energolesokombinat), who met with the Dyatlov group at the logging settlement of District 41 on January 26-27.

> **Mihail Timofeevich Dryahlyh (57)** was born in 1902 in Vyatskaya Governorate of the Russian Empire (as of 1959, Udmurtskaya ASSR; after 1991, Republic of Udmurtia.) Before he was drafted into the Red Army in 1941, he worked as head of the Ivdel district forestry enterprise. He took part in the liberation of Poland and Silesia as an artilleryman and gun commander. He was awarded the order of the "Red Star", "Glory" 3rd degree, and the medal "For Courage". Dryahlyh ended the war in the rank of Guards staff sergeant. After demobilization, he returned to his former job as director of a forestry enterprise. Later he was shifted to the Power Forest Combine.

Gordo had fallen ill and did not go on the search that day. The Yak-12 turned to be unsuitable for the task so that an An-2 was called in from Sverdlovsk as a substitute.

There was as well some positive news. A notification was received from the UPI that a search group led by Slobtsov would arrive at Ivdel the next day, February 22. On its part, the Ivdellag administration reported that all three prisoners who escaped on February 19 from the Shipichnoe settlement had just been captured by a special force. This meant that the searchers would not have to be concerned about dangerous criminals roaming the woods. And, perhaps, additional forces would be detailed to join in the search for the hikers.

On February 22 air search continued. The Yak-12 overflight, in which Blinov took the place of a sick navigator, was uneventful. Dryahlyh, Gordo, and Aleksander Ivanovich Kuznetsov, a ranger at the Vizhay forestry, flew off by helicopter to the yurt of Aleksander Prokopyevich Anyamov at the Northern Toshemka River and the yurt of Bahtiyarov up the Vizhay River. Aleksander Anyamov had not met any hiking groups. The Bahtiyarov men were absent since that night they had gone by reindeer to hunt for meat. The track of the Mansi reindeer-drawn sled was observed from the air in one and a half kilometer to the west from the yurts. Ekaterina Bahtiyarova said that a hiking group stopped for tea at their place more than 2 weeks earlier, but did not stay for the night. It looked likely that she was talking about the Blinov group. No traces of hikers were discovered from the air.

In the middle of the day, An-2 brought the UPI search group to Ivdel from Uktus. The group spent the afternoon at Ivdel preparing for the next day's search. They stayed overnight at the airport hotel.

On February 23 Gennadiy Grigoriev, a staff correspondent of the regional newspaper, The Ural Worker, arrived at Ivdel from Krasnoturinsk to collect materials on the work of the 1st Northern Mine and the Hydrolysis Plant. Upon arrival, he learned about the missing group of hikers and the ongoing search – and could not stay on the sidelines.

> **Gennadiy Konstantinovich Grigoriev (36)** was born in 1923 in an urban type settlement of Atig, from 1924, part of the Nizhneserginskiy district. In 1933 he moved with his parents to the city of Revda. After graduating from school in 1941, he was drafted into the army. Grigoriev served as a private with a separate ski battalion, took part in the Battle of Moscow, which defeated the Nazis at the approaches to the city. However, in 1942 he was heavily wounded and demobilized as a disabled serviceman. Grigoriev was awarded the order of the "Patriotic War" 1st degree and the medal "For Courage". From 1944, he worked at a regional newspaper in Nizhniye Sergy, later at a regional newspaper in Krasnoturyinsk. In 1948, he graduated from the Sverdlovsk party school and in 1957 from the Higher party school under the Central Committee of the CPSU in Moscow.

From 8:30 am to 1:00 pm under conditions of heavy overcast, an air search by An-2 was conducted along the route of Ivdel – Chistop – the western slope of the Ural Ridge – Oyka Chakur – Ivdel. The crew included the pilots of the 123rd flying detachment – Pyotr Gladyrev, Gennadiy Patrushev, and Georgiy Karpushin, with whom we have already met.

> **Pyotr Vasilyevich Gladyrev (37)** was born in 1922 in the Saratov Governorate. After graduating from the Vasilkovskiy military aeronautical technical school, during the war of 1941-45, he fought with the 184th separate Lomzhinskiy Red Banner air regiment in the rank of lieutenant. For his war efforts, he was awarded the orders of the "Red Star", "Patriotic War" 2nd degree, and war medals. In 1946 he met his future wife, who was a nurse at a hospital. After his demobilization in 1948, Gladyrev served as a third class pilot with the Airborne Expedition of the Ural Geological Directorate of the Ministry of Geology, which in 1952 was transferred under the Ural Directorate of Civil Aviation. In 1952 Gladyrev was appointed aircraft commander of the airborne acquisition wing, and in 1953 he was promoted to

a special rank of senior lieutenant of civil aviation. In 1955, he was shifted to the 123rd flight detachment of the Ural Territorial Administration of Civil Aviation, then based at Uktus, to the position of an aircraft captain. He piloted many types of aircraft, while constantly training to improve his skills. When in 1958 his flight detachment received the first helicopters, Gladyrev went through transition training to fly a helicopter. In less than a month after that flight, on March 13, 1959, he would be confirmed as commander of the Mi-4 helicopter.

Gennadiy Vasilyevich Patrushev (26) was born in 1933 in the village of Patrushi of the Sysertskiy district of the Sverdlovsk region. After graduating from the Sverdlovsk Air Force Special School and then from a one-year flying school of primary training, Patrushev was transferred to the Naval reserve (for the reason of reduction of force) while a 3rd year student of the Nikolaev Naval Mine-Torpedo Aviation School in the rank of lieutenant. That was the end of his military career. In 1957, Gennadiy graduated from the Sasov flying school of Civil Aviation with the professional qualification of a 4th class pilot of Civil Aviation. He returned to the Urals and was enlisted as a pilot of the 2nd air squadron of general purpose aviation (small aircraft) of the 123rd flight detachment. He frequently went on long-time missions into remote areas of the Sverdlovsk region. He had been working at Ivdel at least from August 1958, fighting forest fires and helping with afforestation.

Gordo and Blinov were onboard as observers. The total flight time was 4 hrs 25 min. No traces of the group had been discovered. In addition, the search was significantly complicated by numerous deer and elk tracks.

In the afternoon, Vladimir Pustobaev, the commander of the Mi-4 helicopter of the 123rd flying detachment, made two flights with Slobtsov's group to peak Pumsalnel (1023 m), which is on the eastern spur of Mt. Otorten. Local mountain guides Ivan Pashin, a forester of the Vizhay forest division, and Aleksey Cheglakov, head of a separate paramilitary fire department of the Vizhay corrective labor camp division, were sent along with the students. Both were residents of the Vizhay settlement and both lived in the village of Vizhay.

Ivan Fokeevich Pashin (51) was born in 1908 in the Perm Governorate of the Russian Empire. From 1936, he resided in the 2nd Northern, where he was working as a forester and washing gold. For some reason, he was not drafted into the army. From 1942 he worked as a foreman at the "Severniy Mayak" ("Northern Lighthouse") collective farm, where he was continuously elected deputy of the Ivdel village council. Pashin moved to Vizhay after 1951.

Aleksey Semyonovich Cheglakov (35) was born in 1924 in the Kursk Governorate. He served at the Ivdellag at least from 1953, in the rank of MVD junior technical lieutenant. Later, he served as an assistant to the head of a detached militarized fire brigade of the Vizhay forest division; rising to the position of its chief by 1959.

The search group totaled 11 men. Blinov would later recall that the group's assignment was to explore the peak of the Otorten – the northernmost final waypoint in the route of the Dyatlov group. Even though the search party had managed to obtain a 1:100 000 scale map, they, unfortunately confused the peaks. The first team had managed to inspect height 1023 (Pumsalnel) without discovering any traces of the missing hikers and to set up a camp there. About two hours later the second team of the search group arrived. It was already getting dark and they decided to continue the next day.

Meanwhile, at Suevatpaul, negotiations with the Mansi men were coming to an end. They would go on a search together with a radio operator from the Northern expedition, who would be taken with his radio along the ski track allegedly left by the Dyatlov group. Ski tracks and traces of a campsite had been discovered by the Mansi hunters a few days earlier, in 90 km west of Suevatpaul, in the direction towards the Ural Ridge. *"The Mansi have agreed to join the search. Their daily rate for 4 people is 500 rubles,"* reads a radio-telegram sent to Sulman. Egor Nevolin – a radio operator at one of the points of radiotelephone service of the Northern Geological Prospect Surveying Expedition – departed by car along the winter road from Ivdel to Suevatpaul.

At Ivdel, the morning of February 24 began with an air search overflight, which had already become routine. At 11:40 am Vasiliy Titov, the chief mechanic of the Northern Expedition, flew off by Yak-12. On that day there were a few flights, with 5 hours 45 minutes total airborne. The search was carried out in the area of Mt. Otorten, along the Auspiya and Purma rivers. The area behind the Ural Ridge was as well inspected. They were searching in the vicinity of the 2nd Northern settlement and the Toshemka River. Ski tracks were discovered at the Auspiya River, which first went on the river ice, then along its northern bank, in the direction of the mountain ridge. The track was old, in many places snowed up. They also discovered a ski track, which was crossing the Purma River. The ski tracks at the Auspiya River corresponded with the route of the missing group of skiers.

Meanwhile, the Slobtsov group had not discovered anything on the ridges. No traces had been left on the crusted snow. Hence it was decided to search in the lowlands. The group went on exploring the Lozva River head, both up and down the stream. Having examined height 1017, which they confused for Mt. Otorten, and not finding any traces of the movement of the Dyatlov group along the Lozva River, the search party decided to explore the alternative route of the Dyatlov group – along the Auspiya River. Brusnitsyn would later recall that it was he who led the group southwards towards the Auspiya River, at a bearing of 180.

Nevolin got in touch from Suevatpaul. The departure of the Mansi group was planned for the next day, February 25, at 2 pm. Meanwhile, the Mansi people were looking for reindeer as a means of transportation.

"To Sulman. We are planning to leave at 2 pm local time; however, they say that two days won't be enough for the search, since we need to reach the watershed of the ridge, where the hunters had seen them. Stepan Kurikov and three others will go. I have five people total going with me. Nobody saw the skiers, but a fresh ski track and a campsite were observed. By all indications, their group was moving in that direction. Nevolin"

"To Sulman. Shepherd Andrey Anyamov saw the trail about eight or nine days ago. Neither the traces of narrow sports skis nor the number of people has been ascertained. The tracks are running from the headstream of the Auspiya River towards the eastern slope of the ridge leading north to the head of the Lozva. We need to search in that place: the headstream of the Auspiya and Lozva, as well as on the western slope of the ridge along with the sources of the Vanya and Vishera rivers. Nevolin"

The information was immediately transmitted to Sverdlovsk: *"To be delivered to Pervago immediately. In addition to our search for the group of students, today at 11:30 we learned that the hunters saw a fresh ski track and a campsite on the side of the ridge in the direction of Suevatpaul. We have organized a group of the Mansi people led by Stepan Kurikov, to set off together with our radio operator by reindeer following the tracks, with a first-aid kit and food supplies. Sulman. Please inform the Polytechnic Institute about this."*

At the time, this information could already be delivered in person, since Pletnev, Zaostrovskiy, Ortyukov, Vishnevskiy, and Maslennikov were arriving at Ivdel. The Grebennik search group was accommodated at the Ivdel Airport.

At the Ivdel city party committee, a working session was convened under the chairmanship of Prodanov with the participation of Vitaliy Ivanov, Sulman, Spitsyn, Tempalov, and the representatives of the UPI. It was ascertained that there had been no general search plan. Neither there was any clear information about which groups were conducting the search – and where. The Slobtsov group was expected to be in the vicinity of Mt. Otorten, but there were doubts if they had been dropped off in an appropriate place. A Mansi group was to be following from the Suevatpaul settlement on the Auspiya River. Two more Mansi groups, about which they reported from Ivdel to the UPI on February 23, had not gone out on a search.

It was decided to cover all the sections of the Dyatlov group's route. The following day, February 25, it was decided to send the Slobtsov group to the Auspiya River, to drop off the Grebennik group at Mt. Oyko-Chakur and to organize several search groups for subsequent dropping off at the intermediate points on the Dyatlov group route. The plans called for an exploration of the headwaters of the Sulpa, Lozva, Auspiya, Purma, Ushma, Malaya Toshemka, Bolshaya Toshemka, and Vizhay rivers, as well as the headwaters of the rivers on the western slope of the Ural Ridge – by moving radially within the distance of 10-15 km (6-9 miles) from the watershed part of the ridge.

Following the session, Spitsyn was called back to Sverdlovsk. Late at night, inside a hangar at the Ivdel airfield, the Grebennik group was receiving instructions, checking its equipment, and stitching two tents into a single one. They received maps with the route of the search.

In the morning of February 25, the Slobtsov group continued moving southward along the Matveevskaya Parma, as the Russians called the Charkanur ridge, which stretches between the Lozva and the Auspiya rivers. Descending from the ridge into the valley of the Auspiya River, the searchers came across an old ski track on the northern bank of the river. They set up their camp at that location. The discovered ski track was barely discernible. For any reliable identification, it was critical to discover the campsite of the Dyatlov group. The search party was broken into three groups. One of the groups led by Koptelov stayed back at the camp doing the chores. The Brusnitsyn group was moving along the discovered ski track down the Auspiya River; in about 17-20 km (10-12 miles) east of the Ural Ridge it saw the traces of an old campsite. Moving further, in one kilometer from it they came across a relatively recent Mansi encampment. A team of Slobtsov, Sharavin, and Halizov, who were sent to follow the westward leading ski track, lost it at the border of the forest. By the evening, all search parties gathered in their camp.

At the same time, the air search continued: *"On February 25, we took off by An-2 together with a group of the UPI employees; flew along the eastern slope of the Ural Mountains ridge towards the Purma and the Auspiya rivers. Eleven skiers rescue team arrived at the Auspiya River. We dropped a canister with instructions for their further search. That rescue group had come down to the Auspiya River from Mt. Otorten. Titov"*

"Mission plan for the Slobtsov group for the search
of the group of the UPI students (led by com. Dyatlov):
In the area of the Auspiya River headwaters, the campsite of the Dyatlov group was discovered approximately 10–15 kilometers from the top of the ridge on the Auspiya River.

The campsite was discovered by the Mansi men eight or ten days ago.

On February 25, a group of the Mansi men with a radio set departed to the area of the Dyatlov group campsite to search for the Dyatlov group's tracks and then moving along that track further towards the head of the Auspiya River.

You have to go down from the headwaters of the Lozva River to the headwaters of the Auspiya River, discover the trail of the Dyatlov group, its second campsite at the foot of the ridge in the headwaters of the Auspiya River, and meet with the Mansi men.

After getting together with the Mansi group, it is necessary to discuss the results of your search, taking a mutual decision on conducting the subsequent search - jointly with this group or separately. Report on your actions and decisions by radio. Keep in mind that on their way back from Mt. Otorten, the Dyatlov group was to approach the Ural Ridge, and then to move southwards along the ridge up to Mt. Oyko-Chakur.

It is important to pay particular attention to locating the Dyatlov group's second campsite and their cache site in the headwaters of the Auspiya River. In case of its discovery, it is necessary to begin with locating the tracks of the group in the southern direction towards the Oyko-Chakur and then to move along those traces.

In case these traces are not discovered, search for the Dyatlov group tracks going towards the Otorten and then follow them to climb to the top. It is necessary to carefully inspect the vicinity of the peak of Mt. Otorten to locate any signs of a possible accident.

On February 25–26, an airlifted party under the command of Captain Chernyshev will be dropped in the area of the pass from across the head of the Purma River to the head of the Vishera River. Their goal is to cross the ridge along the pass and to locate any traces of the Dyatlov group with a subsequent examination of the ridge in the southward direction and further into the valley of the North Toshemka River. Hence, follow your examination of the head of the Auspiya River and in the event of any traces of the Dyatlov group are discovered along the ridge southward, continue movement until you meet with the Chernyshev group. The latter should leave a note for you at the mountain pass to the head of the Vishera River. You should bring the reconnaissance to a conclusion together with this group and then retire to the huts on the North Toshemka River.

In case of discovering the Dyatlov group, you should light three large bonfires forming a triangle of 30 meters on each side and send off a radio message, if possible.

For your information, a UPI rescue team of six led by Oleg Grebennik has been dropped off in the area of the Oyko-Chakur. In addition, a systematic aerial survey of the entire area of the emergency route is underway.

Leader of the search Colonel Ortyukov"

The Slobtsov group was brought up to date on the latest developments. At 9 am, even earlier than planned, a search party consisting of four Mansi hunters and Egor Nevolin, the radio operator, departed from Suevatpaul on three teams of harnessed reindeer and four sleds. The group was led by Stepan Kurikov.

> **Stepan Nikolaevich Kurikov (61)** was born in 1898 in Suevatpaul. During the war of 1941-45, he led a hunting team and was awarded for his work contribution during the war the medal "For Valorous Labor in the Great Patriotic War of 1941-1945". In various years Kurikov was elected deputy of the Ivdel city council and as deputy of the Sverdlovsk regional council.

The group also included Nikolay Anyamov, Andrey Anyamov, and Timofey Bahtiyarov.

> **Nikolay Pavlovich Anyamov (23)** was born in 1936 in Suevatpaul. He was a Komsomol activist; in 1953 he was elected secretary of the village Komsomol organization – the first Komsomol organization among the Mansi youth. It was Nikolay, who while hunting together with the 20-year-old Andrey Anyamov, discovered the Dyatlov group ski track in the upper reaches of the Auspiya River. Timofey Bahtiyarov also lived in Suevatpaul, and repeatedly took part in the rallies of the settlement's hunters.

The Grebennik search group was dropped off by helicopter in the

area of the peak of Mt. Oyko-Chakur. The group landed in the headwaters of the Vizhay River, along which they were to proceed towards
the Ural Ridge. To be on the safe side, they were given a hunting gun.
The gun and its owner, Tipikin, missed each other, as in the evening
Tipikin arrived at Ivdel as part of the Akselrod group.

At 7 pm a meeting of the search headquarters was convened to
discuss the immediate goals. Its participants included Ortyukov, Maslennikov, Vishnevskiy, Blinov, Akselrod, as well as Yakov Busygin and
Aleksey Chernyshev, the representatives of the command of the 32nd
division of the detainee security of the MVD of the USSR, which was
guarding the local corrective labor camps.

> **Yakov Antonovich Busygin (48)** was born in 1911. He was
> drafted into the army in 1941, and from May 1942 fought in the
> war of 1941-45 as a political commissar in the ranks of senior
> lieutenant and captain – as deputy battalion and regiment com-
> mander for political affairs. Wounded in 1944, he was awarded
> the orders of the "Red Banner" (1943) and the "Patriotic War",
> 2nd degree (1945), the latter for 'heroic deeds,' committed in the
> last two days of the war in Europe. From at least 1957, Busygin
> served as a commander for training in the rank of lt. colonel of
> military unit 6602 of the 32nd division of the detainee security
> of the MVD of the USSR.

> **Aleksey Alekseevich Chernyshev (41)** was born in 1918 in the
> village of Varsegovo of the Verkhoshizhemskiy district in the
> Vyatka Governorate. He completed nine classes of a (10-year)
> secondary school and was drafted into the Red Army in 1938.
> As of 1959, Chernyshev lived in Ivdel, serving as military unit
> 6602 deputy chief of staff for training in the rank of captain–
> with responsibility for combat and physical fitness training of its
> soldiers. An accomplished athlete, he served as a participant, or-
> ganizer, and referee of city shoot matches and ski sports compe-
> titions. Chernyshev was a first category referee in track and field
> athletics, ski sports, and shooting.

Chernyshev was assigned with the organization of a search group.
The next day, February 26, his group was to be ready to be dropped off
by 1 pm; Akselrod suggested for the Chernyshev group to be flown to
Mt. Otorten for a repeated examination of the area.

The Karelin group arrived from Serov at around midnight, but
Karelin still managed to contact Ivdel through the MVD. From Ivdel,
they said on the phone that the search was underway, that two land-

ing parties had already been deployed along the route of the missing group, and that Karelin's group should come to Ivdel, where there was work for it to do as well. Since the leaves of all of them had expired, Karelin requested and obtained a tentative agreement to be issued a validating voucher to present at his place of work. Granin and Gory-achko were exhausted and returned to Sverdlovsk – the remaining participants in the Karelin group took the train to Ivdel.

For the next day, February 26, it was scheduled to deploy the Aksel-rod and Chernyshev search groups and to prepare for the deployment of the Karelin group at Mt. Sampalchakhl in the Komi ASSR, 46 km (28 miles) south of Mt. Otorten.

In the morning of that day, Karelin, Atmanaki, and Skutin flew to the Otorten area for air reconnaissance of the Lozva River valley and the surrounding foothills. It was necessary to select a landing site for the Akselrod group. The searchers from the military unit 6602, including Aleksey Chernyshev, Ivan Vlasov, Grigoriy Sidorov, Sergey Verhovskiy, and Anatoliy Yablonskiy, were dropped off in the area of Mt. Gumpkopay, 25 km (15 miles) from height 1079.

> **Ivan Alekseevich Vlasov (37)** was born in 1922 at Ivdel and completed 7-grade education. In 1945 Vlasov was drafted into the Red Army. Initially, he was sent to a boot camp and then to a reserve unit, shifted to combat forces in 1942, promoted to the rank of sr. lieutenant. He fought with the guards infantry corps in the formation of the Southwestern Front and was de-mobilized in October 1945. As of 1953, Vlasov lived in Ivdel and served as chief of the training section of the staff of the Ivdellag paramilitary infantry guard. Curiously, at the time of the Ivdel-lag transfer under the MVD, someone advised, *"to improve the camp's functioning and to clean up the guards force - to remove the chief of the training section, sr. lieutenant of the MVD Vlasov."* In the six subsequent years, the Ivdellag would not find any "reserve" to replace him. Hence, as of 1959, Vlasov continued to serve, by the time promoted into the rank of captain. Vlasov was a good athlete and was fond of skiing, shooting, and football.
>
> **Grigoriy Fyodorovich Sidorov (42)** was born in 1917 in the Vyatka Governorate. He was drafted into the Red Army in June 1941, after the Nazi attack on the Soviet Union, serving in the Quartermaster forces, at an army surplus store. In August 1944, he was promoted as chief of its warehouse, at the time in the rank of sergeant. For diligence in that service, he was awarded the medal "For Merit in Battle". After the war, Sidorov continued

service as a re-enlistee. As of 1959, he lived in Ivdel and served with the military unit 6602 in the rank of warrant officer. Sidorov was a good athlete, a skiing instructor, and took part in the All-Union ski championship in Sverdlovsk.

Sergey Antonovich Verhovskiy (34) was born in the Urals in 1925 and served in the war of 1941-45, possibly in the quartermaster forces and likely continued in service as a re-enlistee. As of 1959, he lived in Ivdel and served with the military unit 6602, in the rank of staff sergeant, holding the position of the head of its warehouse for ordnance weapons, clothing and equipment supply, and provisions.

Anatoliy Yablonskiy served as a civilian with the military unit 6602. He was a good athlete with 1st category in skiing.

At the time a group of Mansi men was moving into the headwaters of the Auspiya River: *"For Sulman: We are in a settlement in 6-10 km from the mouth of the Auspiya River. We have discovered traces of narrow sport skis at the mouth of the Auspiya River. The ski track is rather well defined, with about eight or ten people having gone along it. The traces are about 15 days old, clearly visible in the forest, but snowed under in the open. We are following along the trail towards the headwaters of the Auspiya River, where we will be searching in the mountains. We spent the night at the mouth of the Auspiya River, and today we are moving along. Nevolin"* Soon the Mansi will find the camp of Slobtsov's group: *"To Sulman. We joined up with the Vizhay rescue squad. The ski track goes to the ridge where it disappears. The rescue team is divided into three groups of which one will search at the ridge. Upon their return we will discuss what is the best approach. There is only one of them who stayed to meet us. Nevolin "*

A group including Akselrod, Sogrin, Tipikin, and radio operators Chigvintsev with Yaburov, landed in the Otorten area amid poor weather conditions. Tipikin would later recall that the helicopter aircrew commander had doubts regarding the assigned landing site on the slope of Mt. Otorten because of the snow cover. He decided to look for a more convenient site and discovered it on a flat, bare rock-rill at a distance of eight kilometers east of Mt. Otorten – the location where the Slobtsov group had been previously dropped off. For some reason, the change in landing location was not reported to the search headquarters.

On Hakimov's instruction, Vladimir Krasnobaev, who served as a preparatory works foreman at the 8th camp logging division, departed to visit the Bahtiyarov's yurts at the North Toshemka River.

Vladimir Aleksandrovich Krasnobaev (39) was born in 1920 in the Dedovichi settlement of the Pskov Pskovskaya Governorate. He completed a 7-year junior secondary school. There is no information on Krasnobaev's family background or on what he was up to until 1943 when he was sentenced to 5 years in a labor camp for grand larceny using his official position. After serving his term at the Ivdel camp, Krasnobaev had stayed in Ivdel. As of 1953, he worked as a technical manager of a logging unit; in 1959 he was a preparatory works foreman of the 8th logging camp. Krasnobaev was not a communist party member, likely because of his criminal record.

According to Krasnobaev's testimony, the Mansi hadn't heard anything about the disappearance of a group of hikers and hadn't discovered any strange traces. The only group of hikers they had seen was a group of nine Muscovites who spent the night in their village about a month ago. Krasnobaev invited Pavel Vasilyevich Bahtiyarov to take part in the search for the missing group, but the latter refused, explaining it with sickness.

However, the main events were taking place at the Auspiya River. In the morning, the Slobtsov group was divided into three search parties. Koptelov had stayed in the camp. Two groups were searching for the ski tracks left by the Dyatlov group in the southern direction, along the right bank of the Auspiya River. Slobtsov, Sharavin, and Pashin were going in a north-western direction up the Auspiya River along the ski track on its left bank and the Auspiya River, and then proceeded from the border of the forest towards a rock pillar at the pass. The weather was improving. The sun came out, but the wind was strong. On the pretext of bad weather, Pashin had remained at the rock pillar. Slobtsov and Sharavin were advancing towards the northern offshoot of height 1079, when they noticed a dark object on their left, in about 50 meters (164 feet) along their path.

The tent was snowed up, except for the entrance, the southern abutting end, which was sticking out from under the snow. The tent's canvas was covered with hardened swelled up snow 15-20 cm (4-6 in) deep. There was an ice-ax stuck near the entrance and a flashlight on the tent's top, closer to the entrance. There was around 5-10 cm (2-4 in) of snow under it; however, the flashlight itself was not snowed up. No other items were noticed outside the tent. Below, to the east from the tent, there was a visible section of snow, which looked as if lowered or blown out or flattened, about 7 m (23 feet) wide.

There is no reliable information regarding the immediate manipulations of the searchers with the tent immediately after its discovery. Slobtsov and Sharavin would later recall that they had dug a groove along the tent, partially removed the snow from the canvas, discovering a cut in its eastern slope. With the help of an ice-ax, they tore the canvas along the ridgepole of the tent, so as to gain access inside the tent. After making sure that there was no one in the tent, Slobtsov and Sharavin headed back to the base camp. According to various testimonies and recollections, they brought the items discovered during the inspection of the tent – the ice-ax, flashlight, storm jacket, which was sticking out near the tent's entrance, photo cameras, and a flask of alcohol – to the camp. For a while, Pashin was returning with them from the pass, but by the end of the route, he was lagging behind. In the camp, they met the Mansi group with the radio operator and received a drop message with new the instructions sent by the search headquarters:

"*Information for the Slobtsov group.*

1. By this helicopter we have dropped the Akselrod and Sogrin group of five, to the peak of Mt. Otorten with the goal of its detailed examination along all the slopes. Therefore, you need not climb Mt. Otorten again, per yesterday's instructions. In the future, when you hear an airplane, try to go out into the open despite the waste of 10 or 15 minutes of your precious time - or quickly light a fire full of smoke. Keep birch bark ready to use. Yesterday we were circling for an hour and a half or more – before we could make you out. There will be a good radio station waiting for you at Mt. O-torten. (A note aside: radio operator Boris Yaburov is sending his greetings to Vyacheslav Halizov).

2. Before noon another helicopter dropped off the Captain Chernyshev group 8 km below the Vishera riverhead. From that point, the group had to climb to the watershed, next cross down to the other side, where they would leave a note, about which you already know. You should catch up with them on the ridge and then continue together.

3. Tomorrow morning, at 6:00 am, the Karelin group (6 men) will be dropped off in the area of Mt. Sampalchakhl, to examine it including both slopes – down to the Vishera and Niols rivers.

4. The Bahtiyarov brothers are proceeding northward by sleds along the eastern slope of the ridge. The hunters from the Komi Republic, starting from several points, have reached the western slope of the ridge. Unfortunately, the Mansi of Suevatpaul have started from the mouth of the Auspiya River only today. We expected that they would have met with you yesterday, but they were delayed. I wish you luck. Greetings E. Maslennikov"

At 6 pm the radio station of the Northern Expedition received a radiogram reporting the discovery of the tent; its further inspection has turned impossible due to the onset of a severe snowstorm. The Slobtsov group has received instructions not to touch the discovered tent; the next morning they were to select a place for the base camp and to prepare a landing site. It was decided to send the Karelin group to the location of the discovery of the tent to assist in the further search.

CHAPTER 7. FEBRUARY 27 - MARCH 10, 1959. DYATLOV FIVE.

In the morning of February 27, near Mt. Otorten, the Akselrod group did not yet know that the day before the tent of the missing hikers was discovered on the slope of height 1079. At 8:10 am Akselrod, Sogrin and Tipikin went on a search. Chigvintsev and Yaburov stayed back in the base camp at the Sulpa River. Tipikin would later recall: *"The day before, following the landing, we did not go on a search and were busy with setting up the camp. We lived in two tents, with one of them occupied by radio operators. The assignment of Yaburov and Chigvintsev, the radio operators, was to establish reliable communication with the airplanes and helicopters operating in the Mt. Otorten area. The efforts failed because both radios turned to be inoperative. Three of the searchers were to make a radial ascent to Mt. Otorten, climbing to its top, then to go round its foot-hill and to return to the camp. The group did not have a map. During the search, the group lost its bearings and was unable to locate Mt. Otorten's peak. The group split and went on examining the surrounding peaks, with each peak, including Mt. Otorten, examined by one searcher. After they had ascertained, which of the peaks was Otorten, all the three made another climb to the summit."*

At the top of Mt. Otorten, they found a message left by a hiking group from the Department of Chemistry of the Moscow State University. It was left back in 1956. No traces of the Dyatlov group were discovered. Soon after, an An-2 airplane dropped a canister for the Akselrod group with a message about the discovery of the Dyatlov group tent with their belongings and skis inside.

Similar canisters were received by the Grebennik and Chernyshev groups. The Grebennik group was instructed to discontinue the search and to go down from the area of Mt. Oyko-Chakur into the valley of the Vizhay River up to the village with the same name. The Chernyshev group was to advance northward along the ridge, in the direction of the discovered tent. On the way, the Chernyshev group was picked up by a helicopter and transported to the area of height 1079.

In 1959, no map or document used the Mansi name of that mountain – Kholat Syakhl, which means Barren or Dead Mountain.

"Mission plan for the joint rescue team led by com. Maslennikov in search of the Dyatlov group in the area of Mt. Otorten.

1. On February 27, 1959, to concentrate the following search groups in the area of Mt. Otorten in the headwaters of the right-hand stream of the Lozva River in the pass between heights 1079 and 880:

a) the Slobtsov group - 9 men

b) the Karelin group - 6 men

c) the Chernyshev group - 5 men

d) the Akselrod group - 5 men (camp at Mt. Otorten)

e) the Northern Expedition group (led by Kurikov) - 5 men

f) the Headquarters group - 4 men

g) K9 team (led by Moiseev) - 2 men, 36 men in total.

2. The mission of the joint team is to locate the Dyatlov group using the discovered tent with equipment, skis, and supplies as a starting point. The search area encompasses the headwaters of the Lozva River, the slopes of the Main Range in the direction of the Lozva River, height 1079, Mt. O-torten, and the lake area beneath Mt. Otorten top.

3. The groups will carry out all their work under the direct supervision of their leaders, with the latter fully responsible for the compliance of safety measures by the group members during their search. The leaders of the groups, namely comrades Slobtsov, Karelin, Chernyshev, Akselrod, Kurikov, and Moiseev, should pay particular attention to meticulous compliance of all safety rules during the groups' movement along the ridge, snowy slopes, and climbs to the peaks.

4. To coordinate the actions of the search groups and to plan their work, a staff of the joint team is assigned under the charge of com. Maslennikov, the Master of Sports. This staff will include the above named group leaders and com. Blinov, the commandant of the base camp.

5. The team's staff will report directly to the leaders of the search and will maintain continuous communication (with Ivdel) via the Northern Expedition radio station – several times a day by mutual consent. To ensure communication with the Akselrod group, the staff should be provided with an additional radio station with two radio operators, comrades Chernousov and Yarovoy.

6. The group will be provided with the equipment needed for an overnight stay, food supplies, and equipment for the search. In case of need, any additional equipment and food supplies will be delivered by helicopter.

7. The evacuation after completing the mission will be organized by helicopters from the base camp under height 1079. In the event of non-flying weather, the team will have to return on its own, moving along the Auspiya River to the 2nd Northern settlement.

8. The leaders of the search efforts are turning to all participants with a request to submit to the strictest discipline, to accurately and quickly follow the instructions of the group leaders and the chief of staff, as well as to strictly follow all the mountain hiking rules during the search.

Colonel Ortyukov, February 27, 1959"

The searchers at the Auspiya River had lots of work to do. The day before, they received an assignment to setup a landing site and to choose a camping spot for 50 people. It was decided to look for the campsite closer to the discovered tent. Sharavin and Koptelov had already reached the pass between heights 1079 and 880 when at the Ivdel search headquarters it had dawned on them that the traces left by the search parties could interfere with the work of the K9 units from the military unit 6602. The dog handlers, led by Sr. Lieutenant Moiseev, were already preparing to fly from Ivdel together with the Karelin group.

"To Nevolin: Try to catch up by deer or skiing with the group gone to demount the tent for the arrival of the dogs. Sulman"

"To Ortiukov and Sulman: We are informing you that the search in the location of the tent of the Dyatlov group started yesterday. Today four men have already left for the search. If we manage to catch up with them, we will tell them to halt the search until the arrival of the dogs. Slobtsov"

They had not managed to catch up with the searchers. Under the cedar, at a distance of about one mile from the tent, which was discovered the previous day, Sharavin and Koptelov stumbled upon two bodies. At 1:00 pm Slobtsov reported to Ivdel the discovery of the first corpses.

From Atmanaki's testimony: *"At 12:00 pm, we boarded a helicopter and landed on the saddle at the height 880. The group included four hikers and two guides with dogs. Our task was to divide ourselves into two groups and to find an appropriate place for the base camp in the basin of the Lozva River, while the second group with the dogs will begin scouring the site from the tent down to the Lozva River. After leaving our skis and equipment at the pass, Borisov, guides Moiseev and Mostovoy, and I went along the slope in the direction of height 1079. At the pass, we met several people from the Slobtsov group, who gave us a tentative location of the tent of the Dyatlov group. The remaining members of the Slobtsov group were at the pass at the rock rills. Subsequently, it became apparent that the discovery of the tent and the bodies of their friends had made such a deep effect upon them, that they were completely demoralized and incapacitated. Together with two men from the Slobtsov team and the guides, Borisov and I have combed the slope below and to the right of the tent. On our way, we met two Mansi men and the chief of the Ivdel fire brigade. They told us that two corpses had been discovered about two kilometers below and then showed us the location of the tent... Following the examination of the tent, we went down, indicating to the Slobtsov men the contemplated place for the base camp and instructing them to go down to that place and to move the equipment to that place."*

On receipt of the information on the discovery of the bodies, prosecutor Tempalov flew to the scene. To maintain communication with the Akselrod group, an additional radio operator named Chernousov was attached to the search party in the area of height 1079; however, his radio proved to be inoperative – similar to the radio brought for the Akselrod group. In view of the decision to send Chernousov to the search area, Skutin was removed from the Karelin group since there was no room in the helicopter.

Tempalov, Maslennikov, Blinov, Yarovoy, Shevkunov, and Chernousov arrived at the pass, where they were told about the discovered bodies and were shown the location of the tent on the slope. At first, the body of Doroshenko was mistaken for Zolotaryov's. The error would be corrected only after some time.

During an external cursory examination of the tent, Tempalov tore a hole in its side. Here is how Yarovoy described this episode in his book: *"The tent was covered with a thick layer of snow compressed by the wind. The rescuers tried to remove the snow from a single spot – with the tent's fabric showing. The fabric was covered with holes, with the items inside the tent visible through them... The prosecutor scraped away as much snow from the tent as he could. We tried to bring the torn edges back together, but the many ruptures were running in disarray – traversing one another, which made it impossible... Two rescuers, armed with ski poles, began to gouge out the snow. First, they pulled out some sack, in which one could hardly recognize a backpack; next came a ski jacket, which was so frozen, that it looked like a wreckage of stone... The prosecutor knelt down and thrust his hands into the tent. Something made a cracking sound. The prosecutor turned red with the effort, then, suddenly, a thick layer of snow gave way, revealing a canvas side. They threw the snow aside. The prosecutor stretched the hole, and the tent opened. What he saw struck with its chaos: blankets, jackets, felt boots – everything was turned upside down, crumpled and mixed with snow."*

At the same time, a free search was conducted. The Mansi men discovered Dyatlov's body on the slope. With the help of a search dog, Moiseev discovered the body of Kolmogorova.

"To Sulman. They did not have enough time to inspect the tent. Prob-

ably everything was buried in snow and under heavy food supplies. The tent was torn open. When the hikers got out, they were blown down the hill by the wind. Akselrod can be brought by helicopter, taking him along with us. The three corpses were partly visible in the snow, with the fourth (a female corpse) discovered by a dog. Maslennikov"

"To Sulman: At 4:00 pm, four people were discovered in various places, lightly dressed and barefoot. This lets us assume that they were blown out in a blizzard. The only one to be identified was Zinaida Kolmogorova. The search is going on. All groups have arrived in the area of Dyatlov's tent. Communication with the Akselrod group has not yet been established. Brusnitsyn, Nevolin, Chernousov"

On their return from the search, the Atmanaki group learned that the camp would be in the valley of the Auspiya River. It was decided not to move it across the pass to the Lozva River, so that not to confuse their tracks with the traces left by the Dyatlov group. The equipment from the Slobtsov's group base camp had already been shifted downstream of the Auspiya River to the new location. The groups of Chernyshev, Slobtsov, and Karelin were transporting their property from the landing site on the pass to the camp. It was already dark when the entire cargo was taken down to the new camp. Two tents were pitched, with one for 30 and the other for 8 people. The small one would be later rolled down.

"To Sulman: The group is all here. We are encamping. Everybody feels well. The strongest part of the Dyatlov group has been discovered, hence the others should be somewhere around. It is necessary to search under the snow. Dyatlov's field bag with all his papers has been found... At the request of the prosecutor, call a forensic expert from Sverdlovsk to come to Ivdel for the autopsies. Maslennikov"

In the evening, Tempalov was examining the documents discovered in Dyatlov's field bag. At the dictation of Tempalov, Yarovoy was writing the on-site inspection report. Citing from that protocol:

"In about one and a half kilometers northeast from height 1079, in the headstream of the right tributary of the Lozva River, starting in the saddle between heights 1079 and 880... traces of a campfire were discovered in a pit under a cedar... At a one meter distance to the north of the campfire, two corpses are lying next to each other, with their heads to the west and feet to the east. They were identified as: Yuri Alekseevich Krivonischenko ... Next to Krivonischenko, there is the corpse of Aleksander Alekseevich Zolotaryov... The corpses have been photographed on the spot. Another corpse was discovered at a distance of 400 meters to the southwest from the above said corpses... (The body will be later identified as Igor

Alekseevich Dyatlov.) A female corpse was discovered in the same area at a distance of 500 meters to the south-west on the slope of height 1079. The body was identified as Zinaida Alekseevna Kolmogorova... The corpse was photographed... The documents and valuables removed from the tent of the missing Dyatlov group by the members of our search team are attached to this protocol."

With the Akselrod group at Mt. Otorten, the search party was comprised of 35 men. All of them were getting ready for the next day's efforts.

By February 28, the aircraft of the 142nd detached mixed aviation squadron (OSAE) of the Ural military district with a base at Aramil (about which Ortyukov was negotiating with General Slobozhan on February 24), had arrived at Ivdel. The An-2 was piloted by Sr. Lieutenant Vladimir Savvich Kuznetsov. The crew included Captain Vasiliy Yegorovich Serebryakov as navigator and Burdasov as a flight mechanic. Victor Vasilyevich Potyazhenko, deputy squadron commander, arrived by Mi-4 helicopter. Its crew included navigator Mihail Ivanovich Novikov and flight mechanic Valentin Petrovich Kovtun.

Victor Vasilyevich Potyazhenko (26) was born in 1933 in the village of Karadonlu of the Azerbaijan SSR. During the war, the family moved to Krasnodar, where he went to school and, while still at school, was simultaneously training at the Krasnodar aero club, flying gliders, and then a PO-2 airplane. Next, he studied at the Military Aviation School of Pilots in the city of Pugachev, Saratov region, from which he graduated in 1954 among the first group of military helicopter pilots. Potyazhenko was sent to serve in Georgia, at an airfield in the town of Telavi. In 1956, he was transferred to the town of Aramil in the Sverdlovsk region. By the time of the search, Potyazhenko had the rank of sr. lieutenant, and would return to Aramil in May in the rank of captain. During the search operation, he met his future wife, Margarita Ivanovna, who worked as a radio operator at the Ivdel airport, maintaining radio communication between the headquarters and the search groups.

Potyazhenko would later recall that they arrived at Ivdel at around noon on February 27. Mihail Gorlachenko, the Chief of Staff of the Air Force of the Ural Military District, arrived with them. After a conference and setting up of the Ivdel-Aramil telephone line, Gorlachenko made an overflight of the search area. On ascertaining the safety of using helicopters, he returned to Sverdlovsk. Appointed as the senior in command, Potyazhenko received an instruction, which obliged him to file applications for each flight and to obtain approval of the route from Aramil by phone. The second Mi-4 helicopter of the 142nd OSAE would arrive at Ivdel on February 28. From that day on, search operations would be conducted only by military aviation.

At 9:20 am Sr. Lieutenant Kuznetsov flew off by AN-2 to drop canisters to the Grebennik and Akselrod groups with information on the group's evacuation procedures with Ortyukov, Vishnevskiy, and Grigoriev, the correspondent of "Ural Worker" onboard.

In the morning, Tempalov, Chernyshev, and about ten more men, including Maslennikov, Brusnitsyn, Sharavin, Lebedev, Karelin, Atmanaki, and Koptelov, went to dig out the tent. Maslennikov instructed Brusnitsyn to make a list of items recovered in the process of digging out the tent, but the latter was continuously distracted by other matters and could not keep a systematic record. There was no thorough examination of the items on-site – they would be properly protocolled only in Ivdel. Soon after they began stripping down the tent: there was an order to wind down the inspection of its contents, to put everything back inside the tent, and to bring it to the landing site. Brusnitsyn and Sharavin dragged the tent with its contents for half a mile towards the rock outlier now known as the Boot rock. Three of the four discovered corpses were as well moved up to the pass under heavy wind. The corpses were taken uphill by eight people so that not to damage the frozen bodies. The body of Krivonischenko would be moved to the pass only on March 1.

"To Sulman: Thus far we have been unable to find anyone else. We have dug out the tent, sorted out their belongings in Dyatlov's tent... There are all the nine backpacks, several storm jackets, 3.5 pairs of felt boots, eight pairs of boots (one pair is missing), and other personal belongings. There is also some part of food supplies, but not all. The remaining part of food supplies should be somewhere else... At the time, they are compiling a protocol. We are moving the corpses up to the ridge to be sent by helicopter. Maslennikov, Nevolin"

From the protocol of the site where the Dyatlov group campsite was discovered: *"The overnight campsite is located on the North-Eastern slope of height 1079 in the headwaters of the Auspiya River. The overnight campsite is 300 meters from the top of height 1079 downhill at 30 degrees. The overnight campsite is a platform of flattened snow, with eight pairs of skis lined up in its bottom. The tent is stretched on ski poles and fixed with ropes. Inside, there are nine backpacks with various personal belongings of group members on the floor of the tent. On top of them, there are padded jackets, storm jackets, and nine pairs of boots at the head. We have also discovered men's trousers, three pairs of felt boots, warm fur jackets, socks, a cap, ski caps, dishes, buckets, a stove, axes, saws, blankets, and the following food supplies: rusks in two bags, condensed milk, sugar, ready-made-food, as well as notepads, pre-planned itinerary and a multitude of other small items and documents, including a camera and its accessories. All discovered items have been handed over to Maslennikov, the leader of the search team, for inventory and submission to the base camp, in which this protocol has been made. No corpses were discovered inside the tent."*

The Grebennik group was transported from the Vizhay River valley. *"The search group has prepared a site for helicopter landing. While on-board the military helicopter, they discussed the discovery of the Dyatlov group tent and the bodies. The group was brought to Ivdel, from where it was sent by train to Sverdlovsk."* Grebennik wanted to join in the subsequent search, but he had to continue his studies.

"To Maslennikov: The Grebennik group has been taken to Ivdel. The second helicopter has arrived at our disposal. Zaostrovskiy, Sulman"

Potyazhenko would later recall that the second helicopter was sent from Kaunas, but its pilot was ill-prepared for winter flights over the Ural Mountains and was soon recalled. In March 1959, the 239th Guards airborne paratroop Belgorod Red Banner Regiment, which was based in Kaunas, was getting ready for transfer to the GDR. From 1952, the regiment had been learning to fly the Mi-4 helicopters, which they had first seen during troop tests. Some of the Mi-4 helicopters have already been transferred into separate helicopter squadrons. As of November 1959, the regiment was already based at the Fürstenwalde airfield.

The probes, ordered for the morning search, were delivered to the pass. Previously, the search was conducted with the use of ski poles. A helicopter with Tempalov onboard flew from the pass to Mt. Otorten area to transport the Akselrod group from Otorten to Ivdel.

Upon their arrival at Ivdel, at the airport hotel restaurant, the Akselrod group reported to the search headquarters on the work undertaken to date. By the time Ivdel had more brass in attendance with the key figures arriving at Ivdel from Sverdlovsk for the investigation: Lev N. Ivanov, the forensics prosecutor of the investigation department of the Sverdlovsk regional prosecutor's office; Boris Vozrozhdenniy, the forensic expert of the regional medical examiner's office, and Genrietta Churkina, the senior forensic expert of the Forensic Laboratory of the Ministry of Justice of the RSFSR.

Lev Nikitich Ivanov (34) was born in 1925 in the Amurskiy region. Later, he moved with his family to the city of Sukhoi Log of the Sverdlovsk region, where his sister Yulia was working at a local fireclay plant on a post-graduate work assignment. From December 1942, he studied at the Frunze Odessa Artillery School, which was evacuated to Sukhoi Log in 1941, and graduated from it in June 1943. Then, for almost a year, Ivanov served with the 9th Guards airborne brigade based in the Moscow region, and from May 1944 he fought in the Guards 107th separate tank destroyer battalion, which fought in the formations of the 2nd Ukrainian Front. In 1945 Ivanov was wounded at the Lake Balaton in Hungary and was demobilized after treatment at a hospital in Romania. He was awarded the order of the Patriotic War 2nd degree and the medals "For Courage" and "For the Victory over Germany". On return to the Sverdlovsk region, Ivanov got a job as a coachman at the Sukhoi Log prosecutor's office. In December 1945, without professional education, he managed to get the job of an investigator at the prosecutor's office – to graduate from an investigators training school in Sverdlovsk only two years later. In 1951 he was promoted to the position of a prosecutor at the investigation department of the Sverdlovsk regional Prosecutor's Office, simultaneously studying extramurally at the Sverdlovsk Law Institute, from which he graduated in 1956. Concurrently, since 1957, he taught criminal investigative techniques at the Sverdlovsk Law Institute. Like Tempalov, as of 1959, he had the class rank of Junior Counselor of Justice.

Boris Alekseevich Vozrozhdenniy (37) was born in 1922 in Gomel, BSSR, in a family of railway workers. After graduating from a 10-year secondary school in 1939, he enrolled at the department of general medicine of the First Kharkov Medical Institute. In 1940, while a second-year student, he was drafted into the Red Army. He fought at the eastern front of WWII from the first days after the Nazi attack on the Soviet Union, first as a medical orderly, then as a company and battalion paramedic in the formation of the Southwestern Front. Wounded in July and August 1941, he was later transferred to the Transcaucasian region, where he served as a military assistant and commander of a sanitary platoon in the cities of Tbilisi, Derbent, Sumgait, and Leninakan. In 1942, he was shifted to Iran as a paramedic with the medical squadron of the 15th cavalry corps. The corpse did not take part in combat, since its mission was to secure communications in Iran and its south-western borders with Turkey.

Arrested in December 1942 in the city of Tabriz, he was tried by court martial in January 1943, charged under the infamous Article 58.10 of the Criminal Code (propaganda or agitation with a call to overthrowing, undermining or weakening of the Soviet power or to misc. counterrevolutionary deeds) to 10 years in a Gulag camp with disenfranchisement for a five-year term and confiscation of personal property. He served his sentence in a Gulag camp in the city of Nakhichevan-on-Araks, the Azerbaijan SSR working as a paramedic. In 1947, his sentence was commuted to 4.5 years with consideration of his character and wartime wounds.

After his release in 1947, Vozrozhdenniy moved to the city of Kurgan, where he reunited with his parents and brother, who had been evacuated from Gomel. In the city also lived his ex-wife with his son. Vozrozhdenniy married Vera Pavlovna Petrunina in 1941 and divorced soon after the birth of their son Valeriy a year later in Baku. Years later, while filling out official personnel forms, Vozrozhdenniy would cover up his criminal record: *"In 1943 I was wounded at the front and treated in hospitals in Stalino and Tbilisi. In 1943 I was decommissioned and transferred into the Office of corrective labor camps and colonies of the Ministry of Internal Affairs, where I worked as a paramedic until September 1947. For health reasons, in 1947 I moved to the city of Kurgan where my family resided."* After working for a year as an engineer-methodologist and personnel training department head at the Ural Agricultural machines (Uralselmash) plant, where his father and brother worked as well, Vozrozhdenniy enrolled as a 1st year student of the Sverdlovsk State Medical Institute. He had no documents in proof of his enrollment at the Kharkov Medical Institute, had not disclosed his criminal record, but still managed to be admitted without entrance exams. While a student, Vozrozhdenniy married for a second time, that time to Rosa Vyacheslavovna Padlovskaya, an epidemiologist at the Sverdlovsk city disinfection station. They had two daughters, born in 1952 and 1958. Since 1950, Vozrozhdenniy simultaneously worked at a traumatology center (of the Ural Institute of Traumatology and Orthopedics) and took an active part in the work of the student scientific circle at the Department of Forensic Medicine, where he went through his pre-graduate internship. In 1954, Vozrozhdenniy graduated from the Institute with the qualification of a physician and got a job as a general forensic pathologist at the

Sverdlovsk regional medical examiner's office.

Genrietta Eliseevna Churkina (29) was born in 1930 in the town of Sysert' of the Sverdlovsk region, in the family of a lawyer and a teacher. In 1954, after graduating from the Sverdlovsk Law Institute, she was hired as an expert at a research forensic laboratory. She was an expert in the field of forensic graphology, technical and forensic examination of documents, as well as trace evidence analysis.

There were rumors that Afanasyi Eshtokin, the second secretary of the Sverdlovsk regional party committee, had also arrived at Ivdel.

Afanasiy Fyodorovich Eshtokin (46) was born in 1913 in the village of Stanovoy, Kursk Governorate, into a working-class family. After graduating from the Donetsk Industrial Institute in 1937, he worked in the coal mines of Stalinska, Voroshilovgrad, and Chelyabinsk regions. Party member since 1943. Since 1948, he held executive positions at the Kopeisk Ugol, Chelyabinsk Ugol, and Sverdlovsk Ugol coal trusts. In 1957 he was appointed head of the fuel industry department of the newly created Sverdlovsk Economic Council (sovnarhoz). Since 1958 - Second Secretary of the Sverdlovsk regional committee of the CPSU. According to the memoirs of Lev Ivanov, it was Eshtokin who supervised the investigation through the regional authorities.

In the camp at the Auspia River, negotiations with the search headquarters at Ivdel were underway until late at night.

"To Sulman: We have not managed to establish communication with Akselrod. Thus far the search has not yielded anything. We have managed to discover the traces of eight or nine people in about one kilometer from the tent along the slope, after which the traces go cold. One man was in boots, one had socks and the rest were barefoot. Further down the slope, the snow is very deep and probing has not revealed anything. The dogs were of no help, as the snow was too deep. We have taken three corpses to the landing site. We will be moving up the fourth one tomorrow. His face was completely snowed in, hence there is an opinion that this is Doroshenko and not Zolotaryov. Both of them are the most portly guys. We have examined the tent site and have drawn up the protocol. The items have been taken down to the landing site. They will be sent to you. In the tent, there were ten pairs of underwear, eight pairs of boots, nine backpacks – all of them the personal effects of the victims. There were food supplies for two or three days. The remaining part of food supplies to last for 8 days had likely been stowed in a cache in the headwaters of the Auspiya River. The whole

group was assembled inside. Thus far, we have been unable to ascertain why had all of them fled the tent while semi-clad. This is incomprehensible. Tomorrow we will be searching for the bodies with probes in the area with deep snow of the size 150 by 500 meters about one kilometer below the tent. The group's belongings have been prepared for transportation. It is necessary to send a helicopter for their transportation. The prosecutor has taken along with him all the documents of the group, except for the sketch maps and personal notebooks. This includes three copies of the route sheet. Maslennikov"

By the morning of March 1, the search participants had reached a consensus: "The disaster occurred in the night from February 1 to February 2. On January 31 the group left the Auspiya in foul weather and climbed up towards the pass, but heavy winds made them turn back. They returned to the border of the forest at the head of the Auspiya River and set up a camp. That was approximately at the site of our camp. In the morning they created a cache and left part of their food supplies there. At 3:00 pm they again went up to the pass towards the Lozva River and climbed up to the site of the discovered tent. It is possible that in a blizzard they had mistaken the slope of height 1079 for the pass from the Auspiya to the Lozva. They climbed up to the mountain crest and, battered by hurricane wind, at around 6 pm decided to set up a camp at that site... The group had supper in a tent and started changing clothes... It was at that moment that something had happened, which made the semi-clad group run out of the tent and rush down the slope. Perhaps, one of them still dressed, ventured out to relieve himself, and was blown down. Those who hurried out to the scream were as well blown down... There was no sense in climbing back from fifty meters down the slope since the tent had been torn down. Possibly, they could go to the forest... to find a shelter there, and maybe they wanted to find the site of their previous night's encampment... They made a campfire. Dyatlov and Kolmogorova went back to look for the clothes. Exhausted, they collapsed. There is a consensus about this version of the tragedy."

There was no longer any optimism about the likelihood of finding the rest: "To Sulman: We believe this day to be the final one. We are going to check with the probes the entire area covered with deep snow. If we do not find anything with the probes, we will have to wait until spring. No one could have made it beyond this place. In some places, the snow is more than two meters deep... Today four men will be looking for the cache site. All the rest are going to search for the missing hikers. Maslennikov"

The opinion at the search headquarters was different: "To Maslennikov: We consider it vital to continue the search now until we discover all other hikers. There is a suggestion to send sappers with mine detectors to *assist you. Give another consideration of the option of sending dogs. The nasty weather will not put the searches at risk. There has been no severe local weather warning for the coming days. Sulman, Zaostrovskiy"*

That optimistic forecast has not turned true. Two helicopter flights were scheduled for March 1 to evacuate the discovered corpses and the property of the deceased group from the pass. It was also planned to send Moiseev, Mostovoy, and Chernousov back from the pass. But due to the deterioration of the weather, they could only make one flight: to transport Lev Ivanov, Akselrod, Sogrin, and Tipikin from Ivdel to the pass.

In the morning, during breakfast in Ivdel, they learned that the Akselrod group was returning to Sverdlovsk. Tipikin would later recall: *"Due to the absence of radio communication, the change of the February 26 landing site at Mt. Otorten, as well as the absence of information about it at the search headquarters, it was reported to Sverdlovsk that the Akselrod group might have died as well. To avoid negative consequences, it was ordered to bring the searchers to the Institute so that to prove to their relatives that they were alive."* Only after lengthy discussions, the Akselrod group was permitted to fly to height 1079 to continue the search.

Sogrin would later recall: *"On the flight to the pass, we met prosecutor Lev N. Ivanov. The helicopter was carrying food supplies. After landing, we saw a tent under the rock pillar, as well as the bodies that the searchers brought up the mountain the day before. The helicopter was met by the members of the Slobtsov group and some people we did not know, most of whom departed with the return flight."* Before joining the search, the Akselrod group had loaded the tent and the Dyatlov group's belongings into the helicopter. Some of the items were left behind and would be sent to Ivdel later.

Maslennikov asked Sogrin to accompany Ivanov and to brief him on the basics of mountaineering. They immediately went to the site of the tent's discovery. There were neither animal nor human traces around, except for the area that had been trampled by the searchers while removing the tent. The same was observed downwards in the area around the cedar. Having examined the tent site, Maslennikov, Ivanov, and Sogrin retraced the Dyatlov group passage all the way to the cedar. Footprints with visible finger-marks were leading down the slope to the ice blister, of around 200 meters in size, which was formed by the discharge of subsurface water. Below the ice blister, one could see barely discernible traces, which had become closely-grouped and short in size. Having approached the cedar, Ivanov paid attention to the fact that the body of Krivonischenko was in a typical position of an exhausted man.

By 4 pm, the search was completed. On the way back to the base camp, the body of Krivonischenko was taken up to the landing site by a group of five or six men, who were pulling it on a drag sled. On the way back to the camp they took with them the food supplies, which had been delivered earlier in the afternoon.

"To Sulman: Today, we have continued the search, despite a sudden deterioration of the weather conditions. We have covered about 1000 meters of a 30-meter-wide zone around the area of the tent site. The search has not yielded anything. The snow is one-two or more meters deep. Today the wind has reached 30 meters per second with no visibility. It is impossible to continue the search in such weather. As far as the advisability of a subsequent search, we may say that even in fine weather the search in this area may turn up useless. It would require at least 100 participants. Had the weather been fine, it would have been possible to check one or two more sections. Maslennikov"

At the headquarters, they were insisting on continuing the search. *"To Sulman: We can continue the search, but half of the group should be replaced with fresh manpower. It is necessary to replace the Slobtsov group and the Mansi men. Sappers will be more useful with probes than with mine detectors since there are no metal objects on the bodies under the snow. We need about 20 pieces of 2.5-meter long probes. According to the current weather forecast, we should expect severe weather conditions on March 2-4. A blizzard is raging right behind our tent, and the weather is getting worse hour after hour. Maslennikov"*

"To Maslennikov: In case of flight weather, a helicopter will arrive at your place at 1:00 pm. Prepare for shipping the corpses and of anyone who may be sick and not needed for work. We agree with your suggestion. Measures will be taken to send replacements for the group up to March 2-3. Sulman, Zaostrovskiy, Ortyukov"

From the morning of March 2, the pass was under a blizzard with no visibility. The arrival of helicopters was questionable. *"To Sulman: Today we will be looking for the cache site at the headwaters of the Auspiya River. We are sending the men on duty to the landing site in case a helicopter arrives. We are also sending a group to go over the pass in search of the victims. We will send Ivanov, Yarovoy, and the four corpses with the first flight. The second flight should take six men from the Slobtsov group... In our and Nevolin's opinion, you should not replace the Mansi men... I deem it expedient to assign Captain Chernyshev as the leader of the search team, particularly that the team is becoming military in composition. The team and Chernyshev are in agreement on this issue. An issue of the removal of*

Blinov, Borisov, and Serdityh has also been raised. Maslennikov"

The weather did not allow any flights. The corpses would remain under the Boot rock near the landing site until March 3. The search participants were coming up with more and more theories of the death of the hikers: *"To Sulman: It would be helpful to ascertain whether a meteorological rocket of a new type flew over the area of the accident on the night of February 1. Maslennikov"*

In the evening, the search headquarters received the daily report: *"To Sulman: Today the search in the Lozva valley has failed. Twenty-two people climbed up the pass and had to return due to a snowstorm. There is no visibility. Instead, they have stored firewood, reinforced the camp, and prepared it for the arrival of the replacement. The search group of Slobtsov and Kurikov has discovered the Dyatlov group's cache 400 meters from our tent, higher up the Auspiya River. The cache was found to contain 19 food items with a total weight of 55 kg, as well as an emergency medicine box, Dyatlov's insulated boots, one pair of ski boots, a mandolin, a set of batteries with bulbs, and a spare set of skis. The coordinates of the cache site have been sent to you. Maslennikov"*

The cache site was discovered 10 meters (32 feet) from the ski track leading from the base camp to the pass. From the protocol of the examination of the cache: *"On this date, in the headwaters of the Auspiya River, below the pass to the Lozva River, the cache of food supplies (labaz) of the Dyatlov group was discovered. The cache is located at the site where the group spent the night. It is reliably covered with firewood, coated with cardboard and spruce foliage. Near the cache, a pair of skis is stuck in the snow, with a torn legging hanging on the point of one ski. The following supplies have been discovered in the excavation of the cache: condensed milk (2.5 kg), meat, canned food (4 kg), sugar (8 kg), butter (4 kg), cooked sausage (4 kg), salt (1.5 kg), sweetened starch drink [kissel] (3 kg), oatmeal and buckwheat porridge (7.5 kg), cocoa (200 gr), coffee (200 gr), tea (200 gr), pork loin (3 kg), milk powder (1 kg), sugar sand (3 kg), rusks (7 kg) and noodles (5 kg). In addition, the following items were discovered: a mandolin, a pair of boots size 41 with worn socks inside, a pair of insulated boots, a set of ski binders, two batteries fitted with a lamp for lighting. According to Blinov, the insulated boots belonged to Dyatlov. Since the food supplies are not of interest for the investigation, they were handed over to comrade Maslennikov, the leader of the search team, as an emergency reserve. All packaging of the food supplies, as well as the mandolin, two pairs of boots, socks, and ski binders, have been removed. Forensic Prosecutor, Jr. Counselor of Justice Ivanov"*

At the base camp, the deliberations over the probable versions have continued: *"To Sulman. While moving from their overnight campsite and the cache site in severe weather conditions, the Dyatlov group might have taken the spur ridge (height 1079) for the pass to the Lozva. However, the greatest mystery of the tragedy remains why did the entire group abandon the tent. Besides the ice ax, the only object discovered outside of the tent was a Chinese flashlight on its roof. This confirms a possibility that one clothed individual might have ventured outside, giving a reason for the rest to hastily rush out of the tent. The reason might be some extraordinary natural event or the passage of a meteorological rocket, which was observed at Ivdel on February 1 and later by the Karelin group on February 17. Maslennikov"*

Preparations were underway for subsequent work and replacements in the search groups: *"To Sulman: Tomorrow we will continue the search together with the new manpower and will organize the transportation of the planned cargo. In the morning we will send the Kurikov group back, with a letter of reference about their work. I am asking to order the sappers to work with probes after working with mine detectors. Except for the three members of the Slobtsov group, the remaining students are about to leave. Blinov has missed lots of classes. I am asking you to summon me to report and resolve the issues involved with the leadership of the team. Maslennikov"*

The snowstorm continued throughout the whole day of March 3, with wind up to 25 meters per second, visibility of 5 to 8 meters. From the morning the Mansi men were returning to Suevatpaul. In the opinion of Nevolin and Maslennikov, their continuous presence was not advisable. Stephan Kurikov was the only one among the Mansi men who was directly involved in the search, the rest of the Mansi men were mainly doing household chores. On Tempalov's instruction, Nevolin was to stay in the camp.

Despite bad weather, two helicopters arrived between 11:00 am and 12:00 pm with an interval of 20-30 minutes. Potyazhenko landed a group of sappers from the railway forces at the pass. The requested long metal probes were not sent. The four corpses and the recovered items from the cache were transported to Ivdel. Ivanov and Yarovoy left as well. The second helicopter damaged its support during the landing and was unable to land at the pass. The students from the Slobtsov group, who were waiting to be sent home, had to stay in the camp for the time being.

When delivered to Ivdel, the bodies were transported from the airport to the central hospital serving the N-240 administration staff and placed in the morgue. The driver of the truck was Stolyarov, the driver of the Northern Expedition, who had been detailed to the Ivdel airport sometime before the beginning of the search for the missing hikers.

By around 2:00 pm Pletnev and Vishnevskiy had completed their list of items brought from the cache site. In the morning, with the help of Grigoriev, they had already completed their inventory of the group's belongings, which were brought to Ivdel on March 1. Grigoriev was copying Kolmogorova's diary for his own use, with Vishnevskiy gathering the letters, a satchel with documents, money, diaries, and watches.

Following the accident with the helicopter at the pass, Gorlachenko urgently flew to Ivdel. The damaged part of the helicopter was taken to Polunochnoe for welding. The Kaunas crew was removed from the search and returned to Sverdlovsk. Due to the ground elevation profile, the airplanes were no longer considered as an option. Potyazhenko was the only one left to take part in the search. As per flight regulations, after doing 25 to 30 flying hours, helicopters had to fly back to Aramil for routine maintenance. Per flying shift, helicopters could make about seven flights to the pass, after which the helicopter had to be replaced. In total, three Mi-4 helicopters were used in the search, with tail numbers 14, 16, and 68. Flight mechanics and navigators were also alternating. Potyazhenko was flying with flight mechanics named Nikolay Nemyko, Valentin Kovtun, and Potegov; pilot-navigators Mihail Novikov, Valerian Ovchinnikov, and Babenko.

In the afternoon, the remaining part of the sappers of the 5th railway brigade was transported to the pass. In total, their group included eight men: Lt.- Colonel Shestopalov, Lieutenant Vladimir Avenburg with the servicemen of the mine warfare platoon of the 2nd company of the 52nd detached railway battalion – sergeant Y. Saveliev, corporal L. Tymkiv, enlisted men M. Mordonov, V. Vasilchenko, V. Kudin, and N. Golubev. The members of the Routing Qualification Commission of the Presidium of the All-Union Tourist Section Kirill Bardin, Master of Sports of the USSR, and Evgeniy Shuleshko, First Class Tourist of the USSR, arrived with the same flight. They were accompanied by the representative of the central council of the Burevestnik voluntary sports society Semyon Baskin, Master of Sports of the USSR, and Vasiliy Korolev, the chairman of the routing qualification commission of the Sverdlovsk city committee for physical culture and sports, 1st Class Tourist of the USSR.

Kirill Vasilyevich Bardin (30) was born in Moscow in 1929. After graduating from the division of Psychology of the Department of Philosophy of the Moscow State University in 1954, he was assigned to the Institute of Psychology of the Academy of Pedagogical Sciences of the USSR. As of 1955, he was already the First Class Tourist, led hikes of the 3rd category of difficulty to the Altai Mountains and the Vetrenniy Poyas (Windy Belt). Bardin had the experience of a winter hike in the Northern Urals of the 3rd category of difficulty. By 1959 he had the title of master of sports in water trekking. Together with Evgeniy Shuleshko, he was detailed by the Union of Sports Societies and Organizations of the RSFSR for investigation of the causes of death of the Dyatlov group.

Evgeniy Evgenievich Shuleshko (28) was born in Kharkov, Ukraine, in 1931 in the family of a Red Army officer. After graduating in 1954 from the division of Psychology of the Department of Philosophy of the Moscow State University, he worked in the laboratory studying younger schoolchild at the Research Institute of Psychology of the Academy of Pedagogical Sciences of the RSFSR. By 1955, he was the First Class Tourist. Shuleshko was a close friend of Bardin from their student days when they went hiking together. Bardin was leading the trek to Vetrennyi Poyas, but the winter trek to the Northern Urals of the 3rd category of difficulty was led by Shuleshko. On that assignment, both of them represented the committee for physical culture of the RSFS.

Semyon Borisovich Baskin (29) was born in 1930 and was an experienced athlete. In 1954 he worked as an instructor at tourist camps in the Caucasus. In 1955 he was the first to climb to the Western Shkhelda along its Northern Face with the 4B category of difficulty. In 1956 Baskin worked as an instructor in mountaineering at the Burevestnik voluntary sports society. As of 1959, Baskin worked as a coach at the Dzhan-Tugan alpine training camp for junior mountaineering instructors. He held the title of Master of Sports in Tourism from 1956.

Vasiliy Ivanovich Korolev (29) was born in 1930 in the Saratov Region. He graduated from a 10-year secondary school in Karpinsk – a copper mining town in the north of the Sverdlovsk Region. In 1949 he was admitted to the UPI Department of Physics and Technology, where he was active as a Komsomol organizer (agitator) of his student group, later a member of his department's Komsomol bureau, as well as his group's labor union organizer. After graduation in 1955, he was employed at a laboratory of his department. As an experienced hiker, Korolev was elected a member of the bureau of the UPI tourist club and chairman of the UPI routing commission. In 1955 Korolev was a member of the Sverdlovsk combined tourist team. It was under his chairmanship that the routing commission was approving the route of the Dyatlov group.

They arrived at Ivdel from Sverdlovsk the day before, on March 2. Vladimir Slobodin, the father of Rustem, flew together with the sports officials. He was still hoping for the better. Korolyov would later tell Grigoriev that Slobodin was questioning him if there were any hunters' cabins or caves in the nearby mountains, where the hikers might be finding a refuge. Slobodin spent several days at Ivdel, talked to Aleksander Deryagin, the chairman of the city council. He had tried to break through to the bodies brought to Ivdel but was not let through the cordon at the Ivdel airfield. Soon he would return to Sverdlovsk, with his son's body discovered at the pass the day after.

On its return flight, the helicopter took onboard six students from the Slobtsov group – Sharavin, Koptelov, Halizov, Devyatov, Krotov, and Strelnikov. From Ivdel, they went home to Sverdlovsk with a transfer in Serov. Slobtsov, Brusnitsyn, Lebedev, and Blinov had remained at the pass on the request of Ivanov so that to clarify the details of the early days of the search. Even further, Ivanov had taken Slobtsov's personal and group diaries, which he was keeping during the search. Later, in Sverdlovsk, they would give official testimony.

"To Sulman: A group of eight sappers has arrived. They have safely reached the camp. The corpses have been sent by helicopter; the prosecutor and the correspondent have also departed. 17 men are taking part in the search. In the morning the weather was better, but now the wind is getting stronger. The search is going on ... The group led by Captain Vlasov has carefully examined the valley of the stream, at the source of which the accident with the Dyatlov group had taken place. The group reached the Lozva River. No traces of the Dyatlov group have been discovered. The stream is the place of snow avalanche from the main ridge, with very deep snow. There is no chance that a part of the group could go to the Lozva through this valley. Moiseev has thoroughly examined the area with his dogs. Another group continued to probe the slope. They have covered two hundred meters of deep snow, one hundred meters wide, along the ravine of the accident up to Kolmogorova's body – without discovering anything. They have once again examined the site around the cedar ... The amount of work done and the places where spruce branches were cut give reason to assume that there might be someone else in addition to the two. Tomorrow we will subject this site to a more thorough inspection. On our way back from the search we met with the passengers of the second helicopter. We are all in

one tent, there are still 30 of us. Tomorrow we will continue our search ... There is a section of one and a half kilometers long and 100 meters wide, which should be examined with probes. With this done, the work will be over, since there is nowhere else to search. This will take three days if the weather gets even worse ... Since the probes, despite our request, have not yet arrived, half of the team will be used for setting a landing site near the campsite ... It is necessary to prepare for the replacement of the remaining students with army personnel. Chernyshev, Nevolin, Maslennikov"

In his draft of the radiogram, Maslennikov assumed that the cut spruce branches might have been *"used for a snow den, in which the rest are sleeping".* However, this guess did not become part of the final radiogram.

On March 4 the weather on the pass cleared. A group of ten cadets from the regimental school of military unit 6602 was sent to height 1079, under the command of Lieutenant Potapov.

> Initially, at the Ivdellag the guarding of prisoners and significant facilities was carried out by the Paramilitary security (VOKhR), as well as by self-protection – the guards, who were selected from among carefully screened convicts and deportees (special settlers). As of April 1, 1956, the Paramilitary security of the penitentiary system of the MVD of the USSR included the following training units: 1 training regiment, 3 training detachments, 18 training battalions, 22 training platoons, 4 schools for training sergeants-guides of search dogs, 25 search dogs training schools. The contingent of the paramilitary search guard was divided into armed guards (67,909 men), supervisors (16,531 men), and paramilitary fire fighting service (2,473 men). Following the party and government decision on reorganization of the MVD system, the decree of the Central Committee of the CPSU and the Council of Ministers of the USSR "On the measures to improve the work of the Ministry of Internal Affairs of the USSR" from October 25, 1956, paramilitary small-arms guard of corrective labor camps and prison camps of the MVD was transformed into the detainee escort of the MVD of the USSR for maintaining security at the corrective labor and prison camps. From 1956, the security of the Ivdellag was maintained by the military unit 6602 of the MVD 32nd detainee escort division, which would be later transformed into the 38th detainee escort brigade of the MVD of the USSR.

The probes had finally arrived, but they were too short. Blinov,

Serdityh, Borisov, Shevkunov, Slobtsov, Brusnitsyn, and Lebedev were sent to Ivdel. They would get back to Sverdlovsk by airplane to return home earlier than the rest of the Slobtsov group, who were sent from Ivdel by train. At the time, Verhovskiy from the Chernyshev group was getting ready to leave – and Ortyukov was deeply dissatisfied with the departure of the students, mostly because it had not been discussed with him.

"In addition to the two military groups of Chernyshev and Shestopalov, a civilian group was organized – to be led by Akselrod. The personnel of the camp totals 34 men. The search went on. 31 men were working from 9:30 am to 6 pm. They had passed a 250-meter long and 300-meter wide territory. Another group began probing the area around the cedar. There they found a handkerchief, two and a half pairs of socks, and a torn sleeve cuff of a gray sweater. There is nothing else to say. Three men were preparing the landing site. Right near the tent, an area of 50 by 50 meters was chopped down. I had climbed to the ridge of the spur, under which the Dyatlov tent was pitched, and then to height 1079. No traces of an ascent were discovered. Mine detectors proved to be useless, hence the lt. colonel had immediately switched to probes. Maslennikov"

The search in the area of the cedar was carried out by five men from the Shestopalov group, who had examined a site of 300 by 150 meters which included both streams. Sogrin, Akselrod, Bardin, Baskin, Shuleshko, and Korolyov, while examining the tent site specified that the slope had no hazard of snow slides. To facilitate the transportation of the belongings from the camp to the landing site, it was decided to move the landing site closer to the base camp. Tipikin would later recall that the site was being prepared in 200 meters (656 feet) to the east of their tent. They had begun to trample down the forest glade even before the arrival of the Akselrod group, but after a few days, the pilots decided it was not a safe landing site.

Maslennikov was told to prepare to report on the progress of the search, with the headquarters meeting scheduled for March 6 at Ivdel, where the inspection of the hikers' belongings brought from the pass was still underway. Among the belongings of the Dyatlov group, they discovered a hand-written issue of the group's satirical leaflet they called The Evening Otorten №1, the last thing they wrote before they died.

TRANSCRIPT OF DYATLOV GROUP COMBAT PAMPHLET

" EVENING OTORTEN " № 1

February 1, 1959   Publication of the trade union
committee of the "Khibina" group

Editorial

GREETING THE 21th PARTY
CONGRESS WITH INCREASED
BIRTHRATE AMONG HIKERS!

SCIENCE

In recent years, there has
been a heated debate around the
existence of Yeti. According to
the most recent reports, the Yeti
live in the Northern Ural, near
Mount Otorten.

PHILOSOPHIC SEMINAR

on the topic of "Love and hiking",
taking place daily on the tent
premises (main building).
Lectures are given by Dr. Thibeaux
and Dubinina, PhD (Love Sciences)

An Armenian Quiz.

Can nine hikers get warm
with a single stove and
blanket?

TECHNOLOGY NEWS

Hiking drag sled

Good while riding by train, car
or horseback. Not recommended
for freight transportation on
snow. For further information
contact chief constructor
com. Kolevatov.

SPORT

Team of radio technicians
including com. Doroshenko and
Kolmogorova has set a new world
record in portable stove assembly
- 1 hour 02 min. 27.4 sec.

The original Evening Otorten is unknown. Only a typewritten
copy remained in the criminal case file.

In the presence of Nikolay Klinov, the prosecutor of the Sverdlovsk
region, and lead investigator Lev Ivanov, forensic experts Boris Vozrozhdenniy and Yuri Laptev conducted the forensic medical examination of the corpses of Dyatlov, Doroshenko, Krivonischenko, and
Kolmogorova at the morgue of the N-240 Central hospital.

> **Yuri Ivanovich Laptev (37)** was born in 1922 in the city of Ufa,
> of the Bashkir Autonomous Republic. In July 1941 he was drafted
> into the Red Army and served in a fighter aviation regiment in
> the rank of sr. sergeant. For his wartime service, he was awarded
> medals "For the Victory over Germany in the Great Patriotic War
> of 1941-1945" and "For the Defense of the Soviet Arctic". From
> 1953, Laptev served as the head of the healthcare office of the
> city of Severouralsk in the rank of a captain of medical service.
> Concurrently, he worked as a forensic examiner of the Sverdlovsk
> regional office of forensic medicine. Before the accident with the
> Dyatlov group, he had been repeatedly summoned to Ivdel to
> conduct the required forensic examinations in other cases.
>
> **Nikolay Ivanovich Klinov (52)** was born in 1907 in the village
> of Malmyzhka in the Kazan Governorate of the Russian Empire.
> He was a railway worker at the Chusovaya station of the Perm
> railway, and then a foreman at the Verkh-Isetskiy metallurgical
> plant. In 1939 Klinov graduated from the Sverdlovsk Law Insti-
> tute, after which he worked as an instructor and head of the
> VCP(b) Sverdlovsk regional party committee, which was super-
> vising the judicial and prosecutorial personnel. From late June
> 1941, he fought as a military investigator of an infantry division,
> which was in the formation of the Kalinin Front. Klinov was
> awarded the orders of the Red Star and Patriotic War 1st degree.
> Heavily wounded, in January 1943, on an order of the Prosecu-
> tor General of the USSR, Klinov was demobilized and appointed
> assistant to the prosecutor of the Sverdlovsk region for special
> cases. From 1950, Klinov served as the prosecutor of the Sverd-
> lovsk region.

The conclusions were uniform: *"On the basis of the findings of the
examination of the corpse... and taking into consideration the circumstances of the case, we believe that the death... resulted from the exposure
to low temperatures (hypothermia)... It was a violent death – a fatality."*

Gordo and K.V. Naskichev served as coroner's witnesses. In fact, Naskichev's name was Filipp Aleksandrovich.

Filipp Aleksandrovich Naskichev (57) was born in 1902 in the village of Yanginichi of the Shapshinsky county, Lodeynopolskiy district of the Olonetsk Governorate. In the early 1930s, the family was dispossessed and deported to the town of Nadezhdinsk in the Urals. There Naskichev found a job as a laborer at the Nadezhdinskiy Mechanical Plant, which produced artillery shells. His wife Mariya Vasilyevna was hired as a tutor at its vocational school. In the mid-1950s, they moved to Ivdel to join their daughter Lydia, who worked at a local school as a primary school teacher. In 1959, Naskichev worked as a stable hand and cartman at the N-240 Central hospital. It was he who was transporting the bodies of the deceased hikers to the morgue and laid them down there. By mistake, an abbreviation of his position was written down into the forensic reports instead of his initials – K.V. (koniukh-vozchik = stablehand and cartman).

The news of the forensic examinations spread across the hospital, with its medical staff trying to peep into the morgue windows. As Zinaida N. Savina, nurse's aide at the hospital, would later recall she saw Yudin crying at the morgue's door. As Yudin himself would later recall, he was summoned to the Sverdlovsk regional prosecutor's office for identification and dispatched to Ivdel. In the morgue, Yuri saw Dyatlov's body under a sheet, and a little later the still frozen corpse of Slobodin, which had just been transported from the pass.

At Ivdel on March 5, Yudin began to identify the belongings of the victims in the presence of Vishnevskiy and Yarovoy serving as coroner's witnesses. The procedure continued until March 7. Yudin remembered only those who owned the larger, more distinguishable items. As to the smaller items, he adhered to the principle that in whichever backpack they were discovered, they belonged to its owner. For this reason, he made some errors in the identification. Earlier, Yudin had managed to compile a list of people with whom the Dyatlov group communicated in Vizhay, and to share with the experts the details of pitching the tent and quartering under canvas. The tent was first hung and stretched at the Ivdel airport, and later taken to the propaganda room (Lenin room) of the prosecutor's office.

"Today, it has again been windy with blowing snow. The wind is 15 m/s, with poor visibility. The team has been working particularly strenuously, covering an area of 500 meters long and from 250 to 150 meters

wide. Halfway between the location of the bodies of Kolmogorova and Dyatlov, the fifth corpse was discovered under a 15 cm layer of snow. That was Rustem Slobodin, who was warmly dressed, in a ski cap, black cotton sweater, pants, long underpants and three pairs of socks – with one foot in a black felt boot... There are several raw sores on the face and a wound on the wrist. He had a "Pobeda" wristwatch, which stopped at a quarter to nine. The body is lying crooked, with the head towards the mountain. A formal note of death was taken. Tomorrow afternoon we will take him up [to the landing site]. There is a 500 square meter plot left [to be searched]. All groups have been unified into a single group; we are walking with probes very close to each other in a 30-men front by separate quadrates along the emergency ravine route. We will proceed in the same manner tomorrow. Maslennikov"

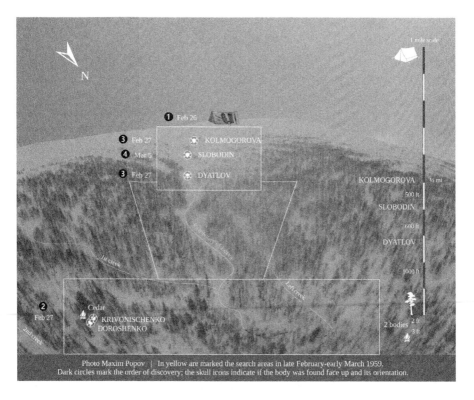

Photo Maxim Popov | In yellow are marked the search areas in late February-early March 1959. Dark circles mark the order of discovery; the skull icons indicate if the body was found face up and its orientation.

The next day, on March 6, Slobodin's body was transported to Ivdel. On the same day, the death of Dyatlov, Krivonischenko, Doroshenko, and Kolmogorova will be registered at the Ivdel civil registration office. In their death certificates the time of death is registered as February 1, 1959, with the place of death given as *"in the mountain area of height 1079 in the Ivdel district"*, and the cause of death as *"hypothermia during a hiking trip"*. Lev Gordo would receive the documents upon presentation of the certificate from the prosecutor of the city of Ivdel.

"[Today] the weather has not been favorable for the search. The search party has covered the entire valley of the creek, which is 250 meters long and 100 meters wide with nothing discovered. I have walked with a small group, along the forest border under height 880, along the ridge above the emergency stream. Any escape of a part of the group from the cedar via this ridge is ruled out, because of the very deep loose snow all over the slope. Tomorrow we will probe the deep ravine 50 meters from the cedar, which is leading to the saddle between heights 880 and 1079. We will also probe for the second time the few sections at the upper part of the slope under the Dyatlov group's tent. There is nowhere else to search at."

Avalanche probes of 2.5-3 meters long (8-10 feet) were delivered to the pass. The probes had to be specially manufactured in Serov. Earlier they had to use ski poles or standard 70-centimeter (2.3 feet) sapper probes with wooden handles. The work on the new landing site near the camp at the Auspiya River was in progress. The makeup of the search party was changing. The six cadets from the regimental school of military unit 6602 in Lieutenant Potapov's group were replaced. Verhovskiy from the Chernyshev's group and Lt. Colonel Shestopalov returned to Ivdel.

On March 8, Vozrozhdenniy was conducting a forensic medical examination of Slobodin's body at the same morgue of the N-240 Central hospital, in the presence of Klinov and Ivanov, with Gordo and Naskichev again serving as coroner's witnesses. By that time, Laptev had already returned from Ivdel to Severouralsk.

"Based on the findings in the examination of the corpse of citizen Rustem Vladimirovich Slobodin, 23 years old, and considering the circumstances of the case, I believe that the death of Slobodin resulted from exposure to low temperature (hypothermia) ... The fracture of the left frontal bone discovered in an inlying examination could result from the fall of citizen Slobodin or a head contusion received from hitting against solid objects, such as stones, ice, etc. The said closed skull injury was caused by a blunt instrument. At the time it was inflicted, it no doubt had caused a state of short-term stupefaction and contributed to Slobodin's rapid freezing. ... Slobodin died a violent death – in an accident."

On March 9, Ivdel civil registry office will note Slobodin's death and issue a death certificate.

The fracture in Slobodin's skull gave grounds for a new theory.

Grigoriev would later recall that there was an opinion that Slobodin might have been injured while climbing to the pass on February 1, which had caused the group to stop for the night on the slope of height 1079.

At the pass, it was a day off. Maslennikov, Bardin, and Baskin flew to Ivdel to report to the emergency commission. From then on, the search party would be headed by Chernyshev.

The day before, on March 7, the work was proceeding according to the plan: *"28 men were continuing the search for the whole day – with no result. A flashlight turned on was discovered 450 meters below the tent. 20 meters from the tent was found a piece of a broken ski. I believe that the search should be suspended until late April. The weather is improving. Maslennikov"*

The search party is 31 men strong. After the replacements made on March 6-8, ten men comprised the group led by Lieutenant Potapov: Potapov, Zauzin, Biryukov, Sautbekov, Syunikaev, Polyakov, Borey, Moiseev, Peremot, and Solovyev.

Based on the outcomes of the conference, the following instructions were sent from Ivdel to the pass: *"March 9, 1959. Today you should continue the search across the strip of 30 by 50 meters around the examined sections of the ravine. Following the four-hour discussion of the findings up to date, it was decided to remove the team's entire available personnel from the search within three or four days. Today, by 12:00 pm, the following comrades should be ready to fly out: Shuleshko, Sogrin, Akselrod, Atmanaki, Karelin, Yablonskih, Chernyshev, and Tipikin. The boarding will take place at the site on top of the ridge. For the evacuation days, comrades Potapov and Korolyov are assigned as leaders of the remaining part of the team. The landing site near the tent has been rejected due to insufficient clearance of the trees for approaching from the east. Take action. The Institute's property should be accepted by Korolyov. The shipment of food supplies and equipment should be done last, and if necessary, left at the camp for subsequent groups."*

The following stayed back at the search camp: Nevolin, Korolyov, ten men from Lt. Potapov's military unit 6602 group, and seven of Lt. Avenburg's railway sappers. Feliks Solomonovich, the chairman of the Ivdel sports committee, would later recall that no one from military unit 6602 was ordered to take part in the search. Most of those sent to the pass were the athletes from among servicemen.

The search went on, with Solovyov from the Potapov group getting injured. *"A 16-men strong search group proceeded along the right side of the ravine, a 20-meter wide strip, from the site of Kolmogorova's body to the cedar. We have double checked the ravine from the creak to the location where Slobodin's body was discovered. The groups of Moiseev and Borei with dogs searched through the nearby passes – with nothing discovered. For the next day, it was planned to survey the creak's bed and the left side of the ravine. Potapov, Korolyov"*

On March 10 at Ivdel, at a conference with the participation of the members of the party regional committee Filipp Ermash, Chernyshev, Vishnevskiy, Ortyukov, Ivanov, and Maslennikov, it was decided to organize two new groups of ten sappers and ten students to completely replace the military search team. The student group was to be ready by March 12-13. It was also decided to replace the radio operator, under the supervision of Captain Chernyshev, to relocate the search camp to the Lozva River's fourth tributary. The camp would be relocated by the Blinov group only in April.

"We have examined the area around the cedar within the radius of 150 meters. We have searched through a section behind the ravine on the right side of the creak, which is 40 meters wide and 150 meters long. The search has not produced any findings. For tomorrow we are considering moving along the left side of the ravine from the location where Kolmogorova's body was discovered and further down. We believe it inadvisable to expand the search any further from around the cedar. Once again, please inform us of the exact date for the evacuation of the group. Potapov"

"Taking into consideration the maintenance of the helicopters, the replacement of the entire team will begin on March 12. Comrade Soloviev and the miners will be removed on the first day, with the remaining men on the second. The search should not be slowed down on those days. Pavlov"

Yudin returned to Sverdlovsk. He helped with transporting the biological tissue samples taken during the forensic examinations of the bodies. He would recall that a helicopter was detailed at Ivdel to fly to Sverdlovsk, with only two passengers onboard – a female expert and himself. In Sverdlovsk, they were met at the airport and taken to the laboratory of the Sverdlovsk regional bureau of forensic examination (SOBSME) on Rosa Luxemburg Street. There the probes were received undersigned receipt written by P.G. Chaschihina, an expert from the division of forensic medical examination of material evidence of the Sverdlovsk regional bureau of forensic examination; she had a long work experience at the chemical examination division of the city department of forensic service, which dated back to pre-WWII time.

Yudin couldn't make it to the funeral of Dyatlov and Slobodin at the Mikhailovskoe cemetery, which took place in the morning. The day before, on March 9, Krivonischenko was buried at the Ivanovskoe cemetery, with Kolmogorova and Doroshenko at the Mikhailovskoe cemetery.

Yuri Bondarev, who in 1959 was a fifth year student of the UPI Department of Engineering, would later recall: *"I was summoned to the Komsomol committee and told that I had to pick up the bodies of the dead from the Dyatlov group from the morgue and bring them to the funeral at the institute, and then to the cemetery. They asked if I might be uncomfortable doing this and that three men had already bailed out. I am not easily unnerved, so agreed. They gave me a truck, and I went to the morgue... I recognized Dyatlov first, although I had seen him only a couple of times before... The bodies in the coffins were loaded onto the open bed and was told to climb into the back and keep the coffins stable during the trip. This is how I rode all the way... There were a lot of people at the ceremony. I remember that Rustik's mother without raising her voice was muttering his name over and over again. His name was misspelled, the plaque having Ruslan, while his name is Rustem. I drew attention to this and asked to correct it. In general, all this made a very strong impression on me – I was absent for a week after... I didn't go to the second funerals, the first ones were enough for me."*

The five were laid to rest, the four were yet to be found.

CHAPTER 8. FEBRUARY 27 - MARCH 10, 1959. THE LEADING AND GUIDING ROLE OF THE PARTY.

Late at night on February 26, the relatives of Aleksander Kolevatov sent a telegram to the Central Committee of the CPSU – namely to its first secretary Nikita Sergeevich Khrushchev: *"We are earnestly asking for your assistance in the urgent search for our children."* The telegram would be registered at the General Department of the Central Committee of the CPSU on the morning of February 27.

The Central Committee's department of administrative and trade-financial agencies for the RSFSR initiated a search for the group and an investigation into the causes of the accident. It is hard to say what was the reason for such efficiency. Possibly it was the March 1 elections to the Supreme Soviet of the RSFSR, the regional and city soviets of people's deputies. On the election day, a radio message was sent from the search camp at the Auspiya River regarding the support for the bloc of communists and non-party members by the search team. The authorities were always considering the appeals of their citizens on the eve of an event like that. On top of this, on February 27, 1959, the Presidium of the Supreme Soviet of the USSR enacted an ordinance, "On the creation of collegiums within the prosecutor's office of the USSR and the prosecutor's offices in the union republics". That ordinance was aimed at changing the prosecution service, with particular emphasis on monitoring the implementation at the prosecutor's office, as well as on the prosecutors reporting on their work at strengthening law and order and organization of crime prevention.

The date of the appeal by Nina Anisimova dovetailed with the top-level discussion of the prosecutor's office. Investigations of the accident were launched with the involvement of the Central Committee of the CPSU, the Council of Ministers of the USSR, the Ministry of Internal Affairs of the USSR, the Prosecutor's Office, the Union of Sports Societies, as well as the agencies at the level of the RSFSR.

On February 28, the Sverdlovsk regional committee of the CPSU resolved to organize an emergency commission of the regional committee of the CPSU. The commission included Vasiliy Pavlov, Deputy Chairman of the Sverdlovsk regional executive committee; Filipp Ermash, head of the science and education department of the Sverdlovsk regional committee of the CPSU; Nikolay Klinov, the prosecutor of the Sverdlovsk region, Mihail Shishkarev, head of the MVD Office for the Sverdlovsk region Mihail Gorlachenko, the first deputy commander of the Air Force of the Ural Military District; Pyotr Pomazkin, head of the department of party agencies of the Sverdlovsk regional committee of the CPSU and Alexander Pozharskiy, chief of staff of the Ural Military District.

Vasiliy Alekseevich Pavlov was appointed the chairman of the commission. He was transferred to Sverdlovsk from Chelyabinsk in 1947 and from 1958 served as the first deputy chairman of the Sverdlovsk regional executive committee.

Filipp Timofeevich Ermash (36) was born in 1923 into a peasant family in the Novo-Nikolaevskaya Governorate (the name of the Novosibirsk region in 1921-25). In 1941, he was drafted into the Red Army and served as an enlisted man, sapper squad commander in the rank of Guards sergeant (1943), and deputy platoon commander. He was awarded the order of the Red Star and the medal "For Courage". After graduating in 1951 from the Department of History of the Ural State University, he served as the second and later first secretary of the Sverdlovsk city Komsomol committee. From 1954, he served as deputy department head and by 1959 as department head of the Sverdlovsk regional party committee. By 1959, he rose from the second secretary of the Sverdlovsk city Komsomol committee to department head of the Sverdlovsk regional committee of the CPSU.

Mihail Nikolaevich Shishkarev (59) was born in Moscow in 1900 into a working class family, earning his living at odd jobs from the age of 13 – until he joined the Red Army in 1918. By 1922, after completing infantry and machine-gun command schools, he rose to the position of a platoon commander. Later in the same year, he began his life-long career in the agencies of state security – the State Political Directorate (GPU) – the Joint State Political Directorate (OGPU) – The People's Commissariat for Internal Affairs (NKVD) – the Ministry of Internal Affairs (MVD), rising from platoon commander of an OGPU border guard battalion at the Black Sea to deputy commander of the Trans-Baikal Front's rear area security (1945), in the rank of major general of security services, to which he was promoted in 1940. In 1946, Shishkarev was appointed head of the MVD Office for the Maritime Territory (Primorskiy Kray) and in 1951 he was transferred to the MVD Office of the Sverdlovsk region – the position he held as of 1959, with a short break in 1953 when he was sent for a few months to Moscow as deputy head of the militia office for the Moscow region. Shishkarev was awarded three orders of the Red Star, three orders of the Red Banner, and the badge "Honored Serviceman of the NKVD".

Mihail Iosifovich Gorlachenko (54) was born in 1905 in a village in the Kherson Governorate of the Russian Empire (now Ukraine.) He was drafted into the Red Army in 1922 (the same year he joined the Bolshevik party.) After graduating from the Kharkov Red Master Sergeants Military School in 1925, he served in the Ukrainian Military District as the commander of an infantry platoon, company political organizer, and battalion commander. In 1935, after training at the Borisoglebsk military pilot school, he began his career in aviation in the Belorussian military region; by August 1937 as commander of a reconnaissance airborne squadron in the rank of a captain. In the same year, he took part in hostilities during the Spanish Civil War and then in the Soviet-Finnish "winter" war of 1939-40. After completing advanced training courses for commanders of air regiments at the Air Force Academy for the command and navigational personnel, from March 1941, he served as a commanding officer of a light bomber regiment, taking part in the Battle of Moscow; from May 1942, he was a commanding officer of an assault aviation division, fighting in the Battle of Stalingrad, and from December 1942 to June 1945 – of an Assault Aviation Corps, which fought at many fronts, particularly in the Battle of Kursk, later in the liberation of Belorussia, Poland, Berlin, and Prague; promoted to Major General of Aviation in March 1943. In 1945, with the war's end, Gorlachenko was appointed deputy commanding officer for combat training of the 4th Air Army. In 1949, after graduating from the department of airforce of the K.E. Voroshilov Higher Military Academy, he was appointed Commander of the Air Force of the Volga Military District. In 1951-53 he was in China on a special mission. In May 1958 he was appointed chief of staff, the First Deputy Commander of the Air Force of the Ural Military District. He would retire in 1961.

Pyotr Vasilyevich Pomazkin (41) was born in 1918 in a village in the Perm Governorate. In 1941-45 he worked at a defense plant in the city of Gorkiy where he joined the communist party in 1944. From 1946 he became a Komsomol functionary, working as a department head, the secretary of the Sverdlovsk city Komsomol committee, and the 2nd secretary of the Central Komsomol Committee of Estonia. From 1952, Pomazkin was promoted to party functionary, first in Estonia, as head of the department of party bodies of the Pyarnu regional committee of the Communist Party of Estonia, and then in the Sverdlovsk Region, as head of the department of party bodies of the Sverdlovsk regional party committee. At the same time, he served as the secretary of the Sverdlovsk city committee of the CPSU.

Aleksander Stepanovich Pozharskiy (54) was born in 1905 in a village in the Polotsk district of the Vitebsk Governorate of the Russian Empire (now the Republic of Belarus). In 1928 he was conscripted and served on active duty in 1928-29; in 1935 he was drafted into the regular Red Army, embarking on a professional military career. In 1944-45 he served as deputy chief of the operations department of the staff of the Trans-Baikal Front. In August 1945 he took part in the Manchurian strategic operation, which liberated Manchuria and Korea at the end of WWII. For his wartime service, Pozharskiy was awarded the Order of the Red Star and Suvorov 3rd degree, and the medals "For the Victory over Germany" and "The Victory over Japan". In 1956, Pozharskiy was promoted to the rank of Major General and appointed as the chief of staff of the Ural Military District.

Information about the search was promptly transmitted to Moscow. A special message from the MVD of the RSFSR under the signature of Nikolay Stakhanov, the Minister of Internal Affairs of the RSFSR, was sent for the attention of Nikolay Dudorov, the Minister of Internal Affairs of the USSR:

"Regarding the death of the students from the Ural Polytechnic Institute, the participants in a hiking trip in the Sverdlovsk region.

During the student winter vacations, a group of student hikers from the Ural Polytechnic Institute (Sverdlovsk) with nine participants went to the Ivdel district of the Sverdlovsk region for a 300-kilometer ski trek along the route from the north of the Ivdel mountain to the Otorten mountain region.

On January 28 this year, the said group departed from the settlement of

Burmantovo, which is 70 km north of Ivdel, with food supplies until Febru-
ary 14. On February 19, the Institute turned to the local party and Soviet
bodies with a request to provide assistance in the search for the missing
students. Until that time, the MVD Office of the Sverdlovsk region had no
information about the trek.

Search groups from among the Institute's expert skiers and the staff of
the Ivdel corrective labor camp [Ivdellag] with search dogs were dropped off
by helicopters in the area of Mt. Otorten. On February 26, the search group
found the tent with abandoned skis, an ice ax, a camera, blankets, and
food on the southern slopes of the mountain, and on February 27, they dis-
covered four snowed in corpses one kilometer from the tent.

The search goes on with the participation of 46 expert skiers, airplanes,
and helicopters. To organize the search and investigate the causes of death
of the students, the Sverdlovsk regional committee of the CPSU has organ-
ized a commission."

Based on these materials, a message was drawn up by the Ministry
of Internal Affairs of the USSR addressed to Frol Kozlov, the First Deputy Chairman of the Council of Ministers of the USSR.

At the same time, the Union of Sports clubs and organization of
the RSFSR and the Burevestnik central sports society had started the
organization of a special commission for consideration of the causes
of the accident. The organization of such a commission was standard
practice in the sphere of hiking. In that case, the decision-making time
was explained by the direct instructions from the Central Committee
of the CPSU. Semyon B. Baskin, the representative of the central council of the Burevestnik sports society, together with Kyrill Bardin and
Evgeniy Shuleshko, the members of the routing qualification commission of the Presidium of the All-Union Section of Tourism were detailed to Sverdlovsk.

According to Semyon Baskin's widow, in Moscow, their mission
was arranged by one Georgiy Eliseev, chief of the department for
physical culture and sports of the All-Union Central Council of Labor
Unions.

Georgiy Ivanovich Eliseev (46) was born in 1913 in a village
of the Tver Governorate of the Russian Empire. In 1934, he was
drafted into the Red Army, and in 1937 graduated from a junior officers' training school in Leningrad. In 1939-1940 Eliseev
took part in the "winter" war with Finland. He fought in WWII
at the eastern front from the very first day of the Nazi attack on
the Soviet Union – until the V-day. Fighting successively in the
formations of the Western, Leningrad, 1st Baltic, and 3rd Belo-

russian Fronts, he served as a commanding officer of an artillery platoon, field artillery battery, and regiment. At the war's end, he took part in the battles in Eastern Prussia and the conquest of Konigsberg. After V-Day, he stayed in the Red Army as an artillery regiment commander, in the rank of a colonel. Following his retirement from the armed services in 1947, Eliseev studied at the Lesgaft Leningrad Institute of Physical Culture and after graduation served as Head of the Department for physical culture and sports of the Central Council of Labor Unions.

The widow of Shuleshko recalled that her husband was woken up at night by a phone call, with only 40 minutes left for getting ready. He grabbed his personal items while a car was waiting downstairs to take him to the airport.

On the side of the prosecution, Lev Ivanov, a forensic prosecutor from the investigation department of the Sverdlovsk regional prosecutor's office, flew from Sverdlovsk to Ivdel. Experts from the Sverdlovsk regional forensic examination office (SOBSME) and from the Sverdlovsk Research Institute of Forensic Science (SNIKL) were summoned. Lev Ivanov would later recall how he was summoned to the regional prosecutor's office and given 30 minutes to get ready. He immediately received new felt boots, a fur cap with earflaps ('ushanka'), and a brand new sheepskin jacket ('polushubok') from the head of the prosecutor's office maintenance and supply department. After another 30 minutes, Ivanov was already onboard the airplane, which would deliver him to Ivdel in a few hours by customer flight.

In early March, the members of the extraordinary commission of the regional committee of the CPSU arrived at Ivdel. Grigoriev would later recall that they were frequently departing from Ivdel and were making allowances for many facts. Nevertheless, in view of Moscow's scrutiny, it was possible to organize speedy and efficient coordination between agencies at various levels and subordination. For instance, a group of hikers, which arrived two or three days behind the schedule, was met at the Rostov-on-Don railway station by an MVD official – to question the group about the UPI group. Earlier they had made phone calls to the group's leader asking about his whereabouts and if there was any information from him.

They were looking for information about that group back on February 27: *"To Maslennikov: Report if in early February Blinov or Karelin met a group of seven hikers from the Rostov Pedagogical Institute. Zaostrovskiy, Sulman"*

For about three weeks, a group of hikers from the Rostov Pedagogical Institute led by Igor Fomenko was proceeding along the following route: the city of Ivdel – the Vizhay settlement – the upstream of the Vizhay River – the Perm region. While in Sverdlovsk, before their departure for Ivdel, they called at the UPI sports club in the hope of obtaining a local map. Along the route, they spent the night in Bahtiyarov's yurts in the upstream of the Vizhay River. Possibly, the hikers from Rostov had heard something about the Dyatlov group, but unfortunately, Fomenko turned to be of no help.

The commission of the regional party committee was abiding by the general line to the letter. The search was to be continued. As much as possible it was necessary to avoid wide news coverage, which was particularly unwelcome in view of the fair amount of foreigners who arrived at Sverdlovsk for the world women's speed skating championship, which took place in Sverdlovsk from February 28 to March 1, 1959.

The parents of the deceased hikers were invited to the regional party committee, where they were told that the funeral would take place at Ivdel. In that period, funerals at the site of large-scale accidents instead of the place of residence were commonplace. That was the case in June 1959, when 56 pioneers from the city of Abakan died in a disastrous railway accident at the station of Minino of the Krasnoyarsk region. The children were buried in a common grave at the Minino station's cemetery, with the parents not allowed to bury their children in the native Khakassia. The parents were had to sign statements vouching for non-disclosure of the reasons for the death of their children. The eyewitnesses of the tragedy were made to vouch non-disclosure of any information about the accident. The monument subsequently erected at the cemetery had no names.

In the same manner, on March 4, the Ivdel search headquarters decided to erect a temporal monument at the pass, which was to be brought by a helicopter and to be fixed with cement. It was planned to install a permanent monument and a memorial plaque with the help of the UPI students. However, it would be done only in 1963 by a group of the UPI students led by Yakimenko.

After the UPI sports club received information that the deceased would be buried at Ivdel, they began to discuss the strength and composition of the sports club's delegation to the funeral. However, after the parents' flat refusal, Vladimir Kuroedov, the secretary of the Sverdlovsk regional party committee, gave permission to bury the deceased at Sverdlovsk.

Vladimir Alekseevich Kuroedov (53) was born in 1906 in a village in the Nizhegorodsky Governorate of the Russian Empire. In 1930 he graduated from the Nizhegorodsky Pedagogical Institute and in 1936 he joined the VCP(b). In the first three decades in his long career, his field was propaganda and agitation – alternatively as party functionary and editor. He served as the second secretary of the Gorkiy regional party committee, then (in 1945-46) as editor-in-chief of the regional paper, Gorkovskaya kommuna (The Gorkiy Commune), after which he moved to Moscow, first, as editor of the science department of Sovetskaia Rossiia daily, then promoted to section and department head of the office of propaganda of the VCP(b) central committee (1946-49). Later in 1949, Kuroedov was sent back to Sverdlovsk as the secretary of its regional party committee for propaganda and agitation (1949-59).

On March 7 information was received that the bodies of the hikers were brought to Sverdlovsk – with the funeral on March 9. Vladimir Pudov, who was Igor Dyatlov's fellow student, would later recall that the bodies were brought in groups of two or three bodies each. At the airport, they were met by the UPI students. The friends of the deceased – Galina Radosteva, 4th-year student of the UPI Department of Radio Engineering, and Igor Shestopalov, a fellow student of Yuri Doroshenko, were asked to come to the morgue for identification. Shestopalov would later recall that he was invited because the mother of Doroshenko was unable to identify her son's corpse. Igor did identify the body: he had been Yuri's fellow student and they had gone in for Greco-Roman wrestling together. The body of Krivonischenko was identified by his father.

On March 8, at the session of the regional party committee at Ivdel, com. Maslennikov first *"laid out in detail the development of the search and its outcomes,"* went on *"to report to the commission the unanimous opinion of the entire search team that the search should be suspended at least until April, waiting for the snow to shrink. The commission resolved that the search should be continued, however, replacing all participants of the search team in view of the rough-duty."* The plan for the continuation of the search work would be discussed at the commission's session on March 10.

According to the available recollections of some of the Ivdel residents, all local candidates for the search mission were to be approved by the KGB officers. There is an opinion that on the bidding of the party bodies, the KGB Office for the Sverdlov Region might take charge of the case of the hikers' death. The UKGB might be providing the profiles of potential search participants and keeping the party city committee informed as to the reaction of the residents of Ivdel to this tragedy and the progress of its investigation.

On March 10 at Sverdlovsk, a session of the Bureau of the Sverdlovsk regional party committee was considering the issue of the death of the hikers from the Ural Polytechnic Institute – with its first secretary, Andrey Kirilenko, attending in person.

> **Andrey Pavlovich Kirilenko (53)** was born in 1906 in the Voronezh Governorate of the Russian Empire in the family of a handicraftsman. He graduated from a village school (1920) and from a vocational school (1925), after which he worked at various enterprises in the Voronezh Governorate and later in the Donbas mines. After two years (1929-30) as a Komsomol, soviet and co-op functionary, Kirilenko joined the VCP(b) in 1931. Following his graduation from the Rybinsk Aviation Institute in 1936, for some time he worked as a designing engineer, but from 1938 shifted to a career of a party functionary – as secretary of the regional party committee in several regions of Ukraine. After the Nazi attack on the Soviet Union, from November 1941 to April 1942, Kirilenko served as a member of the Military Council of the 18th Army in the formation of the Southern Front. From 1955, Kirilenko served as the first secretary of the Sverdlovsk regional party committee; from 1957 simultaneously as a candidate member of the Presidium of the Central Committee of the CPSU.

From the protocol of the session of the Bureau of the Sverdlovsk regional committee of the CPSU from March 10, 1959:

"The regional committee of the CPSU points out to the absence of elementary order in certain athletic organizations of Sverdlovsk in the organization and carrying hiking treks, which results in accidents. For instance, in late January same year, a hiking group of the Ural Polytechnic Institute was sent to the northern Ural area without the knowledge of the directorate and the Institute's social entities, without exercising any control over its movement. The Institute's administration, the party, and soviet bodies learned about the death of this group with considerable delay.

The Bureau of the regional committee of the CPSU resolved:

To pay attention to the Sverdlovsk city committee of the CPSU (com. Zamiryakin) to the lack of control on his part over the organization of the hiking work in athletic organizations, particularly, in the institutions of higher learning.

To suggest to the Sverdlovsk city committee of the CPSU (com. Zamiry-

akin) to thoroughly investigate the causes of death of the hikers from the Polytechnic Institute and to bring those guilty to strict party and government responsibility."

The decisions were implemented very quickly, before the end of the month.

CHAPTER 9. MARCH 10 - MAY 5, 1959. "FURTHER SEARCH TO BE ENTRUSTED TO THE URAL KIROV POLYTECHNIC INSTITUTE."

Following the final decision on the continuation of the ground search, which was taken by the Sverdlovsk regional committee on its March 10 meeting at Ivdel, Konstantin Nikolaev, the chairman of the Sverdlovsk regional executive committee, approved the subsequent plan of the ground search.

Konstantin Kuzmich Nikolaev (49) was born in 1910 in the Kaluga Governorate of the Russian Empire in the family of a rural teacher. From the age of 17, he followed his father by working as a teacher and then as a school principal. Later he worked as an accountant and board chairman of a consumer society in the Mosalsky district of the Kaluga Governorate. In the spring of 1930, Nikolaev moved to Sverdlovsk, where he served as an accountant at the office of public services and utilities of the city soviet and as a technician at the Ural Sanitary-Engineering Construction trust. Simultaneously, from 1931, he studied at the higher sanitary-engineering school and then at the Department of Construction of the Ural Construction Institute, which in 1934 was reorganized as a department of construction of the Ural Industrial Institute. In 1936, Nikolaev received an engineering degree in the field of "water and waste water systems". Upon graduation he was retained at his alma mater, working as an assistant professor and then as deputy dean of the department of construction. In 1940, he joined the VCP(b) and a year later he became the secretary of the Institute's party bureau. In August 1941, Nikolaev became a party functionary – shifted as department head at the Sverdlovsk city committee of the VCP(b). In 1944 he was elected as the first secretary of the Sverdlovsk Leninsky district committee of the VCP(b); in 1946 he was shifted to the position of deputy chairman of the Sverdlovsk district executive committee and in February 1949 he was approved in the position of its chairman.

The responsibility for the continuation of the search mission was entrusted to the Ural Polytechnic Institute (UPI):

"Through the actions taken from February 23 to March 5, 1959, in the vicinity of the height 1079 (to the south from Mt. Otorten) a tourist tent with equipment, food and skis, as well as the bodies of the deceased hikers comrades Dyatlov, Kolmogorova, Slobodin, Doroshenko, and Krivonischenko were discovered.

Continuation of the ground search to be entrusted to the Ural Kirov Polytechnic Institute, for which:

I. To detail a ground search group of 20 participants (in two groups 10 members each)

To assist the UPI in conducting its ground search:

1. For the Ural Military District:

a) to detail 10 sappers until the end of the ground search, providing equipment and food rations;

b) to detail two helicopters for ensuring uninterrupted delivery, procurement, and replacement of ground search groups in the territory of the search.

2. For the Regional Office of Internal Affairs:

a) to detail military escort from the Ivdellag in the strength of 10 until the end of the ground search;

b) to provide other ground search group with the necessary material procurement, transportation, and other needs.

3. For the Northern ground search group of the Ural Geological Office (com. Sulman) to provide two-way radio communication.

For day-to-day supervision of the ground search, to organize an operational group in the town of Ivdel, including:

1. com. Prodanov I.S., the First Secretary of the Ivdel town committee of the CPSU (chairman)

2. com. Ivanov V.A., the head of the Ivdellag office (deputy chairman)

3. com. Ortyukov G.S., an instructor of the Kirov UPI

4. com. Vishnevskiy A.I., the head of the Department of Physical Education, UPI

5. com. Chernyshev A.A., the head of the ground search group.

The work of the regional commission to be continued, to establish liaison with the representatives and all the above listed organizations, to make regular reviews of the work progress and take the necessary decisions."

In May, immediately after the last bodies were located, radio operators of the Northern Geological Survey expedition named Aleksander Temnikov, A.P. Sysoev, Egor Nevolin, and A.I. Kozhushko, were given a citation *"for their qualified and diligent work in radio facilitation of geological surveys of the Northern Expedition."* The order was signed by Sulman on the occasion of the Soviet Radio Day (May 7, in the Soviet Union and Russia, a professional day of communication workers and radio journalists).

Following the approved plan of ground search works, the UPI sports club organized a group of mountain climbers experienced with avalanche probes. The group was led by Abram Kikoin, the founder and chairman of the UPI mountain climbing club – and the head of the emissions laboratory of the IFM of the Ural branch of the Academy of Sciences of the USSR.

> **Abram Konstantinovich Kikoin (45)** was born in 1914 in a Lithuanian settlement of Malye Zhagory. In 1936 Abram Kikoin graduated from the Department of Physics and Mechanics of the Leningrad Polytechnic Institute, majoring in "experimental physics", and was then sent to the graduate school of the Ukrainian Physical-Technical Institute in Kharkov. In late 1939, Kikoin completed his graduate studies and, as an accomplished skier, volunteered for the Finnish front. However, he was rejected as "a valuable scientist". He worked at the Kharkov Institute until its evacuation to Alma-Ata in November 1941. There his application for the Army was again rejected, but instead, given his mountain climbing training, Kikoin was sent to train mountaineers for the army as a junior instructor at a mountaineer instruction school not far from Alma-Ata. Later, in 1943, he was sent to train mountaineer military units in the eastern part of the Kazakh region. In the fall of 1943, Kikoin's life made a sharp turn, when he received an order from the State Committee of Defense to come to Moscow. There he was introduced to Igor Kurchatov, then an organizer of the Soviet nuclear research project, who asked him to join his brother, Isaak, at Sverdlovsk. That was how Abram Kikoin joined the Soviet atomic project. At the time the Sverdlovsk Institute of Physics of Metals was the only institute to work on the separation of isotopes. In late 1945, when the two brothers worked in Moscow, Abram Kikoin was denounced as the last graduate student of 'an enemy of the people' and removed from the atomic project. Not to ruin his brother's career, he returned to Sverdlovsk, where he continued to work low-key at his former laboratory, then became head of the chair of physics at the Ural Polytechnic Institute, simultaneously working at the Institute of the Physics of Metals of the Ural branch of the Academy of Sci-

ences, where from May 1957 he served as head of its emissions laboratory. In 1946, Kikoin organized a section of mountaineering at the UPI sports club, which facilitated the registration of a federation of mountaineering at the city sports committee. By 1954 on five occasions he took part in mountain rescue missions, including as the mission's leader on three occasions. In 1958, Kikoin supervised the UPI training camp at the "Zhan-Tougan" mountain climbing camp.

By that time, a group of the UPI hikers had returned to Sverdlovsk from the "Belala-kaia" mountain camp at the Dombai field in northern Caucasus. Its participants – Vladimir Krylov, Yuri Smirnov, Vladislav Shkodin, and Gennadiy Solovyev – joined Kikoin's rescue group. The UPI military department detailed a car to purchase food for the expedition.

It is likely that students with low academic performance were sent on the early rescue shifts and particularly later since participation in rescue missions was rewarded with some privileges. For instance, Sogrin and Zinovyev took sabbaticals with more than two month long absence from classes, likely no-shows. Slobtsov as well took a sabbatical after he received an unsatisfactory grade in the theoretical foundations of electric engineering in the winter examination session of 1958/59.

On March 13, a group of the UPI mountaineers, including Abram Kikoin, Vladimir Krylov, Pyotr Bartolomey, Yuri Sahnin, Vladislav Shkodin, Stanislav Mertsalov, Gennadiy Solovyev, Yuri Smirnov, and Yuri Kotenev flew from Ivdel to the mountain pass in two flights – as a replacement for the tired soldiers from the groups of Potapov and Avenburg. Bartolomey later recalled that before the flight Lev Ivanov asked for identification of the tent and personal belongings of the Dyatlov group members, which were stored at the Ivdel airport. As Sakhnin would later recall, Zolotaryov's mother was seeing the rescue group members to the helicopter. The nieces of Zolotaryov would later recall that following the news of the death of her son, Vera Ivanovna Zolotaryova was summoned to Sverdlovsk. It was her first air flight. She went alone, since Aleksey Gerasimovich, Zolotaryov's father, had already retired and was sickly.

They could not fly from Ivdel for a few days. The rescue group members boarded the helicopter a few times, but each time they were offloaded due to non-flying weather. Along with the Kikoin group, Ortyukov, Prodanov, and Grigoriev, a reporter from the Urals Worker, were flying to the pass. That morning Grigoriev begged with the staff members to let him fly to the rescue camp at the pass. Prodanov and Ortyukov returned to Ivdel in the evening. Grigoriev stayed back at the camp. In total there were 13 men in the tent: Grigoriev, Nevolin, Korolev, and the members of Kikoin's group.

From Grigoriev's diary: *"We were talking about the deceased throughout the whole evening. About why they had pitched their tent on the mountain, etc. It was said that Igor Dyatlov was very ambitious, prone to domineering. At one point he suggested to his group to cross from one bank of the river to another, without any reason – with no reason at all. At one point the people were so outraged with his behavior that they would not follow his orders. Then he retreated and declared a hunger strike. He was a good and diligent rank-and-file member of the group. All mistakes were attributed to him. Two people who happened to be with him spoke about it in particular. Kikoin as well spoke negatively about him. He said that it was stupid, that the group left at 3 pm when it would get dark here in about an hour and a half or two."*

The next day, Grigoriev, who took part in the search as part of a group of nine, discovered an old reindeer skin in the snow near a cedar. Grigoriev was left alone to dig it out: the students would not help him. Grigoriev was surprised, remarking that the students were searching half-heartedly.

Besides the search works, Kikoin's group was offered to move the camp to the valley of the Lozva River, but they didn't go through with it. Instead, upon their arrival at the pass, the mountain climbers ascended to height 1079. Later the members of the search mission explained their mood by the fact that when one group after another was returning without any result, the students were sincerely and insistently explaining to their higher-ups the uselessness of continuing the search until the final meltdown of the snow. Hence they were not demonstrating great zeal in the search. That mood held until May.

At 11:30 am on March 15, under a heavy snowstorm, a group of military servicemen, a stove, and other camp equipment were delivered for the camp. Grigoriev, Korolev, and Nevolin, who was replaced by another radio operator, returned to Ivdel.

On March 18, the railway sappers of Senior Lieutenant Avenburg returned to search. Savelyev, Tymkiv, Golubev, Vasilchenko, and Mordonov were joined by privates of the mine and explosive platoon R. Hisamatullin, T. Faizov, and Petrosyan. They will remain at the pass until April 9.

On March 22, the third UPI search shift departed from Sverdlovsk by train, including Sergey Sogrin, Vitaliy Malyutin, Rudolf Sedov, Vasiliy Shulyatiev, Victor Meshcheryakov, Victor Eroshev, Valeriy Dubovtsev, Valentin Yakimenko, and Boris Sychev. Before its departure, the group was instructed on safety arrangements at the UPI.

For a few days, the weather at Ivdel was non-flying, hence Kikoin's group could not be removed from the pass. Sakhnin would later recall that in the period of the search there was only a single day without wind. In the remaining time, there was a strong wind or a blizzard. In the period of the search, they inspected the site to the west from the cedar, the slope, and the creek. In the creek, they were sinking neck-deep into the snow but were unable to reach any solid crust in the bottom, with their gauge feelers not long enough. According to the recollections of Nikolay Vasilyevich Tokarev – a civilian serving in the military unit 6602, who was Ivdel's champion in skiing and participant in the Potapov group rescue mission – paid Kikoin's attention to broken fir-trees along the forest edge, however, Kikoin had taken no notice of it. Later, in May, the final four would be discovered in the creek in the vicinity of that site.

Finally, on March 25, the military and civil rescue members were replaced. Borei was replaced by Potapov as the chief of the group from military unit 6602. The group included Victor Klimenko, Nikolay Kuzminov, and Yuri Zauzin, the secretary of the unit's Komsomol organization.

Yakimenko would later recall that at the time of the arrival of the Sogrin's group at the rescue camp, part of the group of mountaineers was still there – to fly with the helicopter's second flight after a few hours. They touched base, cooked dinner together. The students and soldiers kept apart, with practically no intermingling. Someone from among the mountaineers paid attention to the newcomers to the use of the hooks from among the Dyatlov group's equipment on the crossbeam over the fire.

The Mansi men were absent during the ground search. The rescue team was comprised of squads from the 6602 military unit led by Borey with a strength of 6, Avenburg's group of sappers with a strength of 9, and Sogrin's group with a strength of 10. The overall leadership was exercised by Captain Chernyshev. Probing was made along the slope of height 1079 in the direction of the forest, in parallel to the "tent-cedar" line to the south from the site of the discovered tent. The site to the north, closer to the location of the discovered tent, had already been explored by the previous rescue groups. The locations of the discovered bodies were identified with short gauge feelers driven into the snow.

Sychev would later recall how they were walking on the solid crust with 2.5 meters (8 feet) long wire gauge feelers. They were poking the crust in the search of something they might bump into. If it bumped, then they would be digging with shovels. For fear of traumatizing, the members of the rescue teams were forbidden to climb the slope up to the location of the tent and to move away at more than 300 meters (984 feet) from the search zone.

On March 31, the following information arrived at the radio station of the Northern expedition: *"To Prodanov and Vishnevskiy, March 31, 1959, 9:30 am local time: At 4:00 am on March 31, a hiker on duty named Meshteryakov spotted a large flame-colored ring in the eastern direction, which for 20 minutes was moving in our direction and then hid behind height 880. Before hiding below the horizon, a star emerged from the center of the ring, which was gradually increasing up to the size of the Moon, and then began falling while separating from the ring. The entire contingent, alerted by the alarm, was watching the strange phenomenon. We are asking to explain this activity and its security since in given circumstances this is making a disturbing impression. Avenburg, Potapov, Sogrin"*

Soon, on April 5, the Soviet North newspaper published in the village of Gary of the Sverdlovsk region featured an article by V. Granin on the trip of Karelin's group. It as well reported a sighting of a similar celestial spectacle in the morning of February 17, with a suspicion that it might be a meteorite or a rocket.

The members of the search mission had not received any cogent response. On its return to Ivdel, Sogrin's group was met right at the airport by Vishnevskiy, who was accompanied by unknown people. The latter strongly requested not to tell anyone about the sightings on March 31. Sychev would later recall that from that time on students stopped discussing it even with one another.

On April 6, the rescue group of the military unit 6602 was headed by Nikolay Kuzminov. Sogrin's group was substituted by the UPI fourth rescue group shift, including Boris Martyushev, Evgeniy Zinovyev, Valeriy Pechenkin, Mihail Sharavin, Yuri Koptelov, Igor Shestopalov, and Anatoliy Plastun. As Plastun would later recall, enlistment into the rescue group was organized on a notice at the UPI tourist club. The rescue group was a cross-functional team. It was delivered to the pass by a helicopter, with the same helicopter taking the previous group back. Yakimenko used the time to tell him that at night some type of a star was flying over their head.

The weather during the rescue mission was fine. They lived below the river in a large 30-berth tent together with the military rescuers.

An officer from the military group served as coordinator of the search mission. On the slope everything was blown down, however, the traces of the tent site were still visible. The members of the search mission went on the search along those traces. The search was undertaken along the slope closer to the cedar, however, without any result. The snow was deeper than the length of the gauge feelers. Sharavin confirmed that by that time more snow had been accumulated in the lowland due to the snow slide from the mountaintops.

Sharavin would soon get into an accident while skiing to spend three weeks, until May 12, at a hospital in Sverdlovsk.

Shestopalov would later recall that no special instruction had been given. Having landed at the pass, the whole group skied from the Dyatlov people tent site down, along the pass of the traces, until the cedar and further on. That was a superficial examination: the group had not been set the task of a thorough examination of the territory. The track with footprints was clearly visible – leading downwards, to the left from the direction towards the cedar, most likely towards the ravine, but it had not been tracked down to the end. They approached the cedar on skis but did not stay there for a long time. Under the cedar, they saw the remains of a rather large fire.

There was practically no communication with the military rescuers. In the morning the team members were going up towards the path and followed in a chain poking the snow with long metal gauge feelers, in the hope of discovering the bodies of the dead. They were usually moving in the northern direction. The location of the tent of the Dyatlov people would remain on the left, with the fire under the cedar on the right in the lowlands. Throughout the whole time of the search, no discoveries were made.

On April 3, Nikolay Klinov, the prosecutor of the Sverdlovsk region, asked the All-Union Research Institute of Forensics of the Prosecutor's Office of the USSR: *"In February this year there was an emergency in the Sverdlovsk region – a group of 9 hikers died in the region of the Otorten Mountain. In the process of the land search, from February 27 until now, it was possible to discover the corpses of five people, with four of the corpses discovered in the course of a free search, since they were visible at the site, and only one corpse was discovered in the process of probing the territory with steel two-meter long gauge feelers. At present we can confidently assume the location of the remaining corpses – in the valley of two offsets of a ridge measuring 30-50 hectare; however, due to the dense and often very deep snow, the corpses have not yet been discovered. The gigantic expenses of the search may with time become even higher if the search groups do not apply any new methods in discovering the corpses. It is necessary to remark that the use of mine detectors has not been productive, since the corpses are half-undressed and do not have any relatively sizable metal substances. We are aware that one of the VNIIK plans included the development of a device for the search of buried corpses, with the device based on the ultra-sonic properties. There have been oral reports on the positive results of the use of a pilot copy of the device. In view of the situation and following consultations with the search commission of the regional committee of the CPSU, we consider it very useful to test the said device in the search. Asking you, to tackle the issue positively, subject to availability."*

Unfortunately, the Institute did not have the device, which would have facilitated the search for the corpses.

On April 14, servicemen of the 4th company of the 52nd railway battalion joined the search work. Junior Sergeant Zamiraylo, privates Minulin, Krishtafovich, and Mirgorodskiy under the command of Senior Lieutenant M. Starikovskiy replaced the Avenburg group, which on April 10 was sent to work on the construction of the railway. Starikovskiy's group will remain at the pass until April 27.

Late at night on April 15, the next – fifth – UPI rescue shift arrived at Ivdel, including Yuri Blinov, Sergey Arzamastsev, Vladimir Yunyshev, Vladimir Kiselev, and Oleg Sobol. There was to be another member in that rescue team named Igor Alekseev, a student of the Sverdlovsk Law Institute, who was not released by the Institute's director on short notice. On their way, at a restaurant in the town of Serov, while waiting for the train to Ivdel, they surprisingly met Captain Chernyshev, with whom Blynov had already been acquainted, and had a talk. In the evening at Ivdel, the group of Blinov was met by Vishnevskiy who arrived by car. The rescue group members spent the night at a hotel, where they would have to stay for the whole day due to non-flying weather.

On April 17, a group flew to the pass to replace the group of Martyushev. By that time the composition of the group from the military unit 6602 led by Kuzminov had changed as well. Nevolin, who was released for three days to celebrate his birthday, flew to Ivdel together with Martyushev's group.

By that time all the open spaces had been probed, and the search moved into the forest. The rescue headquarters gave an assignment to Blinov's group to relocate the camp closer to the cedar and to undertake a free search, including searching along the Lozva River at three to four kilometers downstream. Zinovyev would later recall that they were inspecting the Lozva's corridor a kilometer up and down from the inflow of its fourth tributary. Sr. Lieutenant Moiseev was working there as well with his dog Alta.

By April 25, the camp had completely relocated to the valley of the Lozva River. Nevolin would later recall that to the north from the searchers' tent at the Lozva River there were two cedars, to which they had to fix the aerial, since communication at the Lozva was noticeably worse than at the Auspiya, on the other side of the slope.

Intensive snow melting continued. Despite the frequent overcast, snow, rain, and fog, daily outings for a free search were continuing. The snow on the mountains had melted, but in the valleys, the mantle of snow was still heavy. By the end of the month, snowfalls had resumed. At the camp, they learned that Ortyukov was again appointed as the head of the search.

On April 27, Blinov's group was substituted by the UPI sixth rescue shift, which included Vladimir Askinadzi, Nikolay Kuznetsov, Vadim Fedorov, Boris Suvorov, and Anatoliy Mohov. Ortyukov and a replacement dog handler arrived together with them.

The UPI party committee appointed Askinadzi as the group's senior. With the approaching test and examination periods, the only ones to agree to join the group from among Askinadzi's acquaintances were Kuznetsov and Suvorov. The rest responded to an ad at the UPI tourist club advertising board with the promise of privileges from the rector and academic leaves with paid stipends. There were girls among the volunteers, but on the instruction of the party committee, they were not accepted. The equipment, boots, and windbreakers were issued at the military department.

The parting words were odd. The UPI rector Siunov believed that because of the melting snow, there could at last be findings at the site of the accident. At the UPI party committee, the searchers were warned that the possible finds might serve as incriminating evidence in confirmation of the plans of the Dyatlov group to go abroad.

Before he departed from Sverdlovsk, Askinadzi talked with the searchers from the previous groups and knew many details of the search – in greater detail than the information that was circulating at the Institute. Besides, following the landing, he had a detailed discussion with Yuri Blinov: both of them were against the participation of the students in the search missions.

In the first days, fearing that the bodies might be taken down the river with the incipient snow thawing, they built a dam at the Lozva's fourth tributary, so that to block any possible flows from the streams. The dam was in the forest zone, about a hundred meters from the first stream, 15 or 20 meters below the searchers' camp. It had taken them three days to build the dam.

The Kurikovs Mansi men appeared at the search site, with Stepan joined by his brother.

> **Grigoriy Nikolaevich Kurikov (52)** was born in 1907 in Suevatpaul. In the 1930s he took part in a ski race along the route from the Sujevat yurt of the Garinskiy district – to Sverdlovsk. He was repeatedly elected deputy of the Bourmantovsky national rural council of the Sverdlovsk regional Soviet. Quite recently, in March 1959, he was elected a deputy of the Ivdel city soviet.

Mohov did not remember the exact time of the appearance of the Mansi men. They were continuously coming and going, sometimes joined by their relatives or acquaintances. Askinadzi recalled that Mansi Sambindalovs were also present in the area of the search; since spring they had been deer grazing in the area. They were even cutting the antlers of a young Siberian stag on Ortyukov's request. The summer yurt of the Sambindalovs was only two kilometers to the northeast from the pass.

The search group got itself settled in two tents at the new camp at the Lozva River. The soldiers stayed separately from the students, and the Ortyukov's students separately from the servicemen. The Kurikovs as well lived in a tent, sleeping right at its entrance. All the camp's fatigue duties were performed by the soldiers. Pilots arrived several times during the search: grouse shooting with their pistols.

The works were undertaken in a free search mode in the forest and along the slopes within the range of up to one kilometer around the cedar by groups of two men each. It was Ortyukov who was setting the routes. The Mansi men followed the students on the search, shooting wood grouses with small-caliber guns. Ortyukov turned evening briefing sessions into a daily progress review routine. The Kurikov brothers took part in all sessions, with Askinadzi and Kuzminov attending wherever required, as the leaders of student and military search groups. It was at those conferences that the plans for the next day's search were approved.

Ortyukov announced May 1-2 to be the days off, since the searchers were very tired. Everybody was getting ready for departure, expecting May 5 to be the final day of the planned stay of the Askinadzi group at the search site. Sogrin was getting ready for his third search mission and was organizing the seventh UPI search shift, with Zinovyev, Martyushev, Pechenkin, Kostrulin, and Victor Lebedev, a fifth year student of the Mechanical Department, already enlisted for the mission.

CHAPTER 10. MAY 5-12, 1959.
DYATLOV FOUR.

On May five, a telegram arrived from the search camp: *"To Prodanov: At 9:30 am on May 5, Kurikov discovered black cotton tracksuit pants without the right leg in 50 meters to the south-west from the cedar, on the location of the chopped spruce grove at the depth of 10 cm. The pants are charred on the backside. The right leg has been cut with a knife. He as well discovered the left part of a women's sweater of light-brown worsted wool. The second part with the right sleeve was cut with a knife and has not yet been discovered. The sweater belonged to Dubinina. At 11 am I decided to excavate the ditch 10 meters to the south-west from the chopped spruce grove. A plot with an area of 20 sq. meters at the depth of 2.5 meters."*

Askinadzi saw firsthand the Kurikovs discussing small thawed out twigs, after which they went to Ortyukov. Mohov would later recall that on their return from the slope to the camp along the ski track laid along the right bank of the fourth tributary, the students came across Nevolin, who told them that in 150 meters to the right from the ski track there were thawed out stubs of small chopped silver firs, as well as a coniferous trace of up to five meters long going down the snow above the stream. An instruction has been given to begin digging after dinner in the area of the coniferous trace, about 200 meters from the search camp. The snow was wet, dense, but digging was easy.

"At the bottom of the excavated plot, they discovered a flooring from the tops of chopped fir trees three square meters in size. On top of the flooring, in a crumpled state, turned inside out, the following items were found: sleeveless gray woolen China made sweater; insulated brown trousers with fleece inside. The upper and lower elastic bands of the trousers are torn. A warm brown woolen sweater with lilac thread; the right leg of the earlier discovered pants; one soldierly foot binding made of junior enlisted military cloth with a stitched webbing about one meter long.

I cannot explain the appearance of the foot binding. The items have been discovered in the course of the excavation at the depth of two meters 30 centimeters from the surface of the snow and 30 centimeters above ground. In the location of the tent pitched by the Dyatlov group, they found an 18 cm long thermazote scabbard from a dagger and one spoon. There is an assumption that the scabbard belonged to Kolevatov. Ortyukov"

Excavations were continued. *"I have decided to continue the excavation of this ditch no matter how difficult it is since the snow is very hard. I am asking you to instruct to send us six very durable sapper shovels with a strong capping piece and two pickaxes. I suppose that the deceased are somewhere near. Excavations will require physically strong and enduring soldiers, about which I am asking to alert the commanding officers. At 5:00 pm, we are going to the excavations. Please report your suggestions and instructions to Nevolin for my execution. Ortyukov"*

In the course of the next probing, Askinadzi detected body fragments on his probe. *"To Prodanov, 6:40 pm: While excavating the ditch, at the bottom of a flowing stream, we discovered a corpse in a grey sweater; the excavation of the ditch continues. The work has to be done in the water. I am going to the search works asking you to prepare for tomorrow's helicopter departure, with representatives of the prosecution and investigation to fly here tomorrow. Ortyukov"*

The body of Dubinina was excavated. Three more bodies were discovered nearby, in the water. The body of Dubinina was removed from the dig since it was blocking access to the rest. They dug out a pit on the left bank of the river, where the body of Dubinina was laid to preserve it, given the above zero temperatures. They made a canopy over the three bodies, which remained in the stream – so that they would not be damaged by the morning sun.

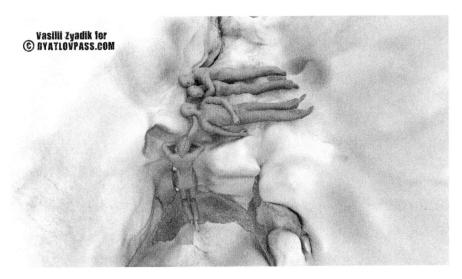

Vasili Zyadik for
© DYATLOVPASS.COM

In the evening, all members of the search team without exception were relieving stress with alcohol, which was left behind by the helicopter crew. Askinadzi, Ortyukov, and Kuzminov were unable to fall asleep.

In the morning Tempalov arrived at the pass. From the handwritten protocol of examination of the location where the corpses were discovered:

"On May 6, 1959, Tempalov, the city prosecutor of Ivdel of the Sverdlovsk region, junior counselor of justice, with coroner's witnesses in attendance..., drew up this protocol of the place of discovery of the corpses, numbering four. On the slope of the western side of height 880, 50 meters from the known cedar, four corpses were discovered in the first stream. Among them, there are three men and one woman. The corpse of the woman has been identified as Dubinina Lyudmila. The male corpses are impossible to identify without lifting them.

All corpses are in the water. They have been dug out from under the snow, which is from 2.5 to 2 meters deep. The two men and the third one are lying with their heads towards the north downstream. The corpse of Dubinina was lying in an opposite direction, with the head upstream. Dubinina has a ski mask on her head, a yellow undershirt, a checked shirt, and two sweaters –one grey and another dark-colored. She has dark leggings and brown ski pants. Her feet: there were two wool socks on her left foot; with her right foot wrapped up in one half of a sweater. The sweater is light beige. According to V.M. Askinadzi, who identified Dubinina, there are traces of damage from a probe on the nape and the back. Her corpse is decomposed.

The first male corpse is dressed in a khaki windbreaker. On the hands: there are two pairs of wristwatches on one hand: one of Pobeda and another of Sportivnye brands. The Pobeda watch shows 38 minutes to nine, and Sporting – 15 minutes past eight. The head and feet of this corpse cannot be seen, since the entire corpse has not yet been excavated from the snow. The two corpses are lying embraced. Both do not have anything on their head. Part of the hair on the heads is missing. One [corpse] is dressed in a windbreaker, and so is the second. It will be possible to determine the remaining clothes only after the corpses are lifted from out of the stream. The feet are not visible, since they have not been completely excavated and are under the snow. The corpses are decomposed. The corpses have been photographed. The corpses should be withdrawn from the stream immediately, since they may get decomposed even further. They may be carried away by the stream since the current is very swift.

Up the stream, at a distance of six meters, along the rows of fir twigs, a flooring was discovered at the depth of 3 to 2.5 meters. This flooring consists of 14 silver fir and one birch tops lying on the snow. The following items were discovered on the flooring.

A drawing showing the items on top of the flooring
1. Leg of black ski trousers
2. Whole woolen light Chinese sweater
3. Whole insulated brown woolen sweater
4. Brown trousers torn at the legs
5. – 20 feet - bodies

The second part of the beige sweater was found under a tree 15 meters to the south from the stream. One half of a pair of ski pants was discovered in the location where fir tops were cut for the flooring, 15 meters from the den towards the cedar. Also under the snow, at the site of the discovery of the Dyatlov group's tent, ebony riveted knife scabbard and a spoon of white metal were found."

The bodies were packed into covers and sleeping bags and shifted to the landing site awaiting the dispatch to Ivdel.

On May 7, Lev Ivanov and Vozrozhdenniy arrived at the pass. As Potyazhenko would recall later, he received a command from the command post to fly for transportation of the corpses. He was met by Ortyukov who said that besides transportation of the corpses, it was necessary to bring a monument to the pass with the return flight, with materials needed for its mounting. His commanding officers confirmed the mission of transportation of the bodies, but not of the monument, hence Potyazhenko refused. Moreover, his commanding officers approved the transportation of the bodies only if in coffins, according to the sanitary guidelines for transportation of corpses.

"To Prodanov: Ivan Stepanovich, it is outrageous that myself, along with fourteen comrades, had carried the corpses to the helicopter in our arms, but the crew, despite my insistent requests, refused to take the requested onboard. As a communist, furious with the behavior of the crew, I want to inform the party city committee and the commander of the military district, Colonel-General Leliushenko, twice Hero of the Soviet Union. For you personally. Corpses are frozen in the state in which you saw them in. This concerns the open body parts. Detailed examination has demonstrated that they are in a frozen state. The forensic expert refused to perform an exception, saying that it was impossible to do. At your request, he will report to you in person about it. Ortyukov"

"I am outraged by the behavior of the crew, which refused to take the specially prepared cargo onboard, despite my imperative requests. Ortyukov"

Mohov would later recall that it had taken very long to resolve the issue with the evacuation of corpses. For two nights, the bodies were lying at the pass near the campfires. Mohov, Suvorov, and Kuznetsov were guarding the bodies against animals and birds.

"To Sverdlovsk, the regional committee of the CPSU, for the attention of Ermash. The regional executive committee for the attention of Pavlov. The Ivdel city committee of the CPSU, for Prodanov. Captain Potiazhenko, the helicopter commander, has refused to evacuate the deceased, explaining his refusal with the order received from com. Gorlachenko, which [order] prohibited any evacuation without zinc boxes. According to the finding of the regional forensic expert, the corpses are frozen. Any expert examination at the site of the accident is ruled out. In the opinion of the same expert, from the hygienic point of view, the evacuation of the corpses is absolutely safe. The corpses have been wrapped and sewn into waterproof tarpaulin covers, which exclude any infection. Asking to request instructions from the Air Force Directorate on the immediate evacuation of the corpses, which have been delivered to the area of the helicopter landing site. Ortyukov 7/5"

"To Ortyukov and Ivanov: I will try to report it, but there is a slim chance that they will agree to transportation without coffins. Zinc-lined coffins have been ordered today. They have promised to send them over tomorrow with the helicopter flight scheduled for tomorrow afternoon. There has yet been no decision in the question of the burial place. I have talked

to Pavlov. He said that the Sverdlovsk city party committee has been instructed to contact the parents. Prodanov"

"To Prodanov: Asking to inform Klinov: the corpses are frozen. For this reason, any detailed examination is impossible. The corpses have been appropriately prepared for transportation to Ivdel, coated with spruce branches and sewn up into tarpaulin. They will decompose if not transported tomorrow. In case of burial at the height, it won't be possible to perform an autopsy, given the absence of any adequate facilities. I have sent Vozrozhdenniy to Ivdel to wait for the arrival of the corpses. There are no traces of any violence. The clothes were cut by the hikers themselves. I am staying in the camp to search for any small items. Ivanov"

Finally, on May 8, the corpses were transported from the pass; and the works on breaking the search camp had begun.

On May 9, at the N-240 infirmary morgue, Vozrozhdenniy with Ivanov and Churkina in attendance, conducted the forensic examination of the bodies of Kolevatov, Zolotaryov, Thibeaux-Brignolle, and Dubinina. Injuries of various degrees of severity were discovered in all of them.

"On the basis of the examination of the corpse of Kolevatov, I believe that his death resulted from the effects of low temperature. The bodily injuries discovered on Kolevatov's head, such as defects of soft tissues, as well as 'bath skin' represent postmortem changes in the corpse, which prior to its discovery had been in water. Kolevatov died by violence."

"On the basis of the examination of the corpse of citizen Zolotaryov, 37 years of age, I believe that his death resulted from a composite fracture of the right ribs with the hidden hemorrhage into the pleural cavity, aggravated by low temperature. The above said composite fractures with the hemorrhage into the pleural cavity had occurred antemortem at the moment of an impact with a great force on Zolotaryov's chest and his fall, compression, or hurl. ... Zolotaryov died by violence."

"On the basis of the examination of the corpse of citizen Thibeaux-Brignolle, I believe that his death resulted from a closed multifragmentary depressed fracture in the area of the calvarium and skull base, with ample hemorrhage under brain tunic and brain substance, aggravated by low temperature. The said vast antemortem multi-fragmentary fracture of the bones of the calvarium and skull base resulted from a high velocity force impact and Thibeaux-Brignolle's subsequent fall, hurl, and concussion... Thibeaux-Brignolle died by violence."

"On the basis of the examination of the corpse of citizen Dubinina L.A., I believe that the death of Dubinina resulted from a major bleeding into the right ventricle of heart, multiple bilateral rib fracture, plethoric concealed

hemorrhage into the thoracic cavity. The said injuries might have resulted from the impact with great strength, inflicting a severe occlusive mortal injury of Dubinina's ribcage. Notably, the antemortem injuries had resulted from the impact with great strength and the subsequent fall, hurl, or impact injury of Dubinina's ribcage... Dubinina died by violence."

Histological examinations would confirm the antemortem type of the injuries; however, Georgiy Gants, the forensic expert of the Sverdlovsk regional bureau of forensic medical examination, would formalize the results of the tests only on May 29.

> **Georgiy Vladimirovich Gants** was born in Odessa in 1930 in a family of a Soviet employee. Soon after the Nazi attack on the Soviet Union, the family was evacuated to Uzbekistan, and in 1942 moved to Sverdlovsk, following the father's new work assignment. In 1948, Georgiy graduated from a 10-year secondary school with a gold medal and was admitted to the Sverdlovsk Medical Institute. Elected as a Komsomol organizer of his group, he was an active member of a student scientific circle at the chair of forensic medicine, where he went through his pre-graduate internship. In 1951, he was simultaneously admitted as a correspondence student in the Leningrad Institute of Physical Culture. After his graduation cum laude in 1954 from the therapeutic department of the Sverdlovsk Medical Institute, Gants worked in the town of Berezovskiy as a district forensic medical expert. From September 1954, he served as a forensic expert and histopathologist at the Sverdlovsk regional bureau of forensic medical examination.

The funeral of Kolevatov and Dubinina took place on May 11 at the Mikhailovskoe cemetery of Sverdlovsk. Zolotaryov was buried at the Sverdlovsk Ivanovskoe cemetery.

Thibeaux-Brignolle was buried on May 12 at the Sverdlovsk Mikhailovskoe cemetery. All of them were buried in closed coffins. The UPI students helped with unloading the coffins at the Koltsovo airport and transporting them to the morgue.

Zinovyev would later recall that the parents and relatives were summoned to the morgue for identification. In the process, they opened only part of the coverlet. The father of Dubinina threw the coverlet off his daughter's body and fainted. The identification procedure was interrupted. Until the last moment, the mother of Alexander Kolevatov had not been told about the death of her son. After his funeral, she had her legs paralyzed. The members of the staff of the

Sverdlovsk city committee for physical culture and sports took part in the Zolotaryov funeral.

It is possible that the investigation believed that the discovered injuries resulted from the impact of a hurricane. Possibly, there were other reasons not to make public the conclusions of the forensic examination. However, the nature of the injuries received by Dubinina, Zolotaryov, and Thibeaux-Brignolle, would become public knowledge only after 30 or 40 years. Previously, the relatives and friends believed that hypothermia was the cause of the death of all of them. For instance, the impact of low temperature was listed as the cause of death in the Zolotaryov death certificate, issued by the branch of civil status registration office of the Kirov region of Sverdlovsk on May 12, 1959.

The criminal case would be closed before long.

"RULING

May 28, 1959, the city of Sverdlovsk

The forensic prosecutor of the Sverdlovsk regional prosecutor's office, junior counselor of justice Ivanov, on considering the criminal case initiated on the occasion of the death of nine hikers at the Ivdel district of the Sverdlovsk region,

has ruled:

On January 23, 1959, a group of backpackers including 10 participants went on a ski track along the following route: the city of Sverdlovsk – the Ivdel Mount. – 2nd Northern settlement – Mt. Otorten – Mt. Oyko-Chakur – the Northern Toshemka River – the Vizhay settlement – the city of Ivdel – the city of Sverdlovsk. The group included: Dyatlov Igor, student of the Ural Polytechnic Institute, leader of the trek; Dubinina L.A., Kolmogorova Z.A., Kolevatov A.S., Yudin Y.E., Doroshenko Y.N., all students of the UPI; Zolotaryov A.A., instructor of the Kourovskaya tourist base; Slobodin R.V., Krivonischenko Y.G., Thibeaux-Brignolle N.V., engineers of the enterprises in Sverdlovsk and Chelyabinsk.

All participants in the trek had good hiking training and were able to take part in a trek of the 3rd category of difficulty. The group had all the necessary equipment and food supplies. The trek was financed by the labor union committee of the Ural Polytechnic Institute. After its safe arrival at the initial point of the trek –the 2nd Northern settlement of the Ivdel district, on January 28, 1959, the group went on its trek. One tourist, Yudin Y.E., returned home from the 2nd Northern since he was unable to continue the trek because of his illness.

It appears from the hikers' diary notes, map sketches, and processed films, that on January 28, 1959, the group was proceeding upstream the Lozva River; on January 30, 1959, the group continued its movement;

on January 31, 1959, the hikers approached the Auspiya River and tried to proceed to the valley of the Lozva River by the pass, however, due to low temperature and strong wind they were forced to get back downhill and put up for the night. On February 1, 1959, the hikers set a cache at the head of the Auspiya River, in which they left their food stock and all excessive equipment. After their return to the Auspiya River valley on January 31, 1959, while aware of the demanding terrain conditions of height 1079, which they were to ascent, Dyatlov, as the group's leader, made a bad mistake, namely that the group began its ascent on February 1, 1959, only at 3 pm.

Subsequently, by the ski track of the hikers, which had survived until the time of the search, it was possible to ascertain that in their movement in the direction of the fourth tributary of the Lozva River, the hikers took 500 to 600 meters to the left and instead of the pass made by heights 1079 and 880, they reached the eastern slope of height 1079. That was Dyatlov's second mistake.

Having used the light hours of the day for the ascent to height 1079, under a heavy wind, which is common in that area, and low temperature of about -25°C -30°C, Dyatlov found himself in a disadvantageous situation of an overnight stop and decided to pitch a tent on the slope of height 1079, so that in the morning of the next day, without losing the height, to proceed to the Otorten Mountain, in a straight-line distance of about 10 kilometers.

One of the photo cameras had a shot (the last made), which showed the moment of digging snow for pitching the tent. Considering that this shot was taken at exposures of 1/25sec., the diaphragm of 5.6, and film sensitivity of 65 units GOST (all-Union State Standard), as well taking into consideration the density of the frame, we may believe that the hikers came down to pitching the tent at around 5 pm of February 1, 1959. A similar shot was taken by another camera. No diary entries and no photos made after that time have been discovered.

According to the protocol of the routing commission, on February 12, 1959, the group's leader, Igor Dyatlov, was to report on the arrival at the Vizhay settlement by telegram to the UPI sports club and the committee for physical culture (com. Ufimtsev). Since the deadline – December 12, 1959 – had expired with no information about the group received, the hikers who had known Dyatlov closely, began to insist on taking steps for the search, and on February 20, 1959, the administration of the Institute sent a search group along the Dyatlov's route, and then a few more groups. Subsequently, soldiers and officers of the MVD of the USSR, airplanes, and helicopters of civil aviation and air force were sent to the search.

On February 26, 1959, the group's tent with all its equipment and food supplies was discovered on the eastern slope of height 1079. The tent and everything inside it had been well preserved. The examination of the tent demonstrated that it had been properly pitched and provided accommodation for the hikers. Inside the tent, there were two blankets spread, backpacks, windbreaker jackets, and pants. The remaining blankets were crumpled and congealed. A few parts of smoked loin's skin were discovered.

The layout of the tent and the items inside it (almost all the footwear, all the outwear, personal items, and diaries) indicated that the tent was suddenly and simultaneously abandoned by all hikers; what is more, as it would be subsequently ascertained in the course of forensic examination, the leeward side of the tent towards which the hikers were lying with their heads, turned to be cut from inside in two places, which allowed for a free passage through those cuts.

Below the tent, along the distance of up to 500 meters, the snow had footprints of people walking from the tent towards the valley and the forest. The footprints were well preserved, numbering 8 or 9 tracks. The examination of the footprints showed that some of them were left by a semi-shod foot (for instance, in a single cotton sock); the others had a typical imprint of a felt boot, of a foot in a soft sock, etc. The tracks of the footprints were very close to each other, converging and then diverging not far from one another. Closer to the forest line, the footprints disappeared – they were snowed in. No traces of fighting or presence of strangers have been discovered in the tent or its vicinity.

On February 26, 1959, the remains of the campfire with the corpses of Doroshenko and Krivonischenko stripped down to underwear were discovered 1500 meters from the tent, at the forest boundary. Dyatlov's corpse was discovered 300 meters from the fire, in the direction towards the tent; then in 180 meters from it the corpse of Slobodin and 150 meters from Slobodin – the corpse of Kolmogorova. The latter three corpses were located along a straight light from the campfire towards the tent. Dyatlov was lying on his back, with his head towards the tent with his arms around a trunk of a small birch-tree. Slobodin and Kolmogorova were lying with their faces down, with their position indicating that they were crawling towards the camp. Money and personal items (pens, pencils, etc.) were discovered in the pockets of Kolmogorova, Dyatlov, and Slobodin. On Slobodin's left hand, which was thrown to the side, there was a wristwatch, which showed 8:45. Dyatlov's watch showed 5:31.

The forensic medical examination established that Dyatlov, Doroshenko, Krivonischenko, and Kolmogorova died from the impact of low temperature (frozen over), with none of them having body injuries, except for minor scratches and bruises. Slobodin had a 6 cm long skull fissure, which had spread up to 0.1 cm, but Slobodin died from hypothermia.

The corpses of Dubinina, Zolotaryov, Thibeaux-Brignolle, and Kolevatov were discovered on May 4, 1959, 75 meters from the campfire, under a 4 to 4.5 meters deep layer of snow, in the direction towards the valley of the fourth tributary of the Lozva River, that is perpendicular to the route of the movement of the hikers from the tent. The clothes of Krivonischenko and Doroshenko (pants and sweaters) were discovered on the corpses, as well as a few meters from them. All the clothes had traces of evenly made cuts since they were removed from the corpses of Doroshenko and Krivonischenko.

The deceased Thibeaux-Brignolle and Zolotaryov were discovered properly dressed; Dubinina was dressed more poorly: Zolotaryov was found to wear her faux fur jacket and cap; Dubinina's barefoot leg was wrapped in wool pants belonging to Krivonischenko. The latter's knife, used for cutting young silver fir trees near the campfire, was discovered beside the corpses. There were two pairs of watches on Tibo's wrist: with one showing 8:14 and another – 8:39.

The forensic autopsy has determined that the death of Kolevatov was caused by the effect of frigid temperature (frozen over.) Kolevatov has no bodily injuries. The death of Dubinina, Thibeaux-Brignolle, and Zolotaryov was caused by multiple bodily injuries. Dubinina has a symmetrical rib fracture: 2nd, 3rd, 4th, and 5th on the right and 2nd, 3rd, 4th, 5th, 6th, and 7th on the left. Besides, there is major bleeding in the heart. Thibeaux-Brignolle has an ample hemorrhage in the right temporal muscle and, correspondingly, a depressed fracture of skull bones of the size of 3x7cm, with a bone defect of 3x2cm. Zolotaryov has rib fractures on the right of 2nd, 3rd, 4th, 5th, and 6th, near the thoracic and midclavicular line, which caused his death.

The investigation has not established any presence of other people, besides the Dyatlov group, on February 1 or 2, 1959 in the area of height 1079. It has also been ascertained that the Mansi people, living 80 to 100 km from that location, are friendly to the Russians, provide night lodging to hikers, and give them assistance, etc. The Mansi consider the location of the death of the hikers to be unfit for hunting and reindeer husbandry in the winter period.

Considering the absence of any external bodily injuries on the corpses, as well as any signs of fighting, the presence of all the group's valuables, as well as taking into consideration the forensic medical report on the causes of death of the hikers, it should be assumed that the cause of death of the hikers was an overwhelming force, which was beyond the hikers to overcome.

For the shortcomings in the organization of the hiking work and lax control, the Bureau of the Sverdlovsk city committee of the CPSU has imposed party penalties on the following: the director of the Ural Polytechnic Institute Siunov, the secretary of the party committee Zaostrovskiy, the chairman of the UPI labor union committee Slobodin, the chairman of the board of the voluntary sports association Kurochkin and the inspector of the union Ufimtsev. The board chairman of the Institute's sports club Gordo has been dismissed from work.

Taking into consideration the absence of any causal connection between the actions of the above listed individuals, who allowed the shortcomings in the organization of the sport work, and the death of the group of hikers, and for the absence of a crime in this case, in consideration of point 5, Art. 4 of the Criminal Procedure Code of the RSFSR,

r u l i n g :

To terminate proceedings in the criminal case of the death of the group of hikers.

Forensic Prosecutor,
Junior Counselor of Justice   IVANOV"

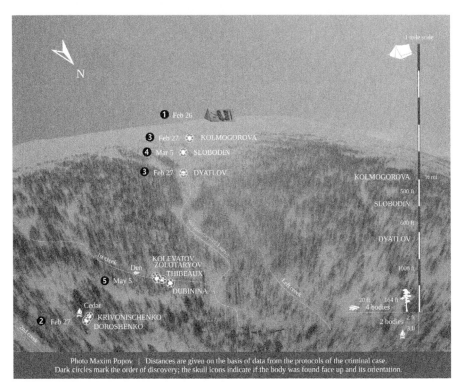

Photo Maxim Popov | Distances are given on the basis of data from the protocols of the criminal case.
Dark circles mark the order of discovery; the skull icons indicate if the body was found face up and its orientation.

CHAPTER 11. MARCH 10 - MAY 30, 1959. PUNISHED BY THE PARTY.

The resolutions of the Sverdlovsk regional committee of the CPSU from March 10 were implemented very quickly, before the end of that month. As soon as on March 16, the issue of the death of the group was discussed at the Sverdlovsk city committee for the physical culture and sports. They pointed to the neglect of documentation at the UPI sports club and the resulting lack of control. The issue "of the death of a group of hikers from the Ural Polytechnic Institute sports club" was discussed on March 27 at the meeting of the city committee of the CPSU with the participation of Pyotr Pomazkin, V.E. Slobodin, Evgeniy Maslennikov; Yuri Ahmin, deputy regional prosecutor on special affairs, and Filipp Ermash. The meeting invitees were Vil Kurochkin, the chairman of the former state committee for physical culture and sports; Valeriy Ufimtsev, Pyotr Repyev, and I.G. Chevtaev, the secretary of the regional labor union council. The meeting was chaired by Konstantin Zamiryakin, the first secretary of the Sverdlovsk city committee of the CPSU.

> **Konstantin Aleksandrovich Zamiryakin (46)** was born in 1913 in Vladimirovka in the Astrakhan Governorate of the Russian Empire. Until 1941, he worked at the Stalingrad artillery "Barricades" plant №221, starting as a metal worker and ending as a shop foreman. In 1942 he was evacuated to the Urals and became a shop foreman at the Urals Machine-building plant in Sverdlovsk, one of the major manufacturers of armored hulls, tanks, and artillery during WWII. From 1952, Zamiryakin became a party functionary, advancing in his career from the second secretary of the party committee of the Ordzhonikidze district of Sverdlovsk to the first secretary of the Sverdlovsk city committee of the CPSU. In 1956 he graduated from the Ural Polytechnic Institute with a qualification in mechanical engineer. Zamiryakin was awarded the orders of Lenin, Red Star, Patriotic War 1st degree and Labor Red Banner, as well as the medals "For Labor Valor", "For the Defense of Stalingrad" and "For Valorous

Labor in the Great Patriotic War of 1941-1945"

From the protocol of the meeting of the bureau of the city committee of the CPSU from March 27, 1959:

"On the death of the hikers from the sports club
of the Ural Polytechnic Institute.

On February 1, 1959, a group of hikers organized by the sports club of the Ural Polytechnic Institute died tragically on the slopes of the Otorten Mountain (the Ivdel district of the Sverdlovsk region)... In the course of the investigation undertaken by the commission of the regional committee of the CPSU (chaired by com. Pavlov V.A., the deputy chairman of the regional executive committee), it has been ascertained that the direct cause of the group's death was a heavy hurricane, which had caught it on the approach to the Otorten Mountain. All the members of the group, who for some reason left the tent pitched on the slope of height 1079, were scattered by hurricane force wind, lost orientation, and unable to return to the tent died of freezing.

According to the conclusion of the commission and experienced hikers (Masters of Sport), pitching the tent on a mountain woodless slope with frequent hurricane strong winds was wrong, with the hikers' leaving of their tent impermissible.

At the same time, based on the materials submitted by the commission, the bureau of the city committee of the CPSU is drawing attention to the fact that while permitting the hiking treks, the leadership of the Ural Polytechnic Institute (comrades Siunov, Zaostrovskiy, and Slobodin), as well as of the former city committee for the physical culture and sports (com. Kurochkin) made serious mistakes, by not setting up personal accountability for the organization, instruction, equipment and conducting of hiking treks, delegating all this work to the Institute's sports club.

The leadership of the sports club of the Ural Polytechnic Institute (board chairman com. Gordo) and its hiking sections have allowed many deviations from the procedure for the conduct of hiking treks, with their formalization and control established by the guidelines. The club's routing commission, neglecting appropriate documentation of hiking treks, was resolving many issues following an oral agreement with the hikers, based on personal trust. The Institute's labor union committee (com. Slobodin) and the board of the sports club did not keep control over the activities of its hiking section, did not request keeping the necessary records, including the necessary information on the hikers, and for this reason, they had no idea of the nominal roll of the hiking groups, their routes, the deadlines for control messages from the hikers on their treks. These shortcomings were manifest in the process of the organization of the Dyatlov group.

The Director of the UPI com. Siunov has not paid attention to the issues of organization of the social and athletic work among the students in the academic and vacation periods. On learning about the death of the hiking group, which had been sent and equipped by the Institute's sports club, he did not take it as a matter of urgency, manifesting indifference and sluggishness in the organization of the search for the group.

The UPI party committee (com. Zaostrovskiy) did not bother with the organization of physical cultural and athletic work among the students and did not insist on keeping high standards by the communist party and Komsomol members.

There are as well serious shortcomings in the work of the former city committee for physical culture and sports (chaired by com. Kurochkin) and the city routing commission (chaired by com. Korolev.) The malpractice of personal confidence, negligence of strict observance of the procedures for hiking treks and their documentation, outlined in the appropriate guidelines – resulting in the lack of control and responsibility by the individuals entrusted with oversight of hiking and excursions.

The organization of the supervision of the preparation of hiking groups for treks with a high degree of difficulty has been unsatisfactory both at the former city committee for physical culture and sports and at the Polytechnic Institute. The details of the hikers' route, the quality, and quantity of their equipment, and feeding have not been addressed in substance, no contact with the sports organizations along the route of the treks have been established.

Com. Lyubimov, the deputy chairman of the executive council of the city soviet, who is in charge of the city committee for physical culture and sports, has been inefficient with the supervision of this committee, attending to its affairs only from time to time. On learning about the death of the hikers, he did not take an active part in the organization of the measures for their search...

The major deficiencies and mistakes in the organization of the hiking work on the part of the leadership of the UPI and the former city committee for physical culture and sports have been manifested in the unsatisfactory organization of the search for the deceased group of hikers in the initial stage of that work.

In the course of the onsite investigation of the causes of death of the hikers it was ascertained that according to all available data, the time of their death had been determined between January 31 and February 1. However, the city committee of the CPSU had learned about this tragic incident only with a great delay and by chance. Only five days after the deadline for submitting a control message from the tourist group (Febru-

ary 15), measures for their search were undertaken, however, on an insufficient scale.

The death of the hikers is a significant and grave lesson for the whole sports community of Sverdlovsk, for the officials responsible for the organization of the work on the development of hiking, as well as for the party, labor union, and Komsomol organization.

The Bureau of the city committee of the CPSU rules:

1. It is necessary to make the point that the leadership of the Ural Polytechnic Institute, namely its director com. Siunov N.S., the secretary of the party committee com. Zaostrovskiy F.P., the chairman of the labor union committee com. Slobodin V.E., have demonstrated irresponsibility in the organization of the hiking work at the Institute as a whole, having delegated this work to the Institute's sports club and its tourist section, without determining personal accountability for the conduct of hiking treks and excursions.

For his unsatisfactory supervision of the work of the sports club, for significant shortcomings in the work of its hiking section, and his procrastination in the organization of the search for the dead hikers, to issue a reprimand to com. Slobodin, chairman of the Institute's labor union committee, with a notation into his personnel record card.

For the significant shortcomings in the work of the Institute's hiking section and violation of the guidelines, "On the procedure of the organization and conduct of hiking treks", to discharge com. Gordo L.S. from his job and to issue a severe reprimand with a notation into his personnel record card.

For insufficient supervision over the activities of sports organizations, the absence of due insistence on high standards in and responsibility for the conduct of hiking treks, to issue a reprimand to the Institute's director, com. Siunov N.S. and to criticize the secretary of its party committee, com. Zaostrovskiy F.P.

2. For serious shortcomings in the organization of the work of the tourist section and its routing commission, to issue a reprimand to the chairman of the council of the city union of sports societies and organizations com. Kurochkin V.F.

To issue a severe reprimand to the former instructor of the committee com. Ufimtsev V.M., as directly responsible for this part of the work.

To suggest to com. Kurochkin to address the issue of the work of the chairman of the routing commission com. Korolev V.I. and Ufimtsev V.M. and to take steps for strengthening the hiking section with qualified volunteer sportsmen.

3. To issue a severe warning to com. Lyubimov, the deputy chairman of the executive committee of the city soviet, in view of his lax supervision of the former city committee for physical culture and sports.

4. To suggest to com. Repyev P.A., the chairman of the regional council of sports societies, to forward the memorandum of the Presidium of the Sverdlovsk regional hiking club, "The criticisms of the existing hiking guidelines" to the All-Russian Council of sports organizations.

5. To oblige the UPI party committee, labor union committee, and directorate (comrades Zaostrovskiy, Slobodin, Siunov) to tighten the supervision of the Institute's sports organizations and to map out concrete measures for normalization and improvement of the work on the development of hiking among the students.

6. To instruct the city council of sports societies and organizations to take a close look at the work of the local hiking sections without delay and to take steps for improvement of their activities.

7. To deem it necessary to submit the hiking routes of the 2nd and 3rd categories of difficulty for consideration of the city council of sports societies and organizations, allowing for the specific recommendation on the organization of the liaison with the groups, control over their movement, providing them with portable radios, weapons, etc.

To request from the organizations, which are conducting treks of the highest degree of difficulty, to check first-hand the readiness of the hikers for the trek (equipment, food supplies, etc.) To request the sports organization to apply for approval of their hiking treks with the leadership of the enterprises, institutions, and institutes of higher learning. To recommend to the city section and the 3rd category trek leaders to request from the trek's supervisors to provide information from the meteorological authority regarding any probable weather changes in the area along the group's itinerary.

8. To obligate the department of propaganda and agitation of the city committee of the CPSU (com. Lesnykh, Kondakova) to provide continuous quality control over the work of the city council of the union of sports societies and organizations, as well as its tourist section.

9. To recommend to the executive committee of the city soviet, together with the UPI directorate to provide material assistance to the families of the deceased hikers and to grant pensions to those of these families, which have been left without a breadwinner."

Extracts from the protocols of the regional and city committees of CPSU on the issue of the death of the hiking group would be sent to the Central Committee of the CPSU on April 7. Earlier, on March 23, a memorandum on the finding of the investigation of the death of the group of Sverdlovsk hikers was received by the Department of administrative and trade-financial agencies of the city committee of the CPSU on the RSFSR:

"The organizational bureau of the Union of sports societies and organizations of the RSFSR is forwarding a memorandum on the findings of the investigation of the death of the group of hikers from the city of Sverdlovsk.

The investigation was conducted by the members of the routing and qualification commissions of the Presidium of the tourist section, who were detailed by the Organizational Bureau: K. Bardin, the Master of Sport of the USSR, and E. Shuleshko, 1st degree tourist of the USSR, who were working together with the commission of the Sverdlovsk regional committee of the CPSU and the regional prosecutor's office.

In accordance with your assignment, we have checked into the issues involved in the preparation for and conduct of the hiking trek of the Sverdlovsk group of hikers and the circumstances of their death… It was ascertained that all discovered people had died from cold and wind."

De facto, following the said decisions, the investigation was closed. For the official confirmation of the causes of death of the hikers, which were now, officially, a hurricane and the mistakes of the hikers, the only thing left was to find the remaining bodies. By April the round-the-clock search headquarters at the UPI sports club was closed; the daily duty at the telephones was discontinued. The Sverdlovsk sports functionaries were punished by party penalties. Despite the insufficient organization of the hiking treks, they did not go as far as instituting criminal proceedings. Lev Ivanov explained it by the fact that the "Resolution of the Plenum of the CC VCP(b) from January 1938 on the mistakes of party organizations in expulsions of communists from the party" was still in effect. A party member may be charged with criminal liability only on the agreement of the party committee. The city and regional party committees had not given the agreement to bring criminal charges against the above mentioned individuals. However, Ivanov did not specify if there had been any request to this effect from the prosecutor's office.

Moreover, the imposed penalties had been mitigated. For instance, Gordo had remained in his office of the chairman of the UPI sports club, despite the decision of the bureau of the city committee of the CPSU. In as much as half a year, along with Siunov and Vishnevskiy, he would be awarded a citation of the central committee of the Burevestnik voluntary sports society for his excellent organization of athletic work at the UPI in the winter period of 1958-1959. A year later, in 1960, the severe reprimand he had received would be as well canceled on Gordo's request.

The control over the treks taken by hiking groups was indeed tightened. Kurochkin would later recall that in late March or early April he was summoned to the meeting of the Presidium of the All-Union sports committee in connection with the death of the Dyatlov group, as well as with the subsequent failure to meet its deadline by the Budrin group from the sports club of the Sverdlovsk "Fakel" ("Torch") plant, which went on a hiking trek from Sverdlovsk to Tien Shan on March 6.

> **Vil Fedorovich Kurochkin (33)** was born in 1926 in the family of a worker of a foundry shop at the Ural machine building plant (Uralmash), who was later elected chairman of the executive committee of the district Soviet of the Ordzhonikidze district of Sverdlovsk. Kurochkin followed his father at the Uralmash in 1940, enrolling in its vocational school, and afterward worked as an electrical fitter at its artillery branch throughout the war of 1941-45. Soon, he was elected secretary of his factory-wide Komsomol committee and then as first secretary of the factory-wide Ordzhonikidze regional Komsomol committee. Later, like his father, he was elected chairman of the executive committee of the district Soviet of the Ordzhonikidze district of Sverdlovsk. In 1951, Kurochkin was sent to the Sverdlovsk regional party school; after graduation he became a cadre party functionary, supervising physical culture and sports. In 1954 he was awarded the title of the Master of Sport of the USSR. He worked as the head of the military and physical culture department of the city committee of the VLKSM, deputy chairman, and chairman of the city committee for physical culture and sports. On March 26, 1959, Kurochkin was elected chairman of the presidium of the board of the Union of sports societies of the city of Sverdlovsk at its first city-wide constituent conference. As of 1959, he was also deputy chairman of the Sverdlovsk city soviet and member of the city committee of the CPSU.

Kurochkin enjoyed the support of Nikolay Romanov, the former chairman of the All-Union committee for physical culture and sports, which was disbanded on March 1, 1959. In the end, the only thing that saved him was the fact that the Burdin group had returned on its own and without incident.

Soon an amended instruction on hiking was issued, which did not include an indispensable prerequisite of passing along the routes in unpopulated areas for the treks of the highest degree of difficulty.

However, this did not solve the problem. Only in the first ten years after the investigation of the causes of death of the Dyatlov group, quite many hikers and mountaineers, who had taken part in the search work on height 1079, died in various parts of the nation.

Valeriy Dubovtsev, a member of Sogrin's search group, died in 1961 while rafting in Transbaikal.

Yuri Kotenev, a member of Kikoin's search group, died in 1961 in the Caucasus while ascending to the top of the Dykh-Tau Mountain.

Georgiy Atmanaki, a member of Karelin's search group, died in 1962 while on a trek in the central Caucasus.

Sergey Arzamastsev, a member of Blinov's search group, died in 1964 while rafting in Transbaikal.

Yaroslav Krotov, a member of Slobtsov's search group, died in 1967 during training exercises in mountaineering.

Boris Martyushev, the leader of the search group, died in 1969 during an ascent in the western Caucasus.

On May 30, 1959, the investigation initiated by the Central Committee of the CPSU on the appeal of the relatives of Alexander Kolevatov, was completed:

"Citizen Anisimova, on behalf of the parents of com. Kolevatov had turned to the Central Committee of the CPSU with a request to assist in the search of the group of hikers from the Ural Polytechnic Institute, which included their son, Kolevatov A.S. In the course of the search for the said group it was ascertained that all participants in that trek had died tragically (their bodies were discovered in a two-month period). To investigate the causes of death of the hiking group of the Ural Polytechnic Institute, the Sverdlovsk regional committee of CPSU organized a special commission; besides, on the assignment of the Central Committee of the CPSU and the Council of Ministers of the RSFSR, com. Urakov, the deputy prosecutor of the RSFSR, traveled to the scene. A criminal case was opened on the death of the hikers; later it was closed since the death of the participants in the hiking trek was caused by a natural disaster.

The investigation has determined that the group of hikers, organized by the sports club of the Ural Polytechnic Institute, including: Dyatlov I.A. (leader), Dubinina L.A., Kolmogorova Z.A., Kolevatov A.S., Doroshenko Y.M., Slobodin R.V., Krivonischenko G.A., Thibeaux-Brignolle N.V., Zolotaryov F.A., died on February 1, 1959, on the slopes of the Otorten Mountain in the Ivdel district of the Sverdlovsk region. The immediate cause of the death of the group, according to the commission's report, was a massive windstorm, in which the hikers lost terrain orientation and died of frost. The bodies of the dead hikers, comrades Kolmogorova, Slobodin,

Dyatlov, Doroshenko, and Krivonischenko, were discovered in March 1500-2000 meters from the location of the tent. The bodies of the remaining dead hikers were discovered in the same area on May 5-6 this year. The findings of the commission on the investigation of the death of hikers were discussed at the bureau of the Sverdlovsk regional and city committees of the CPSU. The resulting resolution singled out the measures for improvement of the organization of hiking in the Sverdlovsk region. The parents have been informed about the findings of the investigation.

Deputy head of the Department of administrative and commercial-financial bodies of the Central Committee of the CPSU for the RSFSR G. Drozdov"

The mistakes made in the initials of the two of the dead hikers, Doroshenko and Zolotaryov, indicate the quality of the investigation.

CHAPTER 12. MODERN FORMULA: OVERWHELMING FORCE = HURRICANE + AVALANCHE.

On May 28, 1959, the criminal case was closed and deposited at the archive of the Sverdlovsk regional prosecutor's office. As of 1959, the Statute on the State Archival Records of the Union of the SSR and of the network of the central state archives of the USSR was in effect. Enacted a year earlier, it said that *"at the institutional archives, the shelf-life expiration for documents of the agencies, organizations, and enterprises of all-union and republican subordination will be 15 years."*

Consequently, the documents of the regional prosecutor's office were to be held for 15 years at the institutional archive, which had been implemented. With the expiration of this term, according to Act № 1 from June 20, 1974, the criminal case files and the materials of the inspective proceedings were deposited for perpetual storage at the State Archive of the Sverdlovsk Region (GASO) – the current location of the Records of the prosecutor's office of the Sverdlovsk Region. In total, this record group has 927 case files from 1922 to 1965. Under Art. 216 of the Russian Federation Code of Criminal Procedure, the right to a public view of the materials of a closed case is limited to individuals with the legal status of a victim. However, in the course of the preliminary investigation of 1959, no victims were recognized in this case.

Only in December 1983, Vladislav Karelin managed to inspect the case files for the first time. Formerly, there had been a single source – Yuri Yarovoy's short novel, published in Sverdlovsk. Based on the story of the Igor Dyatlov group, it described the search work in many details, as well as the discussions at the search headquarters. The first access to the case files became possible with the democratic reforms brought about by Mikhail Gorbachev's Glasnost campaign. In March 1989, the first copies of some file pages were made. In that same time, 1989-1990, the first publications telling about the death of the Dyatlov group appeared in Soviet mass media. These included the reminiscences of Lev Ivanov, the former forensic prosecutor of the Sverdlovsk regional prosecutor's office, and Aleksander Gubin, a former secretary of the Ivdel city committee of the CPSU.

Aleksandr Dmitrievich Gubin (43) was born in 1916 in the Kurgan district of the Tobolskaya Governorate of the Russian Empire. In 1938 he was drafted into the Red Army. After the Nazi attack on the Soviet Union, he was fighting as air service mechanic, in the rank of Guards master sergeant of the 13th Guards fighter aviation Poltava-Aleksandriisky Red Banner division, in the formations of the South-Western, Stalingrad, Voronezh, Steppe, and 2nd Ukrainian Fronts. For his wartime service, Gubin was awarded the Red Star order and the medals "For Valor", "For the Defense of the Soviet Polar Region", "For Combat Service" and "For Victory over Germany". He joined the VCP(b) in 1943, while at the front. From 1951, Gubin worked at the Ivdel city committee of the CPSU as the 3rd secretary for ideological work, then as the 2nd secretary; from 1954, he was supervising the Union of sports societies and organizations of Ivdel. Gubin did not take part in the search itself, but he might be supervising its spring stage.

Only then, 30 years after the tragedy, the families and the friends of the dead had first learned about the heavy injuries received by some of the hikers. In 1959, it was officially announced that hypothermia was the cause of death of any and all the hikers. Due to the restrictions in the access to the archival case file, for a long time, they were unable to receive any detailed information.

In 1996, the case file was retrieved from the archive by the Sverdlovsk regional prosecutor's office in response to the inquiry sent to the State Archive of the Sverdlovsk Region (GASO) by Stanislav Naboychenko, the Rector of the UPI, which said, in particular: *"To keep it as part of the history of the UGTU-UPI, we are earnestly asking you to commit to the archive of the UPI museum a copy of the criminal case file on the death of the UPI hikers in the vicinity of the Otorten Mountain."* The prosecutor's office did not find any grounds for the committal of the materials.

In 1999, Victor Tuflyakov, the deputy regional prosecutor, handed over a copy taken from the criminal case file to a writer Anatoliy Gushchin – resulting in a book, which for the first time made public the copies of the fragments of the case file. In 2000, another writer, Anna Matveeva, published a short novel with additional materials, including the protocols of party meetings. It became clear that in 1959 the causes of the injuries were not determined. The investigation limited its opinion by a single sentence: "... *it should be assumed that the cause of death of the hikers was an overwhelming force, which was beyond the hikers to overcome.*" The prosecutor's office was receiving dozens of letters from public organizations, relatives, and the friends of the deceased with requests to explain the causes of death of the hikers, and in case it might be impossible to do, to resume investigative measures.

In 2000, the Sverdlovsk regional prosecutor's office sent the materials on the death of the Dyatlov group to the Sverdlovsk regional office of forensic medical examination (SOBSME). Subsequent to the review of the expert forensic panel, the reopening of the investigation was found inappropriate.

In 2006, the Office of the Prosecutor General's Office of RF in the Ural federal region informed that "*the case file is in perpetual storage at the State Archive of the Sverdlovsk Region (GASO) and is open for inspection on agreement with the prosecutor of the Sverdlovsk region.*"

In 2007, the Sverdlovsk regional prosecutor's office was considering the question of reopening the investigation – and once again found it inappropriate, since the investigative measures undertaken in 1959 were a sufficient reason for the decision to close the investigation.

In 2009, copies of the major part of the materials of the case file appeared in the public domain – after the prosecutor's office had granted an archival research permit to Evgeniy Buyanov, the Master of Sport of the USSR in tourism, who had developed a version of the group's death from an avalanche. In 2013, under an agreement between the GASO and the Sverdlovsk Dyatlov group memorial foundation, copies were taken from all materials of the case file. In 2017, a compilation of documents was published, which included materials of the criminal case, the inspective proceedings, and certain additional materials regarding the search for the Dyatlov group.

In 2015, on the assignment of the leadership of the Investigative Committee of the Russian Federation, Sergey Shkryabach, 3rd class State Councilor of Justice, a veteran of investigative agencies and criminal investigation, reviewed the materials of the closed criminal case on the death of the Dyatlov group hikers. His goal was to evaluate the completeness and evenhandedness of the investigation undertaken in 1959 and the propriety of the decisions taken at the time. Sergey Shkryabach, with his extensive experience of mountaineering at the Pamir, Tien Shan, Caucasus, Altai, Eastern Sayan, Kamchatka, and The Subarctic, de facto agreed with the 1959 conclusions of the Sverdlovsk regional committee of 1959, as well as with the version suggested by

Buyanov in 2009:

"... The snowstorm continued, and after some time the mass of snow on the slope had become critical. The avalanche took the form of a landslide with a mass of no less than several tons. Had the landslide had time to pick up speed, the members of the group would have hardly managed to get out of the tent... The first to get frozen were, most likely, Doroshenko Y.N. and Krivonischenko Y.G. ... The deaths were caused by the erroneous, however, courageous attempts of Dyatlov I.A., Kolmogorova Z.A., and Slobodin R.V. to reach the tent breaking through the hurricane wind... Most likely, Dubinina L.A., Kolevatov A.S., Zolotaryov A.A., and Thibeaux-Brignolle N.V. made an attempt to settle themselves in the hollow, unaware that they were in fact in the snow over the cove. Likely, the snow and ice neck had fallen under their weight, and they were covered with a crashed down layer of frozen snow with the height of five meters or more, which caused the antemortem heavy injuries of Dubinina L.A., Zolotaryov A.A. and Thibeaux-Brignolle N.V. Most probably, the death of all four of them could be caused both by freezing, as well as by mechanical asphyxia under the layer of snow, which caved them down..."

Shkryabach paid special attention to the fact that *"the circumstances of the death of the hikers had no hidden connotations, with all the questions and doubts resulting from incompetence and imperfection of the work on that case. At the same time, given the years passed, the possibility to fill the gaps in the investigation is limited. It appears that considering the absence of any hard evidence of the complicity of anyone in the death of the members of the Dyatlov group hikers, this work is possible without reopening the investigation – within the framework of an additional official inspection."*

In 2018-2019, such inspection was initiated by the Procurator General's office of the RF upon application of a family member of one of the deceased hikers. Supervision of the scrutiny was assigned to Andrey Kuryakov, at the time the head of the office of supervision over the implementation of the federal law of the Sverdlovsk regional prosecutor's office. In 2020, Andrey Kuryakov privately cited the findings of that inspection, which were not greatly different from the findings made by Sergey Shkryabach:

"... The version of an avalanche has been fully corroborated, however, it was not the only cause of death... Doroshenko and Krivonischenko were the first to die. They were more active than the others in gathering firewood and had exhausted their endurance resource in bitter frost. They stood no chance to stay alive.... Their friends took off clothes from the dead, muffled themselves up with those cloth items, and decided to get back to the tent.

By 3 am the wind chill factor went down to – 46°C, with visibility no more than 16 meters. The snowstorm was heavy and the night was moonless... One by one, Dyatlov, Slobodin, and Kolmogorova started to climb back the slope, however, with hypothermia they had no strength left. The remaining four – Zolotaryov, Dubinina, Thibeaux-Brignolle, and Kolevatov – moved away from the cedar at 50 meters to the south-west from the campfire into the ravine of the fourth tributary of the Lozva River. They shoveled off the snow, made flooring of small-size trees. They settled themselves on that flooring, getting ready for a cold overnight stay. However, the elements interfered with their plans – with the snow movement in the shallows. According to the findings of the comprehensive forensic examination, the fractured ribs of Liuda and Semen were provoked exactly by the snow avalanche with a height of up to three meters. Finally, all four were carried down from their flooring to the ravine bottom and snowed up...

Given the dismal weather, they had done all they could to survive. Simply the frost, snowstorm, and the darkness prevailed."

The official position of the prosecutor's office and the Investigative Committee has not yet been made public. The opinion of the representatives of the agencies is clear – the questions and doubts persist.

PART 2

THE PUZZLE

CHAPTER 13. SIXTH, TWENTY SIXTH OR TWENTY EIGHT?

Even a cursory review of the archival materials raises an immediate question as to when the criminal case on the death of the hikers from the Dyatlov group was opened.. The folder of the case file has the date of February 6, 1959. However, this is the folder of the archival case file. Under the guidelines for processing case files for their delivery into archival storage, the opening date of a case file is the date of its earliest filed document. In our case, this is the protocol of interrogation from February 6, 1959.

"Location of interrogation: Vizhay settlement. The interrogation began on February 6, 1959, finished on February 6, 1959

I, Captain Chudinov, the head of the Polunochnoe settlement militia station, have interrogated as a witness Popov Vasiliy Andreyanovich,... the head of the communications division of the Vizhay logging division."

Vasiliy Andreyanovich Popov (51) was born in 1908 in the village of Kargapolskoe in the Perm Governorate of the Russian Empire. In 1929-31 he served in the Red Army, into which he was drafted again in 1940. From after the Nazi attack on the Soviet Union (June 22, 1941) Popov served in the field army, fighting in the formations of the Kaliningrad and 1st Baltic Fronts, as a commanding officer of a telegraph line-laying company. At least from 1953, he served as the chief of the communications unit of the Ivdellag Vizhay logging division. Popov was a member of the CPSU, had a rank of a reserve captain; resided in the Vizhay settlement.

"The witness has testified the following: In the later part of January 1959, in the settlement of Vizhay, I saw two groups of hikers who were going into the area of the Ural Range. I did not talk to them myself. In the early days of February 1959, there was a strong wind blowing in Vizhay. The wind was blowing heaps of snow and drifting the snow into high banks. In the open spaces, the roads were covered with snow. I have resided in the Vizhay settlement since 1951. I do not recall winds as strong as those we had in early February, 1959."

The record of the interrogation was written three weeks before the date of the decree on the institution of criminal proceedings:

"On February 26, 1959, Tempalov, the prosecutor of the city of Ivdel, on familiarizing himself with the information on the discovery of the corpses of student hikers at height 1079, and taking into consideration that the frozen corpses of Krivonischenko, Kolmogorova Z., Dyatlov and other student hikers from the Sverdlovsk Polytechnic Institute were discovered at height 1079; as well taking into consideration that this fact requires the conduct of the preliminary investigation to ascertain the causes of death of the said individuals, for this reason, guided by articles 96 and 110 of the Code of Criminal Procedure of the RSFSR, ruled:

To initiate proceedings in this case /To institute prosecution into the death of the hikers from the Sverdlovsk Polytechnic Institute and to start an investigation."

Under the Code of Criminal Procedure of the RSFSR effective as of 1959 *"preliminary investigation of criminal cases... should be completed within a two-month term from the beginning of the investigation, with the deed of the committal for trial or termination of criminal prosecution included in this term. Any extension of this term, as well as of the term allocated for the performance of inquiry in individual cases may be allowed for the term of up to a month with the permission of the regional prosecutor, executed as a reasoned decree. The authority of extending the term in an individual case, as well as of the general extension of the terms for certain regions of the Republic, where such extension may be motivated by local circumstances, is vested in the Prosecutor of the Republic."*

The investigation was not completed within two months. The extension of the term required the permission of the regional prosecutor. Lev Ivanov executed a decree on the extension of the investigation term:

"I, Ivanov, the junior counselor of justice, forensic prosecutor of the Sverdlovsk regional prosecutor's office, on consideration of the criminal case on the death of hikers in the Ivdel region, ruled:

In February 1959, a group of nine hikers from the Ural Polytechnic Institute died in the Northern Ural at the height marked as 1079.

In the course of the search, the corpses of five hikers and part of their equipment were discovered. The corpses of the remaining participants in the trek have not been discovered. In view of the non-discovery of the remaining participants in the trek, it is not possible to determine the definitive cause of death of the hikers and the guilty parties; the weather conditions in the area of the accident do not permit undertaking the search at the scale sufficient for the discovery of the other participants in the trek.

The case on the death of the students was opened on February 28, 1959, with its investigation term expiring on April 28, 1959. Based on Art. 116 of the Code of Criminal Procedure of the RSFSR, ruling:

To make an application to the prosecutor of the Sverdlovsk region for extension of the term of the investigation in the case until May 28, 1959"

The application was satisfied. Nikolay Klinov, the prosecutor of the Sverdlovsk region, extended the term of the investigation. On May 28, 1959, one month after the date of the extension *"I, Ivanov, the junior counselor of justice, the forensic prosecutor of the Sverdlovsk regional prosecutor's office, on consideration of the criminal case opened on the occasion of the death of nine hikers in the Ivdel region of the Sverdlovsk region,... and considering the absence of any causal connection between the actions of the... individuals, who had allowed for the shortcomings in the organization of the athletic work and the death of the group of hikers, and for the absence of elements of crime in this case, based on point 5, Art. 4 of the Criminal Procedure Code of the RSFSR,*

r u l e d :

To terminate the criminal proceedings in the case of the death of the group of hikers."

As it happened, the criminal case into the death of the hikers was opened on February 26. But the investigation was extended in the case opened on February 28 and closed on May 28. This discrepancy in the dates may be explained only by one thing: the folder of the archival case file contains materials of a minimum of two criminal cases.

On February 28, the Sverdlovsk regional prosecutor's office opened a criminal case into the facts of the poor organization of the search for the missing group of hikers. It was within the framework of this latter case, initiated by the Central Committee of the CPSU on the application, which Anisimova sent to Moscow, that Lev Ivanov was expedited to Ivdel.

On site it was discovered that on February 26 Tempalov already opened a criminal case into the fact of the discovery of the corpses. Hence, from February 28, two different cases were simultaneously investigated. Tempalov was investigating the case of the causes of death of the hikers, opened on February 26 by the prosecutor's office of Ivdel. Ivanov was investigating the case of potential complicity of sports officials in the admission of the hikers to the hiking trek and unsatisfactory organization of the search, which was opened by the Sverdlovsk regional prosecutor's office on February 28. Within the frame of this case Leonid Urakov, the deputy prosecutor of the RSFSR, was detailed to Sverdlovsk.

Leonid Ivanovich Urakov (53) was born in 1906 in the Ryazan Governorate of the Russian Empire. After graduation from secondary school, he became a secretary of a local rural Komsomol committee and later shifted to secretary of labor inspection in the city of Sasovo, same governorate. From 1926, Urakov worked in prosecution authorities, beginning with the position of an investigator, senior investigator of the prosecution office of the Ryazan Governorate and then of the Moscow region; later promoted to the prosecutor of the investigative department of the Prosecutor's Office of the RSFSR. In 1947 he was promoted to the head of the said investigative department and in 1953 – to deputy prosecutor of the RSFSR when he was supervising its investigative department. As of 1959, he had the civil rank of the state counselor of justice 2nd class.

Within the frame of this case, Tempalov was summoned to Sverdlovsk.

"Vladimir Ivanovich, to report to the deputy prosecutor of the RSFSR on the criminal case into the fact of the death of the hikers, I have been summoned to and I am leaving for the city of Sverdlovsk for two or three days, hence asking to keep an eye here to see that everything is in order... Besides, on an assignment of the regional prosecutor, I have to interrogate Hakimov, the head of the logging division in the Vizhay settlement, on the issue if Dyatlov, the leader of the group of hikers (who is deceased) said that they would return to Vizhay not on February 12, 1959, but on February 15, 1959. This should be done as quickly as possible. I will call you from Sverdlovsk."

The note was written to Vladimir Ivanovich Korotaev, a young investigator at the Ivdel prosecutor's office.

Vladimir Ivanovich Korotaev (23) was born in 1936 in the Romanovo settlement of the Ust-Ishimskiy district of the Omsk region. Following graduation from the Sverdlovsk Juridical Institute in August 1958, he was assigned to work at the prosecutor's office in the city of Verkhoturie, but almost immediately transferred to Ivdel, following his conflict with the regional prosecutor. From September 1958, he served as an investigator at the Ivdel prosecutor's office. On February 4, 1959, Korotaev passed the qualification commission with a conclusion of his adequacy for the job; less than two weeks before, on April 4, and was awarded the class ranking of a junior lawyer.

Within the frame of this case, on April 18, Egor Romanov, a

prosecutor at the Sverdlovsk regional prosecutor's office, interrogated Tempalov regarding the details of the organization of the search at Ivdel.

Egor Yakovlevich Romanov (35) was born on April 12, 1924, in the Chuvash Autonomous SSR. Drafted into the Red Army in 1942, he served with the "SMERSH" (abbreviation for the Russian "Death to Spies") military counterintelligence as a cipher clerk in the SMERSH department of a Guards airborne division, in the rank of guards senior sergeant. He took part in the liberation of the Soviet occupied territories, then in the liberation of Rumania, Hungary, Czechoslovakia, and Austria. He was awarded the medals "For Battle Merit", "For the Liberation of Budapest" and "For the Liberation of Vienna". After demobilization in 1949 in the rank of senior lieutenant of justice, Romanov worked as a district investigator, district prosecutor, and assistant to the prosecutor in the city of Nizhniy Tagil. As of 1959, he served as prosecutor of the investigative department of the Sverdlovsk regional prosecutor's office.

Here is what Tempalov told him:

"On February 21, 1959, I learned from com. Prodanov, the secretary of the Ivdel city committee of the CPSU, that a group of student hikers numbering nine, had not returned to the Sverdlovsk Polytechnic Institute from its hiking trek. I took steps to ascertain where the student hikers were moving and, with the support of the officials of the Central Committee of the CPSU, I sent citizen Dryahlyh by helicopter for the search of the students. So that he located the traces of the hikers and the hikers themselves and determined the direction of their movement. Com. Dryahlyh is very well familiar with the territory of the Ivdel region. For two days he was flying by helicopter in the northern direction from Ivdel. He explained to me that the group of hikers was proceeding through the Vizhay settlement and the yurts of the Bahtiyarovs, which are a few dozen kilometers from Vizhay. He was unable to locate the traces of the hikers themselves.

Soon the officials of the Polytechnic Institute arrived from Sverdlovsk. I set the task for them to immediately organize search teams and to begin the search for the students. From these officials, I learned that the final destination of the students was Mt. Otorten in the Northern Ural. I gave an instruction to send one search team in the strength of five men to Mt. Otorten, another team somewhat to the south of that mountain, and still another team into the mountains 20 to 25 km south of Mt. Otorten. with a view of organizing the search in the mountains of the Northern Ural at a distance of 30 to 35 km. That was how it was done.

I instructed the Institute's staff, directing them to inform me immediately in case they find out anything about the whereabouts of the students in any place. On February 27, 1959, I was informed of the discovery of one corpse on height 1079 and of the tent of the student hikers. I immediately took a helicopter to height 1079. At the same mountain, three more corpses were discovered, which makes four in total, and later the fifth corpse was discovered. Until the present, the remaining four students have not been discovered due to very heavy and thick snow in the mountains. However, the search is actively continued, including at present.

I have taken photos of the corpses, written a protocol of the locus of the accident, and taken the corpses from the discovery site up to the landing site. Over the radio, I requested experienced forensic experts to be sent from Sverdlovsk for the autopsy of the corpses.

On February 28, 1959, in the presence of witnesses, I examined the tent of the hikers, which was 150 meters from the ridge of the offspur of height 1079. The examination of the tent demonstrated that it contained all the personal belongings of the students... On top of the tent, we discovered a Chinese-made flashlight, which was closer to the entrance; at the exit from the tent, I saw a trace indicating that one of the students took a leak. That trace is an old one. Without me present, no one has approached the tent and there were no traces around the tent except for our own. I have not discovered any traces of fighting inside the tent...

...I have taken photos of the footprints. They were leading down from the tent. The footprints have indicated to me that the people were walking down from the mountain at a normal pace. The footprints were visible only within a 50-meter spot, with no further traces, since the snow gets deeper further down the mountain... The five corpses of the frozen students were discovered exactly in the direction shown by the footprints...

In so far as is evidenced by the discovered corpses (numbering five people) and the situation they were discovered in, it has become clear to me that all the students got frozen, any attack against them by any people is ruled out. This is my private opinion. We can arrive at a final conclusion only after the discovery and examination of the remaining students, which means four more people. All the students were able to leave their tent only because at the time when one of them left the tent, he was swept off with a gust of wind and raised a cry. The students got scared, rushed out of the tent, and were as well swept off with wind away from the tent; however, given the heavy wind and blizzard, it was impossible to get back into the tent. So they got frozen. Of course, such a conclusion may be made only judging by the five discovered corpses of the students. I do not know the cause of death of the other four students, since their corpses have not yet been discovered. In case the cause of death of those four students would as well be freezing, then the above stated version would be proved correct."

From all appearances, Korotaev confirmed Ufimtsev's testimony by telephone. The latter on April 13 related the mid-February circumstances to Romanov: "...com. Hakimov of the camp's staff told us by telephone that at the time of their departure the hikers promised to return only on February 15, 1959..." Romanov did not ask Tempalov the question about shifting the time of the group's return.

The fate of the case, which was opened by the Ivdel prosecutor's office on February 26, is not reliably known. We can only say for certain that it had never been extended. The materials of the audit of the Ivdel prosecutor's office indicated that in the nine months of 1959, there were only two cases in which investigation was completed within the term exceeding two months, which two cases did not include the case of the death of the hikers. It is possible to assume that the latter was closed soon after the commission of the Sverdlovsk regional committee of the CPSU had ascertained that the immediate cause of death of the group of hikers was a "superstorm". Under the Code of Criminal Procedure of the RSFSR, which was in effect as of 1959, a prosecutor had a right to terminate criminal proceedings in the cases, "...when any further legal proceedings in the case do not seem appropriate."

Despite the fact that the forensic examinations were more likely concerned with the investigation into the causes of death of the hikers, and not with determining the measure of the guilt of the sports officials, the corpses of Doroshenko, Krivonischenko, Dyatlov, and Kolmogorova had already been examined pursuant to the March 3, 1959 order of the Sverdlovsk regional prosecutor's office. That is, within the frame of the case opened by the regional prosecutor's office on February 28. This is true for the ensuing forensic examinations, which can be explained by the following. In 1953, the USSR deputy prosecutor general requested "...In the future, the people's investigators and the city and district prosecutors should refrain from sending materials for performing forensic examinations to scientific-research forensic institutions, bypassing the investigative department of the superior prosecution authority, the officials of which, in each and every case, must thoroughly check the completeness and correctness of their execution prior to their sending over – as well as the completeness and correctness of the wording of the questions raised by the investigators for consideration of the forensic examination."

This instruction was likely explained by the overall low professional qualification of the lower-level prosecutor's office. To simplify the procedure of sending materials to the Sverdlovsk laboratories for chemical and histological examination, it was decided to immediately execute forensic examinations within the frame of the case of the regional prosecutor's office. Quite possibly, that this was the reason for the appearance of the signature of the regional prosecutor Klinov in the reports (acts) of forensic medical examination.

The comparative documentary examination, which was performed in 2019 within the frame of the audit of the Sverdlovsk regional prosecutor's office into the death of the Dyatlov group in 1959, ascertained that the level of investigation was on a par with the level of investigation in other criminal cases, which were handled by the Sverdlovsk regional prosecutor's office in the period of 1958-63. The preliminary investigation was conducted with non-compliance with the requirements of the Code of Criminal Procedure, which were typical of that time. There were no documents vesting an official with authority to execute proceedings or the rulings to commence a criminal investigation in case of the change of the investigator or the prosecutor, or in case of the absence of the rulings to institute forensic examinations. In individual documents, there are no signatures, the names and initials of the investigators or witnesses, and attesting witnesses.

On March 13, Major Konstantin Bizyaev, the head of the Ivdel city militia division, received the following instructions:

"In addition to the existing assignment in the case of the death of the Dyatlov group hikers, requesting to do the following:

1. Makrushin, chairman of the Burmantovo settlement council, is spreading the rumor that the Mansi Bahtiyarov had, allegedly, seen the hikers falling from the mountain and told about it to another Mansi as early as February 17, 1959. In this connection it is necessary:

a) to check the veracity of the delivered information;

b) to ascertain the current residence of citizen Bahtiyarov P.G.;

c) to check the whereabouts of Bahtiyarov in the period of the death of the hikers.

2. To check into the version of a religiously motivated attack of the Mansi men at the hikers, it is necessary:

a) to ascertain, whose camping ground had the hikers visited and if the Mansi men were aware of that visit;

b) to ascertain if the Mansi men were aware that a group of hikers was moving towards the Otorten Mountain;

c) to ascertain if the Mansi people are considering the Otorten Moun-

tain and its vicinity as a sanctuary (so-called 'sacred' place);

d) to ascertain who among the Mansi men was hunting in the valley of the Auspiya River and in the vicinity of the 4th tributary of the Lozva River around the time of the death of the hikers;

e) to ascertain which of the hunters' ski track the hikers were following. It has been suggested that it was Anyamov's.

The outcomes of operational activities to be reported to the prosecutor com. Tempalov, who is in charge of the investigation in this case.

Deputy regional prosecutor on special cases, senior counselor of justice Ahmin.

Executed by Ivanov
handwritten
12.III-59"

This document makes it clear that as of March 13, Tempalov was still handling the case, which was opened by the Ivdel prosecutor's office on February 26. It is apparent that the case was opened retroactively, since the bodies of the hikers would be discovered only on February 27. There is an impression that it was personally important for Tempalov to investigate the case on his own instead of fulfilling the assignments of Lev Ivanov within the frame of the case opened by the regional prosecutor's office.

The instruction given to Bizyaev is noteworthy for another reason. At first, all interrogations of residents were conducted by the representatives of the Ivdel prosecutor's office and militia. From March 10, Lev Ivanov was actively interfering in the investigation. On that day, he was interrogating Maslennikov regarding the details of the organization of the search. To the question of Ivanov *"What is, in your opinion, the cause of death of the Dyatlov group?"*, Maslennikov answered: *"I believe that the cause of the group's death were some emergency circumstances, which forced the group to believe that staying in the tent was more dangerous than spending the night on the snow, semi-dressed. There is no doubt that group members were consciously leaving the tent. We have discovered the traces of almost the whole group. I cannot explain the circumstances of leaving the tent and the cuts in particular."*

Possibly, this answer given by Maslennikov, along with the injuries in Slobodin's body, which were discovered a few days before, made Ivanov give thought to the criminal version of the death of the hikers. On March 11, Captain Chernyshev was interrogated. After he told about the organization of the search, Chernyshev was forced to answer the unexpected question from Ivanov:

"Question: Where there any traces of other people or animals near the

tent or the corpses?

Answer: There were no traces like these. I have not seen any traces of a dog or a wolf, some were telling about. There was, in fact, a single trace further from the tent, near the stones at the height. But it was the trace left by our search dogs.

Question: Was it possible in those particular circumstances for anyone to approach the tent so that not to leave any traces? In particular, do the Mansi leave traces?

Answer: Had the Mansi approached on their skis, then there would've been no traces. Their skis do not leave traces. The slope above the tent is bare.

Question: Do you entertain an idea of the Mansi attack at the group?

Answer: I refuse even to think about it. I do not know a single case of the Mansi attacking any people in many years. By the nature of my service, I have repeatedly met with the Mansi under different circumstances, talking with them about hunting and life. They always answer willingly, they are hospitable people. They are collaborating with us, assisting in catching fugitive inmates. They have not manifested any hostile attitude towards us. I do not know which religious holidays do the Mansi celebrate – and when; however, in the region, I have not heard that they had any sacred places in the vicinity of mountain 1079.

Question: In your opinion, what are the reasons for abandoning the tent?

Answer: Like everybody, I cannot understand the reasons for abandoning the tent by the group. Something had made them leave the tent in haste, what is more, in such haste that some of them had to leave not through the door, but through the cut, which someone made for that purpose..."

On March 12, Ivanov interrogated Fyodor Zhiltsov, a freight forwarder of the Languro-Samskiy field party, specifically regarding the Mansi, whom Zhiltsov saw the day before at the guest house of the Northern expedition:

"...In the evening two men of the Mansi nationality came to the guest house. Both were dressed in a Russian way: one in a light coat and another in a short overcoat. One of them began writing something; when he finished writing, he sealed the letter in an envelope. He had not written an address and handed the envelope over to the second Mansi. When the Mansi man was writing his letter, I saw the name of Kurikov. I do not know what the letter said. The Mansi men left at once."

On that same day, Ivanov wrote a note to Naskichev with an instruction to hand over to Korotaev the clothes removed from the corpse of Slobodin and formalized an assignment for Bizyaev.

Konstantin Fyodorovich Bizyaev (37) was born in 1922 in the town of Verkhoturie of the Yekaterinburg governorate of the RSFSR. He graduated from a secondary medical school in Nizhniy Tagil on the eve of the June 22, 1941 Nazi attack on the Soviet Union, and volunteered into the Red Army. He fought as a medical attendant within the formations of the Kalinin and later of the Central Fronts and was wounded twice. After the second wound, he served as a medical attendant of the reserve engineer-sapper battalion of the Ural Military District. He was awarded two medals "For Battle Merit" and the medal "For Victory Over Germany" and was demobilized in late 1945. From early 1946, Bizyaev served with the MVD, and in May 1947 he was appointed as a special agent of the Ivdel department of internal affairs, moving to Ivdel with his wife, Vera Ivanovna, and daughter Svetlana. At Ivdel, he worked as a commandant, police deputy chief investigator of the Ivdel city militia department. From February 1957, he served as head of the Ivdel department of internal affairs, serving in that office until August 1962. In March 1959, he was elected deputy of the Ivdel city soviet.

Why did Ivanov formalize an assignment for Bizyaev on behalf of Ahmin? Why was that done? Ivanov might have formalized the assignment on his behalf. Under the 1958 Fundamental principles of criminal procedure of the USSR: *"An investigator in cases under his investigation has an authority to give assignments and instructions to investigative authorities and request their cooperation in certain investigative procedures. Such assignments and instructions of the investigator will be obligatory for the investigative authorities."*

Yuri Nikolaevich Ahmin (41) was born in 1918 in the village of Kyshtym of the Perm Governorate, as of 1959, the town of Kyshtym of the Chelyabinsk region. In 1937, after graduating from secondary school, he enrolled at the Sverdlovsk Juridical Institute, from which he graduated in 1941 when he immediately volunteered into the Red Army. He began the war as an enlisted man and finished in the rank of a captain. He served as a commanding officer of an infantry squad, platoon, chief of battalion staff, the first assistant of the chief of staff of an infantry regiment, taking part in combat in Rumania, Austria, Hungary, and Czechoslovakia. He was awarded the orders of the Red Star, Patriotic War 2nd degree, and three medals. After demobilization from the army in 1946, from June 1946, he served at the prosecutor's office in Sverdlovsk in the capacity of a prosecutor of its investigative department, and in June 1947, he was shifted to the Sverdlovsk regional prosecutor's office in the same capacity. From October 1949, he served as chief of the investigative department of the Sverdlovsk city and from November 1951 in the same capacity at the regional prosecutor's office. In November 1952, he was appointed as the prosecutor of the city of Sverdlovsk and from 1957 he served as deputy prosecutor of the Sverdlovsk region for special cases. He was also a member of the bureau of the city committee of the CPSU.

It cannot be excluded that a formal referral to Yuri Ahmin indicated a conflict between Ivanov, who desired to check into the criminal version of the death of the students, and Tempalov, who adhered to the version of a hurricane. It should be said that Slobodin's clothes, which were to be handed over to Korotaev, for reasons unknown were not presented to Slobodin's relatives at Sverdlovsk for identification. Possibly, Korotaev had simply forgotten about it because of his workload on other cases. From Korotaev's memorandum written for Stepan Lukin, the head of the Sverdlovsk regional prosecutor's office, it follows that in 1959 Korotaev was investigating 52 criminal cases.

The department for special cases of the regional prosecutor's office was involved in reviewing the investigation in the cases of counter-revolutionary crimes, including the cases of special settlers, who were sent to Ivdel, the domain of Tempalov. Ahmin had nothing to do with the investigation of the case of death of the hikers, but Tempalov reported to him on special cases. Ivanov executed that assignment on behalf of Ahmin so as to ensure its implementation. In fulfilling that assignment, investigative measures were undertaken as early as March 14-16. Mihail Mokrushin, the chairman of the Burmantovskiy rural council, and the Mansi Bahtiyarovs were interrogated. It is noteworthy that the interrogations were conducted by Tempalov in person.

Possibly, Tempalov believed that such activity right in front of the eyes of the regional committee's commission would facilitate his career. However, he had not achieved any lift in his career. In his final years before retirement, he worked as an engineer for personnel of shop №32 at a metal-working factory in the town of Verkhnyaya (Upper) Salda of the Sverdlovsk region.

This adds up to an interesting situation. Tempalov opened a criminal case to investigate the causes of death of the hikers retroactively – in all appearances, after the arrival of Lev Ivanov at Ivdel. He adhered to the 'natural forces' version, under which the hikers *"were blown away from the tent by the wind and got frozen."*

Practically all residents adhered to that version.

Aleksey Cheglakov: *"The group of hikers could get frozen because, with the beginning of the superstorm, their tent was blown away and then torn. They wanted to fix it and were even fixing it. Blown by the wind, they were carried down into the ravine, where they lost orientation and were unable to get back to the tent. They died of cold."*

Ivan Pashin: *"I believe that at the time the wind was very strong, and they were carried down from the mountain."*

Egor Chagin, a hunter from the Vizhay settlement: *"It seems to me that the hikers died because there was a superstorm. At the time they were likely sleeping and on hearing the storm they were scared and jumped out of the tent. Then they were swept off and carried down into the ravine."*

Captain Chernyshev: *"I have not been in this area before, but I know that the weather there is very changeable. Frequent winds are blowing with a hurricane force. I have spent 12 days in the camp: throughout that time there were only two quiet days, better say, relatively quiet. Usually, the wind at the pass is no less than 15-20 meters per second."*

Aleksander Deryagin, the chairman of the Ivdel city soviet: *"It is crazy to sent hiking groups to the mountains of Northern Ural in February. Frequently, there are sudden hurricanes, when it is impossible to maintain one's footing."*

Ivan Uvarov, the director of the Ivdel local history museum: *"I consider the deliberations to the effect that the hikers were attacked by the Mansi men because the hikers wanted to approach the Molebniy peak to be wrong; the people who believe and say so are not familiar with the life and daily routine of the Mansi people."*

Nevertheless, pursuing the criminal version, Tempalov was conducting interrogations in person, although it was Bizyaev who was to handle them, on Ivanov's assignment.

CHAPTER 14. WONDROUS ARE YOUR DEEDS.

Thumbing through the materials of the criminal case, one cannot help but paying attention to the behavioral problems of some of the individuals, who to one degree or another were involved in the search for the Dyatlov group.

During interrogation on April 13, Ufimtsev told about the first contacts of the UPI with Vizhay: *"On February 16, com. Blinov telephoned the committee asking if there was any news of the group. They immediately placed a call to Vizhay and spoke to com. Hakimov from the Ivdellag, who said that on January 27 they gave a lift in a truck to the Northern mining camp for the members of the Dyatlov group, who said that they would return to Vizhay not earlier than February 15. Hakimov as well said that the group had not proceeded through Vizhay on its way back…. According to its route, this group of hikers was to return to the Vizhay settlement on February 12, 1959."*

Zakiy Hakimov, the head of the N-240 Vizhay camp division, was slightly confusing the dates and details of the movement of the Dyatlov group. But why on earth was he aware of the group's route and was talking about it without any additional verification? Let us assume that it was Hakimov in person, with whom the hikers had arranged a lift by a truck to District 41. But is it possible that Hakimov could remember such an average event almost three weeks later? After all, a few more groups were passing through Vizhay.

At District 41, they might know about the scheduled time for the return of the group – following Yudin's leaving the trek and subsequent return to Vizhay. However, in Vizhay Yudin was conversing with pharmacist Teodor Gertsen, but for sure not with Hakimov.

The plot was getting thicker. As of 1956, Hakimov was a member of the Ivdel city committee of the CPSU. He likely remained in that position as of 1959. For sure he knew the city party leaders personally. Moreover, he not only knew the details of the Dyatlov group's route back in mid-February, but he had taken an active part in the organization of search groups. The protocol of the interrogation of Aleksey Cheglakov from March 6, 1959, says: *"In the third week of February 1959, following the order of the head of the camp division com. Hakimov, I*

*flew by helicopter to the site of the death of the hikers together with the for-
ester Ivan Pashin."*

Why were mountain guides attached only to the Slobtsov group, which eventually had discovered both the tent and the first bodies? What was the reason for the decision to send mountain guides from Vizhay? Why not send them from among the residents of Ivdel – the point of departure of the Slobtsov group with quite a number of people familiar with the mountains and with the taiga? For instance, why not send any geologists?

From February 23, the Northern expedition was actively negotiating with the Mansi about their assistance in the search, was obtaining approval of their payment, provided a radio and radio operator, and took part in the aerial search. All these activities had taken place before the active involvement of the party and administrative authorities. For all that, Gordo and Blinov had already been at Ivdel, with individual aircraft detailed for the search – even though the geologists had their work overload, which required lots of effort and facilities.

Numerous magnetic, engineering and geological studies, exploratory and prospecting work with the use of mechanical coring, areal magnetic exploration and pit-hole drilling were underway in that area. With the shortage of qualified experts, from the summer of 1958, the Northern group of the Mid-Ural mining party was enlisting charge hands at Ivdel, who would be authorized to perform blasting operations.

From June 1958, the Ivdel Power Logging Works (Energolesocombinat), which was part of the All-Union Power Logging (Energoles) trust of the Ministry of Power Stations of the USSR, was laying the groundwork for the development of logging operations in the headwaters of the Lozva River – in the part of the Ivdel district bordering with the Tyumen and Perm regions and the Komi Autonomous SSR, as well as for the construction of a mast-impregnating factory in the vicinity of the Pershino station for the production of power transmission line supports. Design and survey work in the exploration of the raw-materials base, allocation of logging operations, construction of a factory with workmen's settlements and roads were conducted by the Design Institute № 2 of the Ministry of Construction of the RSFSR. The workmen's settlement (the former District 41) was under reconstruction, with equipment brought in; reconstruction of the road leading from the Vizhay settlement was underway. It was in connection with the said works that Mihail Timofeevich Dryahlyh, the acting engineer of the Ivdel Power Logging Works, was sent on a tour of duty, on which he met with the Dyatlov group in District 41 on January 26-27.

It was Dryahlyh whom Tempalov would send on the air search together with the representatives of the UPI: *"I have taken steps to ascertain where were the students hikers moving and, with the support of the officials of the city committee of the CPSU, I have sent citizen Dryahlyh by helicopter on the search of the students. So that he would find the traces of the hikers and the hikers themselves and determine the direction of their movement. Com. Dryahlyh is very well familiar with the territory of the Ivdel district."* That as well took place on February 21-22, before the interference of the party bodies. For a long time Dryahlyh had been working as the head of the Ivdel district forestry station and in fact, was to know the territory of the district. However, was he the only one to know it, so that it was necessary to pull off an engineer of the Power Logging Works from his job?

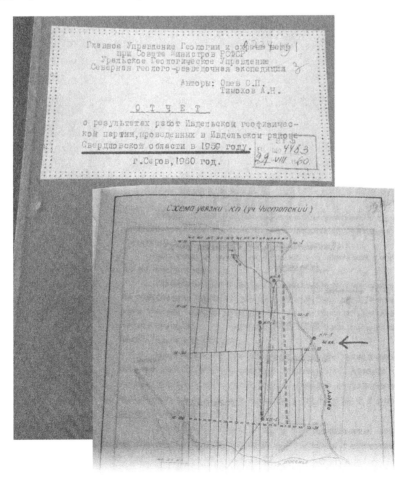

Throughout the whole year of 1959, the said settlement of District 41 was housing a control station №5 of the Chistopskiy section, which served as headquarters for the Ivdel geophysical party of the Serov geophysical group of the Northern geological prospecting expedition of the Ural Geological Survey. After talking to the geologists and workers of the Power Logging Works, Dyatlov decided not to move along the clearings which Rempel recommended to use:

"On January 25, 1959, a group of hikers turned to me as the head of the forest district asking for advice on the best way to get to Mt. Otorten... When I was familiarizing myself with their route, I expressed an opinion that it would be dangerous to walk along the Ural Range in wintertime, given the large ravines and pits one may fall into. Besides, heavy winds are wreaking havoc and blowing people off... At the time, I advised that they should take a shorter route along one of our forest clearings."

For some reason, the group had taken a Mansi trail along the Auspiya River. It is noteworthy that by March 5 laborer Tutinkov and job foreman Evgeniy Petrovich Venediktov had already been fired; it was Venediktov to whom the hikers gave a gift of a book at parting. Valyukyavichus would be shifted to District 100 – to a new job and residence.

The participation of the Mansi men in the search was reported to the UPI as early as February 23. In his testimony, Maslennikov said: *"It was reported to Ivdel that Dyatlov's overnight stop was discovered in the middle reaches of the Auspiya River, that a group of geologists of the Northern expedition was following the Dyatlov group traces and that three groups of the Mansi men had gone on a search along the routes: one group to Oyko-Chakur, another along the ridge and the third towards the Otorten."*

In their report, Bardin and Shuleshko pointed out: *"On February 24, the groups of the Mansi Kurikov (from Suevatpaul) and Bahtiyarov (from the Vizhay area) went on search, with a Komi group prepared to go on a search along the western slopes of the ridge."* On February 26, Maslennikov informed Slobtsov's group that: *"the Bahtiyarov brothers are going northward by sled along the eastern slope of the ridge. The hunters from the Komi Republic have reached the western slope of the ridge from several points. Unfortunately, the Mansi of Suevatpaul have pulled out of the Auspiya's estuary only today"*. In his testimony from March 10, Maslennikov said: *"It is necessary to mention that from the very first days of the search the information on the work of the Mansi turned to be flimsy. The Mansi went out on a search only on February 25, and on February 26 they met with the Slobtsov group. In fact, two other groups of the Mansi, about whom we had heard while at the Institute, did not go on search – at any rate, we have not seen their traces anywhere."*

There is no documentary evidence of the participation in the search of the hunters from the Komi Republic. Most probably, they failed to go on a search before February 26, when after the discovery of the tent, there was no longer any need for the search along the western slope of the ridge. The participation of the Bahtiyarovs in the search is mentioned twice. First, in Slobtsov's testimony, which said: *"I can mention that I saw Mansi Bahtiyarov finding 8 rubles in the snow near the cedar under which the corpses of Doroshenko and Krivonischenko were discovered."* In his diaries, Maslennikov listed the Mansi men from the Kurikov's group: Stepan Kurikov, Nikolay Pavlovich Anyamov, Andrey Alekseevich Anyamov, and Timofey Egorovich Bahtiyarov.

In his testimony, Nikolay Anyamov said: *"In early February 1959, we – that is I, Anyamov Andrey, and another Anyamov, also called Andrey, went hunting. We were hunting in the forest for nine days. While hunting, we saw the traces of narrow skis, which were covered with about 15 centimeters of snow, less in the forest. We thought that some expedition had gone up to the mountains. We saw the traces along the Auspiya River in the second third of February 1959. When we came home, we told about it – that we had seen the traces of skiers. We had not seen the hikers themselves anywhere, and had not heard from them. While we were hunting, the weather was sometimes good, but mostly it was bad. It was windy and cold. Around February 23-24, 1959, we were sent on the search for the hikers, and we went together with the Russians."*

Valeriy Anyamov, who resided in the Ushma settlement, said that his father, Nikolay Vasilyevich Anyamov, took part in the search. The group was led by Stepan Kurikov, the oldest among the participants. The Mansi from Suevatpaul were involved in the search a month after its beginning. A helicopter was sent to their place with a request for assistance in finding the remaining bodies.

There are doubts about the participation of Timofey Bahtiyarov in the search. He, indeed, resided at Suevatpaul, although most of the Bahtiyarov's yurts were in different locations: along the Pelym, Kul, Anchug, Toshemka, and Vap-sos Rivers. However, Stepan Kurikov, the deputy of the Ivdel city council, was married to Praskovaya Vasilyevna Anyamova, the sister of Nikolay Anyamov. It felt better to take one's folks on a search, for which a payment of 500 rubles per day was promised. Pashin confirmed that *"the Kurikov group from Suevatpaul arrived in the area of the search by reindeer of their own."*

Things do not fall into place. Information arrives at Sverdlovsk from Ivdel about the participation of the Bahtiyarovs in the search, notably, at its early stage. However, the Bahtiyarovs would not acknowledge it in any of the interrogations of the Mansi people. Moreover, they refused any suggestions to assist in the search for the missing group.

In his testimonies, Pyotr Yakimovich Bahtiyarov said: *"In mid-February 1959 – I do not remember the particular date – I came to the rural council at the Burmantovo settlement, to the council chairman, to pick up some old newspapers. The name of the council chairman is Mokrushin. While there, we were discussing with him that the reindeer were sick with foot rosary and that many reindeer had died, with the wolves appearing and eating those dead reindeer. Besides we discussed what my father, Bahtiyarov, said when he was still alive, that a man was blown off some mountain. He said that it was dangerous to go to that mountain and he admonished us not to go there. Now I do not remember what mountain it was... Myself, I have been sick with tuberculosis and unable to go hunting for three years."*

In his testimony, Nikolay Yakimovich Bahtiyarov said: *"I have no time to look for the students, since I have to look after 1200 reindeer, and need to shepherd them. There are many wolves. Prokopiy Bahtiyarov can go on a search, but my brother Pyotr is sick. He even does not go hunting."*

The Bahtiyarov brothers – Prokopiy Savelyevich and Sergey Savelyevich – did not receive an invitation to take part in the search. Both of them lived in the Bahtiyarov's yurts in the upper reaches of the Vizhay River. They claimed that they learned about the search for the hikers only on February 22, when some people arrived at their place by helicopter. Those were Dryahlyh and Gordo.

The evidence of Slobtsov and Maslennikov indicate that in the course of the search the discussions about the Bahtiyarovs were so frequent that one of the Anyamovs was mistakenly taken for Bahtiyarov. Why was it so?

From the testimony of Artemiy Gorbushin, senior case officer of the Ivdel city militia station: *"In early March 1959 I was at the militia duty room, with the death of the hikers discussed there at that time.... Kurikov was asked how the hikers might have died. Kurikov said that five Ostyak men were living in the vicinity of the sacred mountain – he did not say where that mountain was. They are like savages, not keeping company with the Mansi, nor with the Russians... Those Ostyak men could have killed the hikers..."*

Artemiy Vladimirovich Gorbushin (47) was born in 1912 in the

Kirov region and had long lived at Ivdel, in its Hydrolysis factory settlement. As of 1953, Gorbushin served at the Ivdellag, as head of the 5th division of its special unit, and as of 1959, he was a senior case officer of the Ivdel city militia department of the Internal Protection Directorate.

Gorbushin left Kurikov's statement without any comment. However, on this account, the testimony of Vladimir Aleksandrovich Krasnobaev, a preparatory works foreman at the Vizhay logging division, comes to mind. Telling about his visit to the Bahtiyarovs yurts at the Northern Toshemka River, Krasnobaev said in particular: *"I have left for the Bahtiyarov's settlement, with five Mansi families residing there..."* We have five Ostyak men and five Mansi families.

Possibly, Kurikov was hinting at the Bahtiyarovs probable complicity in the death of the hikers? Or did he simply dislike the Bahtiyarovs and in that way was trying to get them into trouble? For the Ivdel Mansi, the Bahtiyarovs from the Northern Toshemka were interlopers. There is an opinion that *"the majority of the Mansi who reside at the Ivdel district, are the relatives of the Nyaksimvol Mansi (with Nyaksimvol – a Mansi settlement in the western part of the Khanty-Mansi Autonomous Area.) All of them have one of the three family names: the Kurikovs, the Anyamovs, and the Sambindalovs. Then come to the Bahtiyarovs, who are not typical for the district's territory. The local (Ivdel) Mansi do not consider the Bahtiyarovs as their kin. Some believe them to be incomers from the Pechora, with the others believing them to be some remnants of the Tartar tribes."* This is corroborated by Vladimir Androsov, a Vizhay native: *"The savage Mansi are the Mansi people who have come from the west. In particular, these are the Bahtiyarov kin, who had earlier been referred to as the 'savage people'."*

From the protocol of the interrogation of Krasnobaev: *"Around February 26, 1959, on the instruction of com. Hakimov, the head of the 8th logging division, I went to the Bahtiyarov's settlement, with five Mansi families residing there... At the time, all the Mansi were at home, including Bahtiyarov Timofey, Bahtiyarov Nikolay, Bahtiyarov Aleksander, Bahtiyarov Kirill, and Bahtiyarova Sonya. On the eve of my arrival, Timofey and Bahtiyarov Pavel came from Ivdel, where they had traveled on their private affairs. The Bahtiyarovs Pavel, Timofey, and Kirill said that a week ago they were hunting in the lowlands in the direction of the Ural Range and had not seen any traces left by narrow skis, and neither had they seen any people. As they said, until my arrival, they had no idea of the death of the hikers. Bahtiyarov Pavel Ivanovich said that at the time of the blizzard he was hunting alone, with the rest of the men staying at home. I suggested* to Bahtiyarov Pavel Ivanovich to take part in the search for the deceased hikers, but he refused, explaining that he was ill. Besides, no hikers appeared in the area of their hunting, hence it is not worthwhile to go there... Bahtiyarov Pavel explained to me that if the hikers had died, then only on another side of the Ural Ridge, given the huge snow slides in that area... on March 1, 1959, all the Bahtiyarovs came to District 100, where I met them. They had even stayed overnight at my place; the latter wondered if the deceased hikers had been discovered, themselves, they did not know anything about them."

Krasnobaev told again about his visit to the Bahtiyarov settlement at the North Toshemka River, on Hakimov's instruction. It looks strange that for some reason Dryahlyh and Gordo did not arrive there on February 22, although they had landed quite nearby – at the Anyamov's yurt at the Northern Toshemka. From among the five families of the Bahtiyarovs, the only one to be formally interrogated was the family of Pavel Vasilyevich Bahtiyarov's, whom Krasnobaev named as Pavel Ivanovich: "I live in 20 kilometers to the north from the Bahtiyarov's yurt, at the Northern Toshemka River... I heard that the hikers got lost on March 1, 1959, while I was at the polls – from other people since the search for those hikers had begun. I have no idea about how the hikers got lost and I have no idea of their route... I have never been in the upper reaches of the Lozva River and have always hunted along the Ivdel and the Vizhay Rivers."

Pavel Vasilyevich Bahtiyarov was apparently dodging. He learned about the death of the hikers no later than February 26, when Krasnobaev suggested to him to take part in the search. But what made Bahtiyarov conceal even the fact of his conversation with Krasnobaev? Possibly, this part of Slobtsov's testimony is suggestive of what was the case: "I have seen in person the discovery under the cedar of a dark colored canvas belt with tie strings at its ends. I did not know to whom that object belonged. That object was about 80 centimeters long and about 10 centimeters wide. It looked like a belt or a strap, which the Mansi use to pull the loading. However, that object was not fit to use as a carrying sling, since it was not firm enough."

From Ortyukov's radiogram: "A flooring has been discovered in the bottom of the excavated plot... On top of the flooring were found... one soldierly foot binding made of junior enlisted military cloth with a stitched webbing about one meter long. I cannot explain the appearance of the foot binding."

The report of the Karelin group, which in February met with the Bahtiyarovs at the Northern Toshemka, points out that the Mansi were dressed in clothes made of military cloth...

Summing up, in the materials of the criminal case we can see certain oddities, which for some reason had escaped the eye in the course of the investigation and inspection.

How can we explain the conduct of the Ivdel prosecutor, who opened the case retroactively and was unwilling to relinquish his hold of the investigation?

Why was the Northern expedition using its resources for the organization of the search of the hikers, despite the presence at Ivdel of the UPI representatives with the aircraft detailed for the search works?

Why was the head of the N-240 Vizhay logging division detailing his subordinates for questioning the residents and escorting the UPI search group?

What was the reason for the Mansi Bahtiyarovs to conceal their awareness of the fate of the hikers and to refuse to participate in the search, which was decently paid? At the same time, there was unconfirmed information both on their participation in the search and on their possible complicity in the death of the Dyatlov group.

How can we explain that Dryahlyh, with his excellent knowledge of the Ivdel district, released from his official duties at the Ivdel Power Logging Works and acting as a navigator in the air search, was unable to discover the tent on the slope of height 1079 throughout his participation in the search, beginning from February 21?

Or was he?

CHAPTER 15. THE TENT DISCOVERED FROM THE AIR. COULD THIS BE TRUE?

The materials in the criminal case have no information on the discovery of the Dyatlov group tent from the air. Nevertheless, there are recollections to the effect that it was specifically discovered by the pilots. We are not taking into consideration the account of Victor Vasilyevich Potyazhenko that it was he who had spotted the tent. *"When we were taking off while accelerating to the speed and gaining height, I saw something below – looking like a tent. I pointed it to Ortyukov – have a look! He shook his head… saying, we will take a look tomorrow."* No doubt, Potyazhenko might see the tent during the takeoff on return to Ivdel, however, Slobtsov and Sharavin had discovered it a day before Potyazhenko appeared at height 1079.

Emil Bachurin, who at the time of the search for the group worked as a cook and a stoker at the intermediate base of the Northern expedition, mentioned that *"in the winter of 1959, the corpses of several people and abandoned tents were discovered on the eastern slope of Mt. Otorten from a helicopter, which was making a special flight to one of the parties of the northern expedition."*

Vsevolod Poluyanov, a 1954 graduate of the UPI and a well-known Ural hiker, the friend of Bogomolov and Akselrod, recalled: *"Finally, we discovered from the helicopter a solitary tent at a bare pass near Mt. Otorten. There were no people anywhere near and around it."*

Residents told about it as well. According to Georgiy Novokreschenov *"…they were discovered from the helicopter. Shreds of the tent were swinging in the wind. I heard it all from Vladimir Ivanovich, who was highly regarded."*

Georgiy Vasilyevich Novokreschenov (36) was born in 1923 in Yekaterinburg. After graduation from a factory-and-works school, he worked as a milling machine operator at the Ural heavy machine-building plant. In 1942, he was drafted into the Red Army. Following a six-month training at a mortar battalion of the Omsk infantry school, he was sent to the field army without commissioning and took part in the Battle of Stalingrad. In

1943 he received officer training within the formation of the Steppe Front. Commissioned as a junior lieutenant, he took part in the Battle of Kursk as a squad commander and in 1944 was promoted to the rank of lieutenant. Within the formation of the 1st Ukrainian Front, he took part in the Lvov, Sandomir, Oder, and Dresden operations. Wounded three times, he was awarded the orders of the Patriotic War 1st and 2nd class, the medals "For the Victory over Germany", "For the Defence of Stalingrad", "For the Liberation of Prague". Until December 1945 he served with the Soviet occupation forces in Germany and Czechoslovakia, then shifted to Austria. On return home, he graduated from the Sverdlovsk law school in 1948 and was appointed a judge at the Tugulym district. While working as a judge, he graduated from the Sverdlovsk Juridical Institute (studying by correspondence) and for many years worked in various parts of the Sverdlovsk region. As of 1959, Novokreschenov was a judge in the People's Court at Ivdel. Later, in 1963, he was elected a member of the Sverdlovsk regional court and in 1972 transferred to Sverdlovsk, where he became a member of the Sverdlovsk regional judicial division for criminal cases.

Novokreschenov narrated the account of investigator Vladimir Korotaev. However, Korotaev's own account of that event was extremely brief, *"I am not aware of who had discovered the tent."* In 2004, the above mentioned Georgiy Karpushin, who as of 1959 served as senior navigation officer of the 123rd flight detachment, and later as a staff navigator of the Ural office of civil navigation related: *"we clearly distinguished a tent, which had stuck to the eastern slope. We could clearly see that it was cut through from the northern side. Right near the tent, there was a corpse with the head towards the tent, apparently female. At a little distance, there was one more body... We fixed the position of the tent on the map and contacted Ivdel. We received an order to return to the airport."* It is noteworthy that in the course of the interrogations in 1959, none of the participants in the search or its organizers recalled the participation of the pilots in the discovery of the tent.

From all appearances, Bachurin, Poluyanov, Novokreschenov, and even Karpushin were all retelling some rumors. What could give rise to such rumors? Possibly, there was confusion with another event. By February 18, the search for the strayed geologists of the Bazhenov expedition was completed, with the geologists finally discovered in the vicinity of the Vershina settlement on the Pelym River by the pilots of the 123rd flight detachment.

But what if there was no confusion? Can it be possible that the tent of the Dyatlov group was in fact discovered from the air? If the local pilots were the first to discover the tent on the slope, then why that event had not been anyhow recorded in the materials of the criminal case? Who else, besides the pilots of the 123rd flight detachment, who were based at Ivdel, and the pilots of the Ural Military District, who were attached to facilitate the search, might be flying in the vicinity of height 1079?

In 1959-60, the Northern-Ural party 72/59-60 of the Novosibirsk geophysics trust led by V.V. Bolshakov was conducting a comprehensive aeromagnetic survey of the scale of 1:200000 in the area of the Polar Ural, Pay-Khoy, and the Pechora basin. In their southern part, these works overlapped with the area of the Dyatlov group trek, including the vicinity of height 1079. A summary report on those works has survived. It is noteworthy that according to the "Plan of aeromagnetic works for 1959 of the Northern-Ural party 72/59", it was planned to complete the initial survey within a year. For a number of reasons, the works were extended and continued for two years. Unfortunately, the initial plan has not survived. However, the projected terms of the stages of the work may be reconstructed from the materials of the adjusted report, proceeding from the fact that the work scopes and their terms were the same according to the 1959 plan and upon completion of the works in 1959-60.

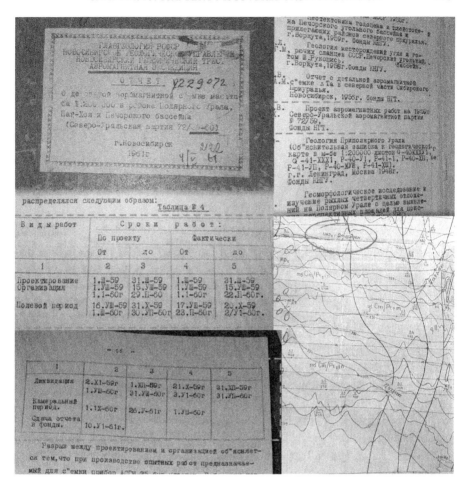

According to the report for 1959-60, on completion of the works their terms were the following: project conception – 1 month, organization – 2 months, field period – 6 months, liquidation – 2 months. Then the planned terms of the works for 1959 looked the following: project conception – January, organization – February-March, field period – April-September, liquidation – October-November; office operations (cameral works) – December.

As early as February, the aircraft of the 6th air detachment of the Western-Siberian Territorial Office of Civil Aviation (which was based at Novosibirsk – leasing the Novosibirsk geophysics trust for its needs) might be flying over the pass. According to established procedures, right before the production survey, they conducted reconnaissance flights to ascertain survey flying heights, rational aerial methods, input/output reference marks, familiarization with the generic character of the magnetic field, as well as to select locations with a normal magnetic field for control strips. With the purpose of aerial photograph navigation, they conducted photographing from control strips vertical to the traverse of airborne geophysical survey.

Following the aerial photograph navigation, the survey (traverse) lines were charted on topographic maps. Production survey was organized in a series of parallel routes at a 2 kilometer (1.2 miles) distance transversally at the height of 300 meters (984 feet).

On February 9 the works had to be interrupted. The entire personnel of the 6th flight detachment was grounded in view of its poor training; however, on February 20 the flights were resumed. It was at that time that Slobtsov noticed the flights over the search area: *"Several helicopters were cruising over the entire area. They were scanning the terrain with an interval of approximately 5 km."* There is a confirmation in Gennadiy Grigoriev's account: *"An area was determined, and it was to be covered on a course line of 3-4 km from each other. That was the task of all aircraft."* On February 25, Ortyukov reported the same to the Slobtsov group: *"For your information reporting that... a systematic aerial survey of the whole territory of the incident is underway."* Koptelov and Sharavin as well were hearing the sounds of the flying search aircraft, since *"there was a mighty air search going on"*.

In April the works of the Novosibirsk geophysics trust were again interrupted. The upgraded airborne prospecting system device (ASGM-25) that was planned to be used in the survey, was lost in the course of the test survey in the area of Novosibirsk. On April 24, a Li-2 airplane of the 5th flight detachment was wrecked near the city of Berdsk while carrying out an assignment of the airborne geomagnetic survey. It was that accident, which served as an official reason for rescheduling the works of the Bolshakov expedition from 1959 to 1959-60. The Novosibirsk geophysicists would appear at Ivdel only in the winter of 1960. Vladimir Povodator, who in September 1959 was hired into the Bolshakov expedition as a young professional, recalled: *"In the winter of 1960, I stayed at Ivdel for a long time. I was processing the instrumental data. I also heard about the death of a group a year ago. Residents were talking about it, saying, 'do not go there.' I had no idea who died – students or geologists. All conversations with the locals were limited to 'don't go there.' But we didn't go, the airplanes flew there."*

As can be seen from the above, the tent of the hikers could indeed be discovered in February from the airplanes of the 6th flight detachment of the Western Siberian Office of Civil Aviation based at several airfields. The flights to the area of height 1079 were carried from the airfield of Ukhta. However, ground services for processing the outcomes were as well at Ivdel. The rumors about the discovery of the tent could have reached Ivdel both through the geophysicists and through the airport controllers.

CHAPTER 16. UNACCOUNTED PEOPLE.

Following the discovery of the tent at height 1079, search teams began to assemble at the site. *"On February 27, groups from other areas were shifted to the pass between heights 880-1079, with a base search camp set below the forest border. In total, the following groups were concentrated in the camp: Slobtsov's group – 5 men, Karelin's group – 5 men, Akselrod group – 5 men, Captain Chernyshev group – 5 men, the group of the Mansi Stepan Kurikov – 4 men, the group of operatives with search dogs led by Sr. Lieutenant Moiseev – 2 men; radio operator of the Northern-Ural expedition G. Nevolin."*

On that same day, Pashin and Cheglakov flew from the search site. From the testimony of Cheglakov: *"On the fifth day of the search four corpses were discovered, including one female. After that, we were taken home to Vizhay settlement by helicopter."* This was as well confirmed by Pashin: *"On the fifth day in our search we discovered 4 people snowed in, and on that same day, we were taken by helicopter and brought home to Vizhay settlement."*

Why did they fly away? Were there enough people at the pass for an efficient search? No, there was a shortage of search personnel. Groups were continuously transported to the pass: *"The following groups arrived later: the group of Moscovites – the Masters of Sport Bardin, Baskin, and Shuleshko, accompanied by Korolev (Sverdlovsk); the group of cadets of the Ivdellag's non-commissioned officers' school, led by Sr. Lieutenant Potapov – 10 men; the group of sappers with mine detectors led by Colonel Shestopalov – 7 men."* But some people were removed from the pass. Here is Sogrin's recollection of the events of March 1: *"The helicopter was met by the members of the Slobtsov group and some strangers, most of whom left with the return flight."* Who could they be?

From the testimony of Colonel Ortyukov, who was one of the leaders of the search, it appears that as of February 26 *"in total, 46 experienced athletes within three landing teams and two groups were sent along the Lozva and Vizhay Rivers."* It is well known that the participants in the search included 11 men from the Slobtsov group, six men from the Grebennik group, five men from the Axelrod group, five men from the Chernyshev group, five men from the Kurikov group, and six men from the Karelin group preparing for the air flight: the total of 38. Eight men, who took part in the search as of the day of the discovery of the tent, are not known.

From Maslennikov's diary it follows that on February 27, 35 men were concentrated in the search camps. Five men from the Karelin group remaining after Skutin's removal from the search; nine men from the Slobtsov group, following the removal of Pashin and Chegla-kov from the search; five men from the Chernyshev group, five men of the Akselrod group, 5 men from the Kurikov group; dog handlers Moiseev and Mostovoy, as well as Maslennikov, Blinov, Yarovoy, and Chernousov.

From Grigoriev's diary it follows that as of February 28, 41 men were engaged in the search. The six men, who took part in the search on that day, remain unknown. It is also unknown from whom did Grigoriev obtain his information. Possibly, he took into account the six men of the group of Grebennik. However, they were removed from the upstream of the Vizhay River on that same day, February 28, and their subsequent participation in the search was not planned.

On the evening of March 1, there were 30 people in the camp at the Auspyia River: *"For Sulman: All participants of the team in the strength of 30 people feel fine."* These included five men from the Karelin group, nine men from the Slobtsov group, five men from the Chernyshev group, three men from the Akselrod group, and four men from the Kurikov group, as well as Nevolin, Blinov, Maslennikov, and Yarovoy. On that day, it was supposed to send Moiseev, Mostovoy, and Chernousov back from the pass. From all appearances, Ivanov was not included in the list of the search team.

From the diary of Grigoriev it follows that on March 2, 34 men were in the camp. Most likely Grigoriev had received information from someone on the number of the search personnel as of March 1, since due to weather conditions, on March 2 there were no helicopter flights to the pass and there could be no changes in the composition of the team.

On March 3, the Mansi Kurikov group left the search camp. Ivanov, Yarovoy, and six men from the Slobtsov group were removed from the pass by helicopter. Bardin, Baskin, Shuleshko, Korolev, and eight sappers from Lt. Colonel Shestopalov group arrived in the search camp, with 30 men left in the camp.

In his diaries, Grigoriev wrote that according to Yarovoy, who had returned to Ivdel, there were 36 people in the search camp. Even taking into account the Mansi men, as of the time when Yarovoy left the camp, there were only 34 men there (according to the official lists).

There were discrepancies in the number of people involved in the search in the period from February 26 to March 3. Compared to official lists of the search groups, from two to eight men remain unknown. On those days strangers might indeed be at the search camps since their composition was continuously changing. In the best-case scenario, search participants knew only the members of their group, and the UPI students did not know each other well, since they were from different departments and classes.

Let us recall the content of the radiogram:

"February 27, 9:00 am... Reporting that the search at the site of the Dyatlov tent started yesterday, with four men having gone there today..."

"March 1, 10:25 am Moscow time... Today, four men will be looking for the cache. All the rest are going on a search for the missing."

In both cases – four men. Can it be a coincidence? The cache was discovered on March 2. After March 3, there were no more discrepancies in the numbers of people in the search camp. Can it also be a coincidence?

On March 3, a group of sappers from the railway troops led by Lt. Colonel Shestopalov arrived for the search. On March 6 the lt. colonel would fly back to Ivdel from the search camp, leaving Lt. Avenburg as the sapper's commanding officer.

Aleksey Mihaylovich Kryukov, Commander of the Railway forces of the Ministry of Defense of the USSR from 1968 to 1983, recalled: *"The Decree of the Council of Ministers of the USSR and the Central Committee of the CPSU from August 6, 1955, on the measures for radical improvement of the timber procurement industry and drawing into an economic turnover of large forest expanses of the basins of the Lozva and Pelym Rivers, the upstream of the Konda and Malaya Sosva Rivers, as well as to provide for the ground delivery of floated wood from the Ob River, provided for the construction of a railway, connecting the Polunochnoe station of the Sverdlovsk railway with point Nary-Kary on the left bank of the Ob."* In February 1957, the Ministry of Forest Industry of the USSR gave an assignment to the Leningrad Planning and Surveying Transportation Institute (Lengiprotrans) to design the Polunochnoe – Nary-Kary railway line as a timber railway. In January 1958, the Ministry of Forest Industry of the RSFSR, which was given charge of the issues involved with railway construction, turned to the Ministry of Railways of the USSR with a request to coordinate the approval of the design and construction of the Polunochnoe – Nary-Kary line by the standards of the MPS; which was done in February 1958. In 1959, following feasibility studies, engineering design drawings for the first 20 kilometers of the line were issued.

The construction of the railway line was assigned to the 5th detached Poznan Red Banner railway brigade, strengthened by the detached units of the 17th, 30th, 35th, and 39th railway brigades. The strength of the 5th railway brigade was doubled. It was joined by three tracks, two bridge, and two maintenance battalions; one auto, one technical and two mechanization battalions; two detached companies, an infirmary, a machine and tractor station and, for the first time in the history of the railway forces, a helicopter wing, based at the Ivdel airport from the spring of 1960 was. The official green light for the construction of the railway line was given in March 1959, with the beginning of the construction of a bridge over the Ivdel River.

In February 1958, 12 hikers died in Transcarpathian Hoverla height. Regular military forces were as well called for the search of the bodies. The participation of the military servicemen in the search is nothing unusual. However, the arrival of a senior officer, in the rank of lt. colonel, as a leader of a group of seven sappers, raises questions.

> **Mihail Fyodorovich Shestopalov (43)** was born in Moscow in 1916 in a large family of a railway worker. His parents died, when he was seven, leaving eleven children orphaned, to be brought up in orphanages of Moscow and Volokolamsk. From childhood, he demonstrated an excellent memory. With his many talents, he tried to study at several institutions but had not completed higher education. In 1937, Shestopalov was admitted to the Moscow military railway school. In 1941-42 he served as a senior lieutenant and squad commander of the 64th detached railway battalion. In 1942-45 Shestopalov served as the head, later as an engineer of the blocking service of the 6th railway brigade. At the end of the war, he had the rank of captain. For his wartime service, he was awarded the order of the Red Star, the medals "For Battle Merit", "For the Defense of Moscow", "For the Capture of Koenigsberg", and "For Victory over Germany in the Great Patriotic War of 1941-45". After the war, he served with the 5th detached Poznan Red Banner brigade, rising to the rank of major by 1950 and lt. colonel by 1959. He was part of an athletic committee of his military unit.

Why did Shestopalov arrive in person for the search at the height of bridge-building works?

Possibly, he wanted to see for himself that his subordinates were safe. He would fly away on March 4 after his group had searched through the 300x150 m site in the vicinity of the cedar, including both streams. Was it by pure chance that they had not discovered anything? In May the final four bodies of the deceased would be discovered in one of those streams.

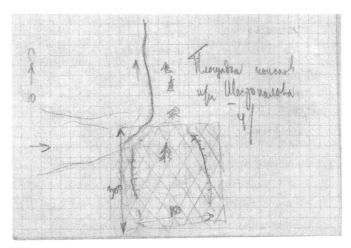

Search site for the group of Lieutenant Colonel Shestopalov on March 4.
From Maslennikov's diary.
In the center is the cedar, on the sides are drawn streams. The last
four bodies will be found in the left (western) stream in May.

From the troop orders, it appears that in the period of the search for the Dyatlov group Shestopalov stayed at Ivdel on at least three occasions. He was first dispatched for the period from March 2 to March 15, from which it appears that immediately upon arrival he went to the pass. Shestopalov returned to Serov on March 13, two days before the scheduled time. It is noteworthy that exactly on the day of his departure from Ivdel, the Sverdlovsk regional soviet executive committee accepted a plan for conducting a subsequent search.

The next mission of the lt. colonel lasted from March 18 to March 23. He returned to Serov at the time when the Kikoin search group was preparing to fly away from the pass.

Shestopalov appeared at Ivdel for the third time on March 31. It was in the night to March 31 when the members of search groups, including the railway servicemen, were observing the anomalous phenomenon in the sky over the pass. The lt. colonel would return to Serov only on April 30. It was on that day that the resolution on extending the term of investigation in the Dyatlov group case was issued. It is a known fact that railway officers, as well, were dispatched to Ivdel for demolition works to allow the ice to flow through the Lozva River.

However, can there be so many coincidences in the dates of the key events in the search?

It is noteworthy that in January 1959, Shestopalov was appointed as chief military inquiry officer of the staff of the brigade management headquarters. A military inquiry officer is an officer authorized to conduct an inquiry in criminal cases involved with servicemen of the military unit. He conducted an inquiry under the supervision of an investigative agency and with the oversight of a military prosecutor. Then in which capacity did Shestopalov appear at the search: as a commanding officer of a group of sappers – or as a military inquiry officer?

One may as well wonder about Prodanov, who flew to the pass on March 13 and, possibly, on May 6. What was the need for the city committee's first secretary to appear at the search site in person?

What do we know about how the first bodies were discovered on February 27? In the morning, four men left the search camp to take down the tent and to search in its location. Possibly, Yuri Koptelov and Mihail Sharavin were among those four. However, they had never said that they were searching as part of any group. Koptelov recalled that it had taken them 45 minutes to reach the pass from the camp. At 12:00 pm local time a helicopter with the search party and the dog handlers flew from Ivdel. Yakimenko recalled that the helicopter flight time from Ivdel to the pass was approximately an hour and a half. That means that the helicopter was to arrive at the pass around 1:30 pm. By that time, Koptelov and Sharavin had discovered two bodies under the cedar. Virtually without taking a look around, they returned to the camp.

Sharavin would later recall that *"...Yuri went along our route to meet the guys so that to apprise them of what happened; simultaneously I went to the rock outlier because the helicopter had already arrived. The helicopter brought dog handlers with their dogs. I met and informed them of what had happened."* As can be seen from the above, Sharavin met the helicopter, which delivered the first team of the Karelin's group and dog handlers, while Koptelov went back to the camp to report on the discovery of the bodies.

From the testimony of Atmanaki: *"At the pass, we met several people from the Slobtsov group, who gave approximate directions to the location of the Dyatlov group's tent... Borisov and I, together with two men from the Slobtsov's team and the dog handlers, combed through the slope below the tent, and on the right from it, they met two Mansi men and the head of the fire department of the city of Ivdel. They told us that two corpses had been discovered in about two kilometers below and showed the location of the tent...*"

This means that at the time of the arrival of the helicopter, besides Sharavin, there were at least two Mansi men, Cheglakov and someone 'from the Slobtsov's team' at the pass. Once again this makes four men. At the time, Koptelov was on the way to the camp. Slobtsov would later recall that someone had come to the camp and told about the discovery of the bodies near the cedar. The prosecution team would arrive pretty quickly.

Soon a helicopter landed at the pass with Tempalov, Maslennikov, Blinov, Yarovoy, Chernousov, and the second team of the Karelin group onboard. Koptelov recalled that while on the way to the search camp he saw an approaching helicopter and met its arriving passengers.

Here, again, were some anomalies. It had taken Koptelov about an hour and a half to come to the camp, to report the discovered corpses, and to return to the pass. The radio telegram about the discovery of the bodies under the cedar was sent from the camp no earlier than at 2 pm, after which Slobtsov ordered those who remained at the camp to go to the pass for the search. Koptelov met the helicopter at around 3 pm, while the helicopter was to fly from Ivdel around 1:30 pm.

According to the recollections of Blinov: "*The first radio telegram on the discovery of the bodies arrived around 11:00 am Moscow time*", that is around 1:00 pm local time, which is compliant with the helicopter's takeoff time. The question is who could report on the discovery of the bodies if Koptelov arrived at the search camp not earlier than 2:00 pm? Moreover, Tempalov flew to the pass after he had received the report on the discovery of one body, and not two: "*On February 27, 1959, I received a report that one corpse was discovered at the mountain 1079 and that the tent of the student-hikers was discovered. I immediately flew by helicopter to height 1079. At the same height, three more corpses were discovered, which makes four total. Later, the fifth corpse was discovered.*" This checks in the notation in Grigoriev's diary: "*We found Dyatlov. Gathered at the pass. The helicopter arrived.*"

Blinov recalled that immediately after the arrival at the pass, they were informed about the discovery of Dyatlov's body. The remaining participants in the search received that information late in the afternoon. Blinov saw with his own eyes the body of Kolmogorova, which was not yet fully dugout, and two bodies under the cedar. Koptelov, who was detailed for setting up a new search camp, would later recall that throughout the day at the camp they heard that Dyatlov's body was discovered by the Mansi men. Kolmogorova was discovered by a search dog.

It appears that someone had discovered Dyatlov's corpse before Sharavin and Koptelov discovered two corpses under the cedar. This may be possible since Dyatlov's body was not completely snowed in – same as the bodies under the cedar: *"For Sulman... As of 4:00 pm, four people were discovered in different places... Three corpses were partially seen from under the snow. The fourth was discovered by the dog."* In the materials of the criminal case information that Dyatlov's body was the first to be discovered can be found only in the testimony of Tempalov, who on April 15 was summoned to Sverdlovsk to report on the criminal case into the death of the hikers to the deputy prosecutor of the RSFSR; on April 18 he was interrogated by Romanov regarding the details of the organization of the search at Ivdel.

Probably, Lev Ivanov might have noticed the oddities in Tempalov's testimonies; however, from mid-March Tempalov had little if anything to do with this case.

CHAPTER 17. LIGHT PHENOMENON IN THE SKY.

By the end of March, the investigation into the case of the Dyatlov group had been de facto closed. In the period from March 10 to March 27, the commission of the Sverdlovsk regional committee ascertained the cause of death of the hikers. To confirm the causes of death of the hikers – which were, officially, the hurricane and the mistakes made by the hikers themselves – on a proforma basis, it was left to discover the remaining bodies. The degree of guilt of each of the officials had as well been determined, with appropriate party penalties imposed.

This may be the reason for the absence of the conclusions of the chemical and histological examinations of the first five of the discovered bodies in the materials of the case. The forensic medical examination reports say that *"part of the internal organs of the examined corpse has been removed for chemical and histological examination and forwarded to the laboratory of the Sverdlovsk regional forensic examination office (SOBSME) for analysis."* At the SOBSME the specimens were received on March 10 against written acknowledgment of P.G. Chaschihina. Up to two weeks were allocated for the examination. After the cause of death of the hikers was ascertained by the commission of the regional committee, there was no longer any need in the examination: they could either be interrupted or if completed their final reports would not be officially registered. In the register books at the archives of the SOBSME there is no mention of any documents connected with the Dyatlov group.

Such things happen even at present. For instance, after the reports on the forensic examination of corpses and the conclusion of the expert of the Khabarovsk city department of forensic examination for 2006, in 74 cases the cause of death was considered to be hypothermia or the impact of low temperature. In all the 74 reports there are indications of the removal of the organs for forensic histopathological examination, however, the reports on the histological examinations were attached only in 58 cases.

The forensic expert examination of the tent was not needed at all.

On March 16, in his order on the criminal proceedings, Lev Ivanov pointed out that *"the determination if the tent was cut or torn is important for the case."* Most likely, that order was formal and was needed only for filing the forensic examination report. Churkina concluded that the tent was cut from inside still in Ivdel since the information found its way into Bardin and Shuleshko's report on the outcome of the investigation of the death of the Sverdlovsk hikers. On March 23, the Organizational Bureau of the Union of the sports societies and organizations of the RSFSR sent the following to the Department of administrative and commercial-financial bodies of the Central Committee of the CPSU for the RSFSR: *"The experts have determined that the tent's wall was initially cut open from inside with several strikes of a knife."*

The tent was received at the Sverdlovsk Research Institute of Forensic Science (SNIKL) only on April 3, two weeks after the date of the order. Under the Ministry of Justice of the RSFSR 1958 Instruction on conducting official forensic expert examinations, an examination was to be completed within a ten-day term in case of an insignificant number of its subjects and with no complicated methods required for their examination. Besides Genrietta Churkina, there was another participant in the examination – SNIKL's young expert Evgeniy Grigoriev, who was detailed in her assistance.

> **Evgeniy Vasilyevich Grigoriev (29)** was born in 1930. For five years he served at the Pacific Fleet as an artillery forward observer; after his release from active duty, he enrolled at the Sverdlovsk Juridical Institute, from which he graduated in 1957. His post-graduate work assignment was at the SNIKL as a forensic expert. His fields included trace evidence and ballistic data analysis, as well as dactyloscopy.

Churkina was also assisted by another SNIKL expert – T.I. Mihailova. Tipikin recalled that his uncle, Boris Kretov, who was the SNIKL's head, consulted him in person about how a tent should be properly set up.

> **Boris Fyodorovich Kretov (38)** was born in 1921. In 1940, he was drafted into the Red Army, serving in the field army from October 1941 as a company commanding officer in the rank of lieutenant. Heavily wounded in December 1941 in the Battle of Moscow, he had his right foot amputated and was demobilized in 1943 (as a Patriotic War invalid, 2nd group.) In 1945, while a student of the Sverdlovsk Juridical Institute, he was awarded

the order of the Patriotic War, 2nd class. Kretov was among the first post-war graduates of the Sverdlovsk Juridical Institute and the first head of SNIKL, who took part in its organization in June 1951.

Despite the overall simplicity of the expert examination and the involvement of a considerable number of experts, its deadline was not kept. The expert examination lasted for 14 days and was completed a month after the order. The tent itself was no longer of any interest to anyone, and it had stayed in the laboratory's cellar until the mid-1980s when it was disposed of following the flooding of the cellar with a pipe burst.

By the end of March, the overwhelming majority of interrogations of the participants in the search and the relatives of the victims to ascertain the details of the organization of the search were conducted by prosecutor Romanov. He would be the one to interrogate Tempalov. It was also Romanov, who most likely dealt with the identification of the victims and issuing their personal effects to the relatives. Ivanov only signed the protocols. Under the Code of Criminal Procedure, personal effects could be issued to the owners only after the case was closed. Accordingly, the case from February 26, which Tempalov opened retroactively, was most likely closed before March 30, when issuing the personal effects of the victims to their relatives began.

Vasiliy Shulyatiev, who was sending the identified personal effects of Yuri Doroshenko to his younger brother Vladimir in Aktiubinsk, would later recall that he received those personal effects from a prosecutor's assistant. It was that same assistant who was giving various assignments to students on behalf of the investigation. Evgeniy Grigoriev, the SNIKL's forensic expert, recalled that initially the case was handled by Lev Ivanov, but later it was passed to someone else.

Around the same time, in late March, the UPI students were invited to the laboratory of the Sverdlovsk regional prosecutor's office for printing photos from the films of the deceased members of the Dyatlov group and the members of the search groups. There were plans to give the photos to the relatives of the deceased. This fact appears in the recollections of Chubarev, Yudin, Bienko, Sogrin, Shulyatiev, Brusnitsyn, Plastun, and Yakimenko. Boris Bychkov, a student of the UPI Department of Construction, took part in printing photos together with them.

As to Lev Ivanov, he was declining from communication on the Dyatlov group case with everybody, including Maslennikov. Sogrin recalled that approximately in early April Ivanov suddenly closed up, cutting off all contacts. Among the materials of the criminal case, there are protocols of only four interrogations, which Ivanov conducted in April-May 1959.

On April 7-8, Atmanaki testified: *"On February 17, Vladimir Shevkunov and I got up at 6:00 am, so that we could make breakfast for the whole group. Having set the fire and done all the chores, we were waiting for the meals to cook. The sky was grey; there were no clouds, but there was a light mist, which usually clears away after sunrise. By chance, while sitting with my face towards the north, I turned my head to the east and saw a milk-white blurred spot in the sky at the height of 30 degrees; with the size of about 5-6 lunar diameters, it consisted of a few concentric circles. Its shape resembled a halo, which can be sometimes seen around the Moon in clear frosty weather. I pointed to my partner how the Moon had become embellished. He thought and said that, first, there was no Moon, and besides, it should be on another side. One or two minutes passed since the time we spotted this event. I don't know how long it had lasted before that and how it had initially looked. At that moment a little star flashed right in the center of that object; for a few seconds it remained in its original size, but then it began growing rapidly in size – moving westward with lightning speed. Within a few seconds it had grown to the size of the Moon, then, bursting through the smokescreen or the clouds it appeared as a giant milk-colored disk with the size of 2 or 2.5 lunar diameters, surrounded by the same pale-colored circles. Then, staying in that same size, the sphere began to pale until it merged with the surrounding halo, which in its turn spread throughout the sky and died out. It was dawning. The watch showed 6:57 am. The spectacle continued less than a minute and a half and left an indelible impression.."*

On April 24, Akselrod testified: *"It is my firm conviction that nothing and nobody could strike panic in the guys from inside. Meaning in the tent itself. Hence, they were forced to run by some external forces. If the tent is asleep and closed - then it is either a very bright light, or a very strong sound, or both of them."*

On that same day, Sogrin said under interrogation: *"The group, frightened by something, fled the tent… The influence of the external factor, which forced the group to leave the tent, was, likely, for an extended period."* Sogrin was short-spoken, even though he had seen this type of external factor during the search: *"On March 31, at 4:00 am, we noticed a large fiery circle, which for 20 minutes was moving towards us and then hid behind height 880. Before hiding below the horizon, a star emerged from the center of the circle, with that star gradually growing in size to the size of the Moon, then began falling, separating itself from the circle…*

We are requesting to explain this phenomenon and its security since in our situation it is leaving an uneasy impression. Avenburg, Potapov, Sogrin."

On May 15, Brusnitsyn testified: *"Something extraordinary, not seen before, had forced the hikers to leave the tent in panic. To escape undressed, in bad weather, at night from the only warm nook would be only possible under pain of death. That strange phenomenon (the light penetrating through the tent, the sound and, possibly gases) was in place during a rather extended period, rushing the hikers to their feet."*

All four interrogations, which were conducted by Ivanov, were involved with the sightings of strange celestial phenomena or with assumptions of their connection with the death of the hikers. It is noteworthy that the criminal case has abundant material involved with witnessing such phenomena.

On February 18, 1959, "Tagilskiy rabochiy" ("The Tagil Worker") daily published a paragraph by one A. Kissel, deputy head of the Vysokogorskiy mine, which said: *"Yesterday, at 6:55 am local time, a luminous sphere with the size of the visual lunar diameter appeared in the direction of east-southeast at the height of 20 degrees."* Ivanov recalled that the editor of the newspaper was penalized for publication of that paragraph. Publications about the phenomena appeared not just in Nizhniy Tagil, but as well in the papers "Za kommunizm" ("For the Communism") in the city of Turinsk, "Leninskoe Znamya" ("Leninist Flag") in the village of Verkhoturie of the Sverdlovsk region, and "Ulyanovskaya Pravda" ("The Pravda of Ulyanovsk").

About ten people were interrogated regarding the observation of the phenomena, including Atmanaki and Karelin; the servicemen of military unit 6602 named Aleksander Savkin, Igor Malik, Aleksander Novikov, Anatoliy Anisimov; Valentina Piguzova, the head of the Ivdel meteorological station, and technician-meteorologist Natalya Tokareva; Georgiy Skoryh, the head of the "Karaul" section of the truck farm of the paper mill of the Novo-Lyalin district of the Sverdlovsk region.

What did the event of February 17 have to do with the death of the hikers? In the materials of the criminal case, one can find references to the observations of similar phenomena on other days as well.

From the testimony of the father of Lyudmila Dubinina: *"At around seven o'clock in the morning of February 2, the flight of a projectile was observed in Serov. In the accounts of the UPI students, it was observed by a certain group of tourists, which at the time was on a hiking trek to Mt. Chistop."*

From the testimony of the father of Georgiy Krivonischenko: *"...the participants of two groups said that in the evening of February 1, 1959, they were observing striking luminous phenomena to the north from the disposition of those groups: an extremely bright luminescence of some missile or projectile... The students said that they had observed that phenomena twice: on February 1 and 7 of 1959."*

From the testimony of Rimma Kolevatova: *"On those days, in the first days of February, a group of hikers from the Department of Geography of the Pedagogic Institute, which was at Mt. Chistop, observed some fireballs in the area of Mt. Otorten. Similar fireballs were as well recorded later."*

Where did the information on the observation of such phenomena in early February come from? At the search camp, discussions of a possible flight of a projectile or a missile on February 1 began in early March: *"For Sulman, March 2, 1959... It could be caused by some extraordinary natural phenomena or a flight of a meteorological rocket, which was observed at Ivdel on February 1 and by the Karelin group on February 17... It would be a good idea to ascertain if a meteorological rocket of a new type flew over the area of the accident on the evening of February 1. Maslennikov"*

There are recollections of Evgeniy Okishev, who as of 1959 served as deputy head of the investigative department of the Sverdlovsk regional prosecutor's office, to the effect that on their return from the cinema in the evening, the personnel of one of the N-240 camps, saw flashing from the side, where the hikers died. Possibly, this is what was discussed at the search camp.

Evgeniy Fyodorovich Okishev (40) was born in the city of Perm in 1919 into a working class family. Until 1932, the family lived in the town of Koungur, then the family moved to Sverdlovsk, where his father was given a new job. However, at that time the Sverdlovsk regional committee of the VLKSM sent him to the military Chkalov aviation school, but he ended at the Aramil pilot school of the Society for the Promotion of Aviation and Chemical Defense, from which he graduated in 1938, commissioned as jr. lieutenant and sent to reserve flying squadron in the Amur region. Not long before the Nazi attack on the Soviet Union, his reserve squadron was made part of a newly organized regiment and expedited to the Soviet western border. On July 27, 1941, his fighter plane was shot down in combat and he was wounded in the head and was eventually sent to the hospital in Ufa. Upon release, he was found unfit for flying and was detailed to the court martial of the Ural military district as an "expert in aviation". Soon he was further detailed to Tyumen to take part in the formation of the 175th infantry division, to become secretary of its court martial. In November 1941, the division was sent to the South-Western front, where he took part in combat in the failed Kharkov operation, managed to escape from surrounding and eventually sent to a two-month infantry mortar course; commissioned as a lieutenant he was sent to a guards infantry regiment, with which he fought in the Battle of Stalingrad, the Battle of Kursk (when he joined the party) as a commanding officer of a mortar battery. He was heavily wounded in February 1944 and after long treatment was commissioned in the rank of a captain as a first-degree invalid. For his wartime service, he was awarded two Red Star orders and the medals "For Courage" and "For Defense of Stalingrad". On return to Sverdlovsk from the hospital, Okishev enrolled at the Sverdlovsk Juridical Institute. After his second year, he was detailed to the Sverdlovsk district prosecutor's office and continued education by correspondence. After his graduation in 1947, he worked as an assistant to the district prosecutor and as prosecutor of the Nizhnaya Salda district until in 1950 he was detailed to the Sverdlovsk regional committee of the VCP(b) as an instructor in its administrative department. Following training at the instruction courses for senior-ranking officials under the Prosecutor's Office of the USSR, in 1954 he returned to the Sverdlovsk regional prosecutor's office as a prosecutor in its general supervision division, then as a prosecutor for the supervision of militia bodies and chief of division for the supervision of militia bodies. In 1956 he was appointed deputy chief of the investigative division. It was Okishev who signed the renewal of the investigative term and the closing of the case instead of Stepan Lukin, the chief of the investigative department of the Sverdlovsk regional prosecutor's office. In 1960 Okishev was seconded at the disposal of the Prosecutor of Moldavian SSR, and since that time lived in the city of Kishinev.

Stepan Petrovich Lukin (36) was born in 1923 into a peasant family of the Sverdlovsk region. From 1939 he worked as a teacher at a rural school. In September 1941, he was enrolled at the Chkalov aviation school, but was soon shifted to a reserve artillery regiment and eventually to a three-month junior lieutenant school and from May 1942 served as artillery battery deputy commanding officer, then a commanding officer at the North-Western front. In April 1944 Lukin was heavily wounded in the battle for the city of Pskov and in November 1944 he was demobilized. For courage and heroism, he was awarded the orders of the Red Star (1943), the Patriotic War 1st class (1985), and the medal "For Victory over Germany" (1945). On return home, he first worked as military training instructor of a secondary school, but in April 1945 was detailed to the prosecutor's bodies as an assistant prosecutor of his native Slobodo-Turinskiy district, from 1946 as assistant prosecutor at Verkhnaya Salda, from March 1948 as prosecutor of the Kamenskiy district, simultaneously studying at the All-Union Juridical Correspondence Institute. After graduation in 1950, from December 1952, he served as head of the investigative department of the Sverdlovsk region – the position he held until 1964 when he became deputy prosecutor of the Sverdlovsk region; from 1974 to 1985 he served as the prosecutor of the Sverdlovsk region, advancing to the class rank of the State Counselor of Justice 3rd class.

In Sverdlovsk, the luminous phenomena in the sky over the Ural Range were described by the students of the Sverdlovsk Pedagogical Institute, who took part in the trek led by Shumkov.

Second-year students Anatoliy Shumkov, Mihail Vladimirov, Georgiy Klein, Faina Abramova, and four-year students Vyacheslav Serdityh, Anatoliy Burakov, Galina Ryazanova, Zoya Shilova, Svetlana Shmetter, 10 in total, departed from Sverdlovsk in late January. After staying overnight at the home of the Klein family in Polunochnoe settlement and then going on an excursion of a manganese mine, the group headed in the direction of Burmantovo settlement. After covering 12 kilometers they spent the night at the Northern logging section. In the morning they hitched a logging truck to make the remaining 50 kilometers to Burmantovo. After an evening concert, they spent the night at a local school and then headed towards Lyamyapaul, namely to Peter Anyamov's yurts at the Lyamya River, 25 kilometers from Burmantovo.

In the morning, after the group had spent the night in the yurts, Anyamov gave them a lift to Suevatpaul. The girls with the backpacks were taken by two sleds, with the men covering the 50 km distance on skis. After an overnight stop in the tents of geologists, the group headed towards Mt. Chistop. They spent the next night in the vicinity of the Verblyuzhya Mountain, 30 km (18 miles) from Suevatpaul. At night, their tent was snowed up.

The next day they approached Mt. Chistop, walking along the valley of the Toshemka River. Late at night on February 5, in the dark of the moon, they were already at the mountain top. Between the Chistop and the Otorten Mountains, in the direction from west to east, they witnessed a short flight of a luminous object, which resembled a signal rocket.

At night, the temperature went below -40°C. After a few dangerous alarming experiences, which included an encounter with a pack of wolves and the rescue of Svetlana Shmetter, who had fallen through the ice, the group skied along the Ushma and Lozva Rivers to the barracks of District 41, from where it was taken to Ivdel.

Now we know that many of the observed phenomena had something to do with the Soviet rocket launchings.

On February 2 there was an aborted launch of an R5-M rocket from the Kapustin Yar test range. Due to the early engine cut-off, the rocket fell short of 280 km from its estimated range of 1167 km. On February 17, at 4:45 am Moscow time and 6:45 am Sverdlovsk time R-7 rocket was launched from the Tyuratam test range. The rocket flew a distance of 6307 km. The fiery circle, which frightened the search group in the night from March 30 to March 31, as well had something to do with rockets. That event coincided with the aborted rocket launch from the Tyuratam test range on March 31 at 1:52 am Moscow time. The rocket fell in Yakutia, in the vicinity of Ust-Nera, 4800 km from its launching site.

The aborted launches of Soviet rockets were reported even in the Voice of America broadcasts. Gennadiy Solovyev recalled that after the mountaineers' search group returned to Sverdlovsk, his friends told him that they had heard such a broadcast. Nevertheless, Ulyanovskaya Pravda daily explained the appearance of the fiery circle in the eastern part of the sky in the morning of February 17 by a flight of a fireball. The Ivdel paper, Severnaya Zvezda (Northern Star), wrote about long-lasting northern lights to the north-east from Ivdel in the night from February 16 to February 17 from 11:00 pm to 5:30 am local time.

There is no unequivocal explanation of the sightings from the top of Mt. Chistop in the night from February 5 to February 6. No rockets were launched on that day. We know that in the evening of February 5, Sogrin's group was observing northern lights in the vicinity of the top of the Sablya peak. Individual flashes of lightning looking like searchlights went very high up in the sky. On that same day, northern lights were recorded in the log of the Burmantovo meteorological observation station. Possibly, it was that phenomena that the hikers from the pedagogical institute were watching.

Quite possible, that following the reports on the abnormal phenomenon in various areas of the USSR in early 1959, the Department of defense of the Central Committee of the CPSU or the Commission for military and industrial issues under the Presidium of the Council of Ministers of the USSR decided to gather additional information on such sightings. Within the framework of that decision, the USSR Prosecutor's Office gave assignments to its offices in the regions where abnormal phenomena were observed. At the Sverdlovsk regional prosecutor's office, the assignment to collect information on the observed celestial phenomena was given to Lev Ivanov. It was rumored among the participants in the search that in mid-March Lev Ivanov was summoned to Moscow. Ivanov would later recall: *"As a prosecutor, who at the time was already dealing with certain secret defense issues, I discarded the version of an atomic weapon test in that area. That was when I began to deal directly with the 'fiery balls'."*

Back in 1952, the order of the USSR Prosecutor General instructed *"...the investigators to keep the files of suspended proceedings and to consistently use reasonable efforts for detection of hiding criminals."* Indeed, the case of the death of the hikers was not suspended but closed. However, there is a feeling that even at the Sverdlovsk regional prosecutor's office they were not ready to put up with the official cause of death. Ivanov might assume the connection between the abnormal phenomenon and the death of the hikers. Evgeniy Okishev recalled that the case against the leaders and organizers of the trek was closed. However, the prosecutor's office was ready to continue the investigation into the causes of death if given appropriate permission. This may explain the rumors of the participation of the KGB in the investigation of the case of the death of the Dyatlov group.

Leonid Drapkin, who in 1959 served as a senior investigator of the Sverdlovsk regional prosecutor's office, recalled that KGB operatives were supervising the case.

Leonid Yakovlevich Drapkin (35) was born in Tyumen in 1924. In June 1942, he volunteered into the Red Army and was sent to the Chelyabinsk air war mechanics school, from which he graduated in early 1943, after which he served as an aviation technician in the legendary 20th guards Sevastopol regiment of long-range bombing, which was destroying Nazi fortification along the Dnieper River, at Kiev and later bombing Koenigsberg, Berlin and other Nazi strong points. For his wartime service, Drapkin was awarded the medals "For Service in Battle", "For Victory over Germany", "For Liberation of Warsaw", "For Capture of Budapest", "For Capture of Berlin". After demobilization in 1949, Drapkin enrolled at the Sverdlovsk Juridical Institute, from which he graduated cum laude in 1953, after which he worked as a defense lawyer in the Omsk region. From 1956, Drapkin served as an investigator at a Sverdlovsk district prosecutor's office, and from March 1959, he was appointed senior investigator of the Sverdlovsk regional prosecutor's office.

Vladimir Lyubimov, a radio operator of the geological party, said that in mid-June 1959 a captain from the Tyumen Office of State Security was interrogating observations of "fiery circles" in the vicinity of Mt. Yaruta.

Evgeniy Grigoriev, a forensic expert from the SNIKL, recalled: *"Neither the KGB nor the military took an active part in the investigation. However, it was rumored that the prosecutor's office was passing the conclusions of the examinations somewhere."*

In 1959, under the auspices of the committee on meteorites of the Academy of Sciences of the USSR, an expedition was sent into the impact zone of the Tunguska meteorite. Its thematic priorities included questioning residents, field radiometrics, collection of samples for spectroscopic analysis, testing the methodology of examination of the zones of tree clearing caused by a shock wave.

There is a radiological examination report amongst the materials of the Dyatlov group case files; a forensic expert, describing the injuries in the hiker's bodies: *"The said injuries, namely given the impression and the absence of any deformity of the integrity of the soft tissues of the ribcage, look very much like an injury resulting from an air blast"*, as well as questioning regarding the observation of the abnormal celestial phenomenon.

Quite possibly, Ivanov relied on the methodologies of the committee on the Meteorites of the Academy of Sciences of the Soviet Union, which were developed for the study of the nature of the Tunguska meteorite.

Korotaev, who had a recollection of his mission trips to Severouralsk, Nizhniy Tagil, and about how he was visiting the Mansi yurts for several days, might have taken part in questioning the residents. According to him, the archival case files were missing the protocols of interrogation of the Anyamovs, Sambindalovs, Kurikovs, and Bahtiyarovs, who told Korotaev about their observation in the sky of an "arc of flame". On the other hand, a protocol of an interrogation conducted after the criminal case was closed, has survived:

"Novaya Lyalya, May 29, 1959. The prosecutor of the Novo-Lyalin district, junior counselor of justice Pershin, interrogated Skoryh Georgiy

Ivanovich as a witness. ...Regarding the questions asked I have to say that approximately in mid-February of 1959, I was in my apartment in the village of Karaul of the Novo-Lyalin district. Approximately at 6 or 7 am my wife went out into the street and immediately knocked in the window, shouting to me through the window, 'Look, there is some ball flying and turning around.' On hearing her shouting, I jumped out to the porch and from the second floor of the house I live in, from its porch, I saw a large luminous ball, which was moving away in the northern direction – with alternations of red and green light every now and then. The ball was moving away with a very quick speed – I was observing it for only a few seconds, after which it disappeared below the horizon..."

What had the testimony on the abnormal phenomenon over the Novo-Lyalin district to do with the death of the hikers of hypothermia in the Ivdel district? Still, Georgiy Skoryh was interrogated by the local prosecutor.

A number of other documents from the closed criminal case and its supervisory proceedings are noteworthy. On May 16, 1959, the Sverdlovsk regional prosecutor's office recorded a motion from the deputy chief of the Office of criminal investigation of the USSR Prosecutor's Office A.D. Kamochkin: *"You are requested to inform on the outcomes of the investigation and the resolution taken in the case of the death of the nine student skiers."* In just two days, a ruling on the performance of physic-technical examination was executed: *"May 18, 1959, the city of Sverdlovsk. I, Ivanov, the forensic prosecutor of the Sverdlovsk regional prosecutor's office, on consideration of the criminal case on the death of the students of the Ural Polytechnic Institute and taking into consideration that to ascertain the causes of death of the hikers it is necessary to conduct a radiological examination and to settle the issue of radioactive contamination of the clothes of the hikers, and in consideration of Articles 63 and 171 of the UPK RSFSR, ruled: to commission physic-technical examination to resolve the following issue: If there is radioactive contamination of the clothes and parts of the corpses of the deceased hikers."*

What is the connection between the death of the people of hypothermia during a superstorm and the radiological examination? No connection of this sort has been traced. What is the connection between this examination and the assumption on the connection between an unidentified flying object and the death of the group? The connection is direct.

The prosecutor's correspondence continued in June 1959, after the criminal case opened by the Sverdlovsk regional prosecutor's office and the party investigation, instituted on the complaint of Anisimova, were closed.

"June 10, 1959. Telegram. To Sverdlovsk regional prosecutor Klinov. Send information on the decision taken on the case of the death of student skiers NR 3/2518-59=depgenproksoyuz Terebilov"

Vladimir Ivanovich Terebilov (43) was born in 1916 in Petrograd. After graduating from the V.N. Krylenko Law Institute in 1939, he worked as an investigator and prosecutor in the district prosecutor's offices of the Leningrad region and Leningrad, as the head of the investigative department of the Leningrad city prosecutor's office. In the first months of the Great Patriotic War, he became a commissar of a 56-men strong militia force, with which he fought at the frontline in October 1941. In 1949-1957 he worked at the Moscow Institute of Forensic Science. In 1957 Terebilov was appointed Senior Assistant to the USSR Prosecutor General, Deputy Head of the Investigation Department of the USSR Prosecutor's Office.

"June 15. 1959. Moscow, the USSR Prosecutor's Office for Terebilov. The case file on the death of the students was sent on June 15 with airmail to Urakov Klinov"

What could stir the interest of the union and republican prosecutor's offices in the closed criminal case? There is an assumption that the case was reexamined in response to the complaint of Vladimir Slobodin, the father of Rustem, however, there is no documentary evidence that Slobodin indeed applied to higher-level prosecutor's offices. The case file was returned from Moscow on July 1. Quite possibly, they were reviewing the materials, which were collected by the regional prosecutor's office on the unidentified celestial phenomenon over the Sverdlovsk region.

It is noteworthy, that according to the recollection of Okishev, the file was taken to Moscow by Urakov in person, who was sent to Sverdlovsk for that particular purpose. There is no document to support this. We know that Urakov was in Sverdlovsk in April, and in June the case file was sent to Moscow by airmail.

Under current procedures, a prosecutor's office must submit quarterly statistical reporting no later than on the 10th of the next month. Doubtful, if these procedures are significantly different from the procedures in effect in 1959. The Sverdlovsk regional prosecutor's office was to submit its report for the first quarter no later than April 10, 1959. It was that report that Urakov might take along on his return to Moscow in April. This may serve as an explanation of the recollections of Okishev, who simply confused the documents.

We do not know about the outcome of the investigation into the nature of the abnormal phenomenon. Most probably, the materials on the phenomena, which could not be explained at the time, happened to be sought-after in Moscow. The information on the events, which could be explained by rocket launches and other obvious reasons, was kept locally.

That was why among the materials of the closed case on the death of the hikers there were materials explained by the rocket launches on February 2, 17, and March 31, as well as the radiological examination, which had discovered traces of radioactive contamination on the clothes of Krivonischenko, which had remained from the time of the 1957 accident at the combine of complementary industrial plants №817, now known as PO Box "Mayak". Those documents were of no use in the study of the abnormal phenomenon. No connection between those phenomena and the death of the hikers was found.

Lev Ivanov was of a different opinion. In 1990, he wrote: *"At present, the examination of the case is absolutely convincing; at that time I as well maintained the version of the death of the student hikers from the impact of an unknown flying object. On the strength of the accumulated evidence, the role of a UFO in that tragedy was apparent."*

Was he onto something? Had Lev Ivanov solved the actual cause of the death of the Dyatlov group?

CHAPTER 18. "ON THE NINTH DAY GO TO UPPER LOZVA"

Let us get back to January 28, when the hikers took the route from the second Northern settlement. For reasons unknown, Dyatlov decided against using the clearances, which were recommended by Rempel. Possibly, while at the District 41 settlement, Igor received information that proceeding along the clearances would not be safe because of some work activities.

Vladimir Kuskov, a geologic engineer, who lived at Ivdel from 1961, said: *"Even in field parties, certain services work year round. These are profile fellers, who mostly work in winter. The same is true of the geophysicists, who take measurements along these profiles at any time of the year. Profile fellers on skis were cutting profiles for the geophysicists. Then topographers were running the profiles and plotting them on the map. Only afterward the geophysicists were following along the profiles with the measurements. In winter, it is convenient to work in the marsh."*

Andrey Alekseevich Anyamov said under interrogation that he *"...saw the traces of the hikers – along the road there were tracks left by narrow skis. It was impossible to determine how many people had passed. I saw the traces along the Lozva River, 1.5-2 kilometers above the Auspiya River. The traces led to the Auspiya River and further towards the Ural Mountains."*

Whose traces were those? The Dyatlov group was proceeding from the 2nd Northern settlement up the Lozva River and then turned to the west along the Auspiya River. Their traces could not appear along the Lozva River anywhere above the inflow of the Auspiya River.

However, experienced hikers, who had repeatedly been round there, noticed: *"Auspiya is flowing into the Lozva by two spill-streams. Notably, the first, which is downstream, is unnoticed for all practical purposes, since it is very narrow and is falling at a very acute level to the Lozva bed. The second spill-stream is also hardly noticeable, particularly in winter. In the forest administration chart, copied at the Vizhay forestry section, the estuary of the Auspiya River is designated as a single bed. Hence, it cannot be ruled out that the Dyatlov group might have proceeded along the Lozva above the Auspiya estuary, and then reached the Auspiya along one of the foot passes of the Mansi hunters."*

It is difficult not to agree with this. Most probably, the hikers indeed had not noticed the estuary of the Auspiya River, and for some time continued their movement upstream the Lozva River. After 1.5-2 kilometers, the group understood its mistake and turned back. According to the testimony of Anyamov, they were not returning along the Mansi trails, but directly along the river bed of the Lozva River.

When they discovered the estuary of the Auspiya River, the group continued its movement in the western direction. Due to continuous ice-built, the hikers were forced to cross into the left bank of the river, with the Mansi trail leading in the direction of the Ural Range. At the upper reaches of the Auspiya River, the group turned north, moving towards the pass between heights 1079 and 880, along the Auspiya's left tributary, which was designated in the maps of the time, including in the chart of the Vizhay forestry, which was in the possession of the hikers. That tributary served as a good landmark. Hiking groups are still taking it on their way to the pass.

Yuri Sahnin would later recall: *"In our search from the camp until the pass and back, we were taking the Dyatlov ski track. It has a highly definitive direction indicate – the Auspiya's tributary. Dyatlov was a reasonable man: he had chosen a reliable foot-path, which took him straight to the pass."*

According to the trek's plan, on January 31 the goal of the group was to top into the upstream of the Lozva River. Having faced a heavy wind at the pass, the hikers went back south, to spend the night in a forest zone, retracing their own ski track. In 1959, the search team made attempts to reconstruct the events of the next day from the perspective of the tent, which was discovered on the slope of height 1079. Ultimately, the key question was posed as follows: *"...Why had the entire group, semi-dressed, left the tent? ...The major mystery in this tragedy has remained the departure of the entire group from the tent..."*

But is this statement of the question adequate? It should be noted that experienced hikers, who in 1959 took part in the search, had no doubts regarding the Dyatlov plans for February 1.

Akselrod, who was the only Sverdlovsk hiker with an experience of four winter hiking treks of the highest category of difficulty behind him, testified among other things: *"...I believe that the group set out... from the place with one of the two goals: 1) to top from one forest to another, from the valley of the Auspiya to the valley of the Lozva Rivers, or 2) ... to advance as further to the forest border as possible.... so that they can reach Otorten by the next evening."*

And here is the explanation of setting the tent on the slope of height 1079 given by Evgeniy Maslennikov, who became the Master of Sport in hiking back in 1955: *"Probably, at the time of the blizzard, they took the main ridge of height 1079 for the pass from Auspiya to Lozva... In nasty weather, the Dyatlov group might have taken the spine of the spur of the mountain 1079 for the pass to Lozva."* Maslennikov was as well sure that the hikers were proceeding to the forest zone in the Lozva upstream, but made a mistake in choosing their direction in a blizzard.

This opinion found its way into the ruling on the termination of the case. Ivanov wrote: *"...moving towards the valley of the fourth tributary of the Lozva River, the hikers had taken at 500-600 meters to the left and instead of the pass made by heights 1079 and 880, they took to the eastern slope of height 1079."*

Aleksander Efimovich Berman, the Master of Sport of the USSR in ski hiking, said: *"In the first winter treks, by the end of the second day through the unpopulated country, the fatigue begins to increase rapidly. Very quickly, it goes beyond any normal limit, with its increase accelerating continuously. On the 3rd-4th day, a group of beginners needs to come to some lodging. With gaining experience (on the 5th-6th winter trek in succession) the situation changes fundamentally: on the 4th-5th day of the trek the accumulated fatigue begins to slow down."*

Taking into consideration the winter treks of the group participants, the fatigue was to be accumulated by the fourth day of skiing – that is, on January 31. Dyatlov and Zolotaryov were the only ones with four winter treks behind, the rest had less. On February 1, the group was scheduled to have a restful day. According to the trek's plan, Dyatlov wanted to spend it in the headwaters of the Lozva River:

– 3 –

Trek route by day

202

Day	Date	Section of the road	Means of transport	Km	Note
1-2		Sverdlovsk . Polunochnoe	Train		
3		Polunochnoe . Vizhay	Truck		
4-5		Vizhay . 2nd Northern	Ski	55	
6		——— " ——— " ———			
7-8		Up Auspiya river		38	
9		Pass in the upper lozva river		14	
10		Ascent to Mt. Otorten		20	
11.		Otorten - upper Auspiya river		18	
12		Pass to the upper Unya river		18	
13.		To upper Vishera river		22	
14		To upper Niols river		22	
15		Ascent to Mt. Oyko-Chakur		18	
16		Along North Toshemka to the hut		25	
17		Along North Toshemka -			
18		– Vizhay.		50	
19		Vizhay – Polunochnoe	Truck		
20-21		Polunochnoe – Sverdlovsk	Train		

In the course of the investigation, it was speculated that on February 1 the group reached the pass after a half-day halt in the Auspiya headwaters. However, it is difficult to call it a rest, since according to the version of the investigation, the hikers were busy with setting up the cache site.

Why did Dyatlov decide to leave the cache in the valley of the Auspiya River, when originally it was planned to set it up above the forest border? Why did Dyatlov decide not to keep an appropriate full-day halt? The group was indeed tired. The day before, on January 31, Dyatlov made a notation in the diary: *"We are going down in the southern direction – into the valley of the Auspiya... Tired and whacked to the wide, we got down to setting up the night's stay... We were setting the fire on the logs, unwilling to dig a pit."*

What could be the reason for such a significant change in the trek's plan? Lagging behind the schedule for just one day would not be a great problem. There are no other explanations. From the films, which were discovered in the cameras of the deceased, it is apparent that on February 1 the group approached the pass with a tent, which was practically not rolled down. It was impossible to walk that way for a long time. Hence, the hikers were contemplating a very short passage. It is logical to assume that Dyatlov was not going to change the plan of the trek and that on February 1, after the morning packing up, the group made the passage to the forest zone of the Lozva upstream, where it stopped for a day's halt.

Andrey Yurievich Korolev, the Master of Sport in sport hiking and the Honored traveler of Russia, was judgmental: *"In the winter period in the mountains of the Northern Ural above the forest zone, the main danger is a strong wind. The best escape from the wind is to organize an overnight stay in the forest zone. In the Northern Ural, the forest goes up to the height of 700-800 meters above sea level, when the ridges are usually at the height of below 1000 meters. This means that the difference in elevation from the camp to the axial line of the ridge, which is convenient for moving along the route, won't be great and won't involve any great loss of time and effort. Hence there is no sense in organizing an overnight stay above the forest zone, particularly in the wintertime."* At the time when Korolev said this, he had 28 years of sport hiking behind him. He had visited the Dyatlov pass ten times in winter, summer, and fall in the course of ski and walking treks of the 2nd to 4th categories of difficulty.

The reason why the members of the search team began making assumptions of the reasons for an overnight stay on the slope of height 1079 was the tent discovered on that slope.

CHAPTER 19. FIRE IN THE HOLE.

One of the specific tasks of the Northern-Ural party of the Novosibirsk geophysical trust was to ascertain the anomalies from the point of view of prospective iron-ore deposits. The ASGM-25 (upgraded airborne prospecting system) integrated station, which according to the plan was to be used in the course of aerial photography, had four-channel recording units to record the radioactivity, the magnetic field, the terrain clearance, and reference marks.

It is quite possible that simultaneously with the aerial photography it was planned to conduct aero-radiometric surveys in the search for uranium deposits. There is information that in 1959 massive prospecting for uranium was underway in the Alapaevskiy, Krasnouralskiy, Nevyanskiy, Rezhevskiy, Sysertskiy, and Kamenskiy districts of the Sverdlovsk region, under the territorial auspices of the Central-Ural party of the Shabrovsky expedition of the First Main Geological Directorate.

The front office of the Northern-Ural party, which was supervising the works, might have been located in the Polunochnoe settlement. Vladimir Nikolaevich Kuskov recalled that at least from 1960 two parties of geophysicists were based at Polunochnoe.

In the very first days of the reconnaissance flights, a magnetic or a gamma anomaly might be discovered upstream of the Lozva River. That area is characteristic of magnetic declinations within the range from 29 grades east to 7 grades west. Observations like that appear in the current reports of the hikers: *"In its geomorphology, the area of Otorten is interesting with its three magnetic anomalies. One of them is in the upstream of the Auspiya – with a 'western' declination. The masses of ferromagnetic materials, which cause the anomalies, are of no industrial value."* And here is a record from the area of Mt. Chistop: *"We were proceeding to the mountains along the bed of the Tosemya River, with a hut of the geologists on its bank. The river is of interest: its bed is blocked by stones, with the water flowing underneath. Such rivers are called 'disappearing.' We were trying to find our bearings by reading the compass, but failed – the arrow was rotating like mad. That's what magnetic anomaly is about."*

In 2013, a group of hikers from the Perm State National Research University led by the above mentioned Andrey Korolev encountered a magnetic anomaly to the south-west from Mt. Kholat Syakhl. *"When the group was a few kilometers to the south-west from the pass itself, a mist fell while the group was passing along the mountain ridge in the area of Mt. Khozyatalyakh Syakhl. Sometime later, we noticed an increasing declination of the compass needle from the northern direction. Compass anomalies continued for about 500 meters along our route."*

In 2020, local magnetic anomalies were discovered on the eastern and southern slopes of Mt. Kholat Syakhl.

Aleksander Vinogradov, a mining engineer and geological prospector, who worked in various capacities in expeditions in the North of the Krasnoyarsk region, the Nether-Polar, and Northern Ural explained: *"One of the goals of the aeromagnetic survey is the search for the deposits of raw materials. It results in a map of the terrain with indications of the geomagnetic and gamma anomalies. Afterward, ground groups of geophysicists with portable equipment are delivered to those places. They make more accurate measurements of the anomalies and detail their geographical bearings. In case of serious anomalies, mining exploration and drilling works are planned and conducted in such locations."*

Vladimir Zenchenko, who in 1955 was a geologist with airborne prospecting party №325 of the Sosnovskaya expedition, recalled: *"In the airborne party the structure and methodology of the search are integrated. The first thing is to chart the most promising projected space. Usually, the next is the organization of the base and the airfield. Then, to avoid turbulence, – early morning flights at the height of 50-70 meters. Flying above 100 meters would be a waste. Flying lower is dangerous, but the quality, that is a possibility to discover a radioactive anomaly, would, of course, be higher. Flight crews consist of former war veterans. Load-masters are the men of the people. The sequence of works is determined by experience: identification of an anomaly and indication of its location by dropping a pendent, usually by paper cutting. Next comes testing it by a ground 'visiting group' or a preliminary review team. In case of an anomaly with mineralization – evaluation by a team for a detailed check. In that case, it is performed with the required complete set of mining geophysics methods. The outcome will be a rejection or recommendations for further evaluation of the ore occurrence and a reconnaissance survey of the recommended site."*

A similar account is given by Vadim Kirillov, a representative of a younger generation of geologists: *"The airborne party №35, in which I had worked until 1995, was the most mobile field division – a sort of a 'direct-action corps' in the geological survey. Its work was as follows: multi-channel spectrographic and magnetic surveys of the most prospective areas were performed with equipment onboard helicopters. Then groups for pre-liminary examination were dropped at the airborne anomalies; in case of any exploration outcome, the ore feature would be dealt with by a large team for a detailed check, including getting access to the ore bodies by dig-ging gutters and sometimes by drilling."*

In the early 1950s was suggested *"to give a year for processing the airborne data, after which the airborne anomalies would be passed on to the ground parties for their check and evaluation. This had been tested in practice, but with negative geological results and involving organizational difficulties. Most importantly, many geologists started doubting airborne exploration."* Hence they turned to *"operational assessment of the air-borne anomalies on the ground in the same field exploration season."* If anomalies were detected people were dropped off for ground inspec-tion.

In case of checking a gamma anomaly, given the limited capabil-ities, the works might be done with a method borrowed from the practice of the leasing system of excavation of the radioactive ore by the MVD of the USSR in 1945-48: *"The works were conducted in the most primitive way – by manual short-hole drilling. Next, blasting out, collect-ing, and sifting chlopinite (aka hlopinite) – a pitch-black mineral contain-ing uranium. Antimagnetic anti-tank mines weighing up to 5 kg were used as explosives."*

Air blasts could be used should there be any need for seismic sur-veying. Vladimir Ustyuzhaninov, who in the 1950s worked as a geo-physicist in the Western Siberia, recalled: *"To avoid a great waste of time and material assets in well-drilling, in the 1950s the Kolpashevskiy expedition came to utilizing a method of earthquake ground excitation by air blasts. The charges that were selected by trial were placed in the trees at a certain height."* Blasting operations could be employed as well in case of a need for ditching and prospect holes drilling.

Back in 1945-47, aeromagnetic surveying with simultaneous groundworks became the leading method in Karelia. That was how large iron-ore deposits of Gimolskoe and Kostomukshskoe were dis-covered.

The Northern Ural party did not have sufficient manpower and re-sources for ground check of the anomalies. Hence, at Novosibirsk, they turned to the local Ivdel organization for assistance, which agreed to help. In Moscow, the extraordinary 21st party convention was under-way. A chance to make a gift to the convention by opening a promising deposit would be an excellent occasion to shoot to fame, to advance in one's career, and to make money. Under the Decrees of the Council of Ministers of the USSR №722 from May 30, 1956, and №92 from January 22, 1959, "On state monetary rewards for the discovery of new mineral deposits", a new system of payment of government monetary rewards for the discovery of mineral deposits was introduced; it was based on the evaluation of the economic significance of the discovered deposit. The list of individuals submitted for a monetary award was compiled by an appropriate ministry (agency) based on the materials submitted by a geological or a mining industrial organization, which was involved in the exploration of the deposit.

The N-240 administration had an abundant experience of interaction with geologists. Back in 1941, the geological parties looking for the bauxite-aluminum ores in the Ivdel district were provided with manpower from among the inmates of the "Toshemka" zone of the Ivdellag. In 1944, a permanent scientific research station was organized in Ivdel, to lay the groundwork for an iron ore base in the Northern Ural, with the station as well using the Ivdellag workforce in case of need. In 1949-51, the Ivdel station was conducting geological surveys in the area of the Sosva and Taltiya Rivers, under the supervision of the Ural Geological Office and the Mining and Geological Institute of the Ural Branch of the Academy of Sciences. In 1954, the Ural station of the Ural Branch of the Academy of Sciences was moved to the city of Salekhard.

On the instruction of Vitaliy Ivanov, the head of the N-240 office, and Abram Sulman, the head of the Northern geological exploration expedition, members of the N-240 staff and the Northern expedition were detailed in assistance of the Novosibirsk geophysical trust. In case of any need for blasting works, Ivan Prodanov, the 1st secretary of the Ivdel city committee of the CPSU, negotiated the detailing of the sappers from the 5th railway brigade, which was occupied with preparations for the beginning of construction of the Polunochnoe – Nary-Kary railway line. All decisions might be approved at a meeting of the Ivdel city committee of the CPSU.

Aleksey Mihaylovich Kryukov, Commander of the Railway Forces of the USSR Ministry of Defense of the USSR from 1968 to 1983, wrote: "We can cite thousands of examples of friendship and mutual assistance between the army and civilian personnel. These are joint Saturday or Sunday voluntary work tasks and recreational evenings; visits of factory shops and kolkhoz fields by military personnel; visits of military units by workmen delegations, war veterans and veterans of labor at military sites;

oath-taking ceremonies by young soldiers in factory shops and at sacred places of military and labor heroic deeds; formal, flag-flying presentation of Komsomol cards to young people; visits of, and warm meetings with, soldiers' parents at military units, etc. Such events are abundant in the life of any military unit of our gallant Armed Forces. This is also true of the subunits and elements of the railway forces. This is a source of our strength and the pulse of our might.

However, we, the military railwaymen, have one more, peculiarly professional feature in our relationship with the local party and Soviet bodies and labor collectives. It goes down to the nature of our work. After all, we had to rail, build bridges and settlements in the territory of certain districts, regions, and republics, to obtain construction materials, building blocks, and all kinds of equipment from many enterprises. The local party and soviet officials have always assisted us in all kinds of ways, facilitating the rapid delivery of the newly built railway lines. The secretaries of central committees of communist parties and the chairmen of the councils of ministers of the union republics, the secretary of the party district and regional committees, the heads of all kinds of local agencies visit the construction sites. They are assisting the builders of steel railways in word and in deed."

Wherever possible, military railwaymen as well willingly responded to the requests from local leaders.

Quite possibly, such ground inspections might take place in several locations. Karelin pointed out that *"at present large-scale geological exploration works are underway in the area."* By all appearances, such work as well continued later on. For instance, on March 22, the Chelyabinsk hikers from the Voluntary sports association "Locomotive" led by S.S. Poutonen, spotted a helicopter in the vicinity of the mouth of the Ushma River, which made two circles over the group and fired colored flares, three green and one red.

This is what most likely happened. A circle over the discovered people and one fired green flare meant "I see you." Going down and to the side with firing two green flares meant requesting direction and location of landing. The hikers did not understand the signals and in response gave a rousing cheer to the helicopter. Assuming that the group was asking for assistance, the pilot made a horizontal 'eight' and fired one red flare, which meant, "Wait for assistance at site, a helicopter will come for you."

The pilots, confusing the hikers with geologists, might have asked for the direction and location of the landing at the base of the ground party. Of course, we may also assume their participation in the airborne search for the crew of the Mi-4 helicopter of the Tyumen air group of the Operational Air Group of the Civil Air Fleet, which crashed the previous day, that is on March 21, 1959, in the vicinity of Sosva during the flight on the assignment of expeditionary team №2 along the route of Sosva cultural center – site №72 of sector 200 – Sosva cultural center. Onboard there was a freight of 500 kg and five men to conduct a seismic survey. However, the emergency route ran much further to the north, in the territory of the Khanty-Mansi Autonomous Area.

A cross-functional combined preliminary survey team landed at the site of the discovered anomaly upstream of the Lozva River. The very next day after the works started, the militia station at the Polunochnoe village received some disturbing news: strange objects had been spotted from a flight over the Main Ural Ridge south of Mount Otorten. They looked like human bodies.

CHAPTER 20. SO TURNS THE WHEEL.

In 1959, more than 50 hikers and mountaineers died in the USSR. There were hundreds of tragedies in the previous years. Let us recall some of these.

Yuri Menzhulin, director of the Gorelmik school, which was under the All-Union committee for physical culture and sports and the People's Commissariat of Defense chain of command, and was training mountaineer scout saboteurs, said: *"In 1943, Colonel Gorin fell from a peak and plunged to his death right in front of me and my adjutant. We were in a state of shock for a long time. We were unable to evacuate the body across two passes. We were continuously called on the carpet for negligence, but it was wartime, and that quickly came to an end. The body was retrieved by a large group only after a month."*

On February 4, 1946, Oleg Vavilov, the son of Nikolay Vavilov, died at Mt. Dombay.

Nikolay Ivanovich Vavilov – was a Russian and Soviet scientist and statesman, chemist, and geographer, particularly famous as a genetic scientist, botanist, and plant breeder. He was born in Moscow in 1887, was an Academic of the Academy of Sciences of the USSR, the organizer and first president of the All-Union Academy of Agricultural Sciences. From 1921, he served as director of the All-Union Institute of Plant Science and from 1930 as the director of the Institute of Generic Science of the AN USSR. In 1926-35 Vavilov was a member of the Central Executive Committee of the USSR – the Soviet supreme agency of state power. He was an organizer and participant of botany and agronomic expeditions across most of the continents, in the course of which he uncovered the ancient seats of intermutation of cultivated plants. Vavilov formulated the teaching of the immunity of plants, made an important contribution to the development of the teaching of biological species. Under his supervision, the world's largest collection of seeds of cultivated plants was assembled. He laid the foundation of the system of official tests of field crop seeds for the major national center in agrarian sciences and organized a network of scientific institutions in that field. In

1940, he was arrested following a conflict with Trofim Lysenko, a Soviet agronomist, and biologist, who was a founder of a pseudo-scientific field in biology, known as the Michurin agro-biology. Elected academic of the Academy of Sciences of the USSR in 1939, from 1940 to 1965 Lysenko served as the director of the Institute of Genetic Science of the Academy of Sciences of the USSR and was the Hero of Socialist Labor, winner of three First Class Stalin Prizes. Most of the methods advanced by Lysenko had been criticized at the time of their large-scale implementation in Soviet agriculture. Lysenko's name is infamous for the crusade of ostracism against genetic scientists and against Lysenko's opponents, who had not recognized the "Michurin genetic science". At the peak of this campaign, Vavilov was sentenced on charges of subversive activity, assistance to bourgeois organizations, preparation of imminent crimes or non-reporting on the said, and was sentenced to execution. Subsequently, his death sentence was commuted to a 20-year prison term. Vavilov died in 1943 in a prison in Saratov.

It was that same Lysenko's campaign that caused the repressions against the parents of Rustem Slobodin. His parents, Vladimir Mihaylovich and Nadezhda Fyodorovna had taught at the Timiryazev Agricultural Academy and were sacked in 1947 for their criticism of Academic Lysenko and banished from Moscow to Sverdlovsk, where they managed to find teaching jobs at an agricultural institute.

Oleg Nikolaevich Vavilov was born in 1918. After graduation from the Department of Physics of the Moscow State University in 1941, he worked as a research associate at the laboratory of cosmic rays of the Institute of Physics of the Academy of Sciences of the Soviet Union. In December 1945, he qualified as a Candidate of Sciences. Following the defense procedures for the degree, he went to the Dombay with a group of mountaineers, where he fell off a cliff into an abyss. To warn the local authorities of the tragic accident and to arrange for the transportation of the body, a few members of his group went on skis from the Dombay to the Teberda. The rest were trying to organize a search, but their attempts were obstructed by a snowfall.

Later, after a new search group was organized, there was unrest among it. The mountaineers were furious with poor meals and suggested postponing the search into a period when the snow would start melting. It was impossible to conduct any search with six meters deep snow. In 1959, it was as well suggested to postpone the search into the spring period. An agreement to bury Oleg Vavilov in the Caucasus was reached. In 1959, there were also plans to bury the dead at Ivdel.

It was decided that after the body would be discovered, it would be photographed from all sides and then taken down to the Dombay, where experts would arrive. Letters were sent to the secretary of the Kluhori's party district committee and the district prosecutor with a request to dispatch a forensic expert and an investigator to the Dombay. Veteran-mountaineers explained: *"In case of the death of some brass, sports officials were always trying to initiate a criminal case; however, with no one convicted in those cases."*

After the body of Oleg Vavilov was discovered, it was wrapped into a tent and then it took an hour to take it down to the foot of the mountain. They went on horseback to Teberda to bring over militiamen. The latter gave a death certificate, which was based on the deed of the mountaineer's death, to Vavilov's widow. S.G. Zhgenti, the Kluhori's forensic expert, would examine the bodies together with a physician-in-chief of one of the Teberda hospitals only in case when the cause of death raised suspicion. The examination would be followed by executing an Act for Internment with the description of injuries.

Oleg Vavilov was buried at a local mountaineer cemetery. The cause of his death raised no suspicion: the injuries he received in the fall were fatal. No criminal case was opened.

The case of the death of mountaineer Ivan Vasilyevich Miroshkin in the Western Pamir in 1948 as well as limited to a medical report, with no criminal case opened. The only investigation conducted was by the All-Union committee for physical culture and sports and the Nauka (Science) sports society.

In February 1959, it was necessary to start with checking up on what the pilots had observed. Leonid Chudinov managed to arrange with the geologists for sending a search team. Closest to the site of the presumable location of the bodies happened to be the team performing a ground check of the anomaly discovered by the Novosibirsk geophysicists. Vladimir Alekseevich Cheglakov remembered his father saying, that *"…there was the first group, about which nobody knew anything…"*

In his testimony, Atmanaki said that *"the Slobtsov group… proceeded along the third tributary of Lozva River to the slope of height 1079, where it discovered the tent of the Dyatlov group."* The Slobtsov group had never proceeded along the third tributary of Lozva: it was moving towards the Auspiya to the east of the said route, along the Charka-Nur ridge. It was the ground check team that might be moving towards height 1079 exactly along the third tributary. Some of the members of that group might have stayed at the search camp at the Auspiya River, where they might have told about the route of their movement. There was nothing unusual that Atmanaki mistook the first search team with the Slobtsov group.

According to different recollections, the first bodies – the number of which differs depending on the source – and the tent were discovered either by the Mansi or by Pashin. Pashin spotted the tent by the pennant, and he saw two bodies under the cedar, of a man and a woman, who were frozen in a squatted down position. Some geologists, who were based five kilometers to the east from Mt. Otorten had discovered five corpses in the vicinity of height 1079 and reported the finding along their chain of command. The leader of the ill-fated group was discovered 15 or 200 meters from the tent, or even possibly as much as a kilometer away. Moreover, he was pulling some girl along. *"The perished were dragging and crawling, one by one, down the slope in a semicircle through the deep snow. Only two of them, a young man and a girl, were dragging together, helping each other, and they moved at a greater distance than the rest – at more than a kilometer from the tent. The bodies of the rest were 400 to 800 meters from the tent."* The bodies were carried over either by geologists or by the military. But nobody attached any importance to the confusion with the routes of the search groups or the details of the discoveries.

The Polunochnoe militia station had begun its preliminary investigation. According to available recollections, besides Chudinov, Boris Yanashpolskiy, who at the time was a young officer at the Polunochnoe militia station, was dealing with the issues involved in the death of the hikers. Soon it became clear that there was no reason to suspect foul play. The case was handed over to the Ivdel prosecutor's office.

Under the Code of Criminal Procedure effective at the time: *"...In any case, a preliminary investigation may be initiated by any investigative agency... On completing the necessary procedures, the initiating agency is to submit the case to the investigator without waiting for the investigator's instruction or until the expiration of the month's term. After the case has been handed over to the investigator, other investigative agencies may undertake any investigative activities only on a special commission of the investigator."*

The still outstanding problem was involved with the removal of the corpses from the site of the accident. The Ivdel prosecutor's office did not have its own facilities for transportation of such a number of corpses from a hard-to-reach area. Tempalov was turning for assistance to the party city committee and the heads of the major city agencies.

It follows from the archival documents of the Ivdel city soviet executive committee and the Department of Internal Affairs for the year of 1959, that the Ivdel daily life at the time was one of drunkenness, thievery, and adultery. Everyone, from factory worker to party official, drank. A reason for not being admitted into the party was cited as *"she has abandoned one man, mixed up with another and is sleeping with still another."* In two years, the chief accountant of the Ivdel city committee embezzled 27 thousand rubles. It cannot be ruled out that Vasiliy Ivanovich Tempalov shared his problem with his drinking pals. Quite probably, besides Tempalov, Prodanov, Vitaliy Ivanov, and Sulman, there would as well be some military railwaymen.

– Vasiliy Ivanovich, what do you say has happened? Did the hikers freeze in the taiga?

– Yes. In the sources of Lozva, their tent was snowed up while they were asleep. Some were crushed, some managed to get out. However, without fire and in panic they could not survive for a long time. It was too cold on those days.

– In the sources of Lozva? Was it where they sent a team to check the anomaly?

– Tough luck. Couldn't they be crushed by an explosion? There should be some works underway nearby, shouldn't there?

That was followed by dead silence at the table. Safety rules were very seldom observed in the logging camps: *"...Suddenly, ten meters away, explosions began, and lumps of earth and pieces of stumps flew all around me - hurtling up and crashing like a ton of bricks. I threw myself down, curled up, and thought of only one thing – not to be hurt. It turned out that the blasting men usually loaded two or three dozen stumps, then set them on fire all at the same time, and fled themselves. They did not put up any fences or flags, since there were usually the only people in the field. And so they lit up, ran away and suddenly saw me, who had almost entered the zone of explosions on the opposite side from them..."*

– The things are not simply bad – they may end up very bad for us all – too bad. We have a colonel serving in the railway forces, a war veteran. He had fought in the war with the Finns, later at the Voronezh and the Belorussian fronts, serving as a regimental commanding officer; was awarded as the Hero of Socialist Labor. That was not because he had been wearing out the seat of his trousers at the staff office, but for his deeds. I had served with him in Mongolia, where he was chief of the production department at the Trans-Mongolian trunk-line. He is a good fellow and a smart one too.

– Now listen. In around 1950, more than ten men in his regiment were burned to death in a fire. He was sentenced to a 25-year term, although at the time of the fire, he was not on the grounds of his regiment. He was stripped of all his ranks and awards, including that of the Hero. he was lucky that in 1953 he was released in the general amnesty. It was the USSR Prosecutor General himself who filed the motion.

The man in question was Iosif Mironovich Shapovalov.

Iosif Mironovich Shapovalov (55) was born in 1904 in the town of Kazatin in Ukraine in the family of a railway worker. After finishing three years of primary school in 1920, he went to a local depot to train as a locksmith. In 1924 in Kiev he completed two years of an evening school and later a workers' prep school. After that, he worked as a train stoker, a fireman, and an engineer. Following graduation in 1932 from the bridge-building department of the Kiev Polytechnic Institute, he worked as a foreman and as deputy head of a railway station line service. In 1933, Shapovalov was drafted into the Red Army. After completing a single-year course of leadership training in the Ural Military District, he served as a senior technician in the staff of the 6th railway regiment in the Kiev Special Military Region. In 1934 he joined the VCP(b). From 1939, Shapovalov served as assistant commanding officer of a bridging battalion of a railway regiment. In late 1939, during the war with Finland, he served at the front as senior engineer of the western section in the construction of the Petrozavodsk – Suoyarvi railway line. In 1941 he had the rank of captain and served as a commanding officer of the 7th detached bridging railway battalion; in early 1942, he was restoring bridges over the Volga River during the Red Army counter-offensive in the Battle of Moscow, for which he was awarded the Order of Red Star. In 1942 and 1943, Shapovalov as a commanding officer of the 4th bridging railway regiment was restoring bridges during the Battles of Stalingrad and Kursk, for which he was awarded as a Hero of Socialist Labor. From August 1943, Lt. Colonel Shapovalov served with his regiment at the Belorussian front. In the summer of 1944, Shapovalov was awarded two Orders of Lenin. In the fall of 1944, he served as the commanding officer of the 15th detached bridging railway special purpose regiment and met the war's end in the rank of a colonel.

After the war, Shapovalov continued his service in the railway forces and was awarded two Red Banner orders and three Red Star orders. In 1943, by a Decree of the Presidium of the Supreme Soviet of the USSR, Lt. Colonel Iosif Mironovich Shapovalov was awarded as the Hero of the Socialist Labor with the Order of Lenin and the "Sickle and Hammer" medal, "for special merit in facilitating frontline and civilian transportation and for outstanding achievements in the recovery of the railways in wartime hardships". Only in summer 1944, in the Kremlin, Colon Shapovalov was awarded two orders of Lenin and the gold Sickle and Hammer medal, which he could not receive earlier in view of 'working at a great distance'.

In 1950, 15 servicemen of Shapovalov's regiment died in a fire. The court martial of the Moscow Military District sentenced Shapovalov to 25 years of prison with disenfranchisement and deprivation of his military rank as a colonel. The Military College of the Supreme Court upheld the sentence, and on August 21, 1951, Shapovalov was deprived of all his combat awards and the title of the Hero. After Stalin's death, in April 1953, following the motion of the USSR Prosecutor General, the Plenum of the Supreme Court commuted the sentence to 10 years with no disenfranchisement and deprivation of his military rank. Later in that same year, he was released in the general amnesty and returned to the railway forces. He served as chief of the production department in the construction of the Trans-Mongolian railway, where he was awarded the medal "For Labor Valor" and a Mongolian order. Only as late as in 1968, the Presidium of the Supreme Soviet of the USSR would restore his title of the Hero of Socialist Labor and his rights to battle awards.

– That is how you have failed us. We have detailed sappers in your assistance, but you would not care to think of safety procedures. If it is acknowledged that my sappers have wrecked [drove to death] the hikers, then it may end up in the death sentence. This amounts to habitual negligence by a member of the commanding staff of the Workers' and Peasants' Red Army in case of particularly aggravating circumstances – under Article 193 of the Criminal Code. As to me, as I've heard of Iosif Mironovich, and now I know the whole Criminal Code by heart. Your life will pretty much go down the drain. Including those, who are now working at the anomaly site. The complicity of civilians in military crimes entails a similar liability. It is up to all of us now the case not to see the light of day.

Fatal casualties were not unusual for the geologists and the N-240 administration. In the period from January 1957 to February 1958, 435 cases of work-related injuries were registered at the Ivdellag. Among them, 10 resulted in death and 5 in severe health issues. Eight members of the staff were called to account, including two of them convicted.

In December 1961, a female cook at the base of the ground team of geophysicists of the party of A.A. Latypov died upon the breach of safety procedures in unloading an aircraft. The body would be taken to Ivdel by reindeer sled. There would be no investigation and nobody would be punished.

It was decided to prepare the discovered bodies for burial at Ivdel with the execution of the Acts on the death of the hikers from freezing, with compliance of all other formalities, and with notification of the UPI and the relatives of the deceased.

The instructions of the USSR Prosecutor General of that period were crystal clear: *"The cases of violent death, apparently resulting from causes not entailing criminal liability of anyone, in particular as a result of violent acts of nature, such as floods, earthquakes, etc., do not require the institution of criminal proceedings."*

First thing was to make sure the bodies of all the members of the group were discovered. There was information that a hiker had left the trek and returned to Vizhay. Someone, with frostnip, came out to the barracks of District 41. Who were they? How many people in total were there in the perished group? Chances were of a later discovery of a body with the injuries, which would be impossible to write off as freezing.

However, there was no need to hurry. It was necessary to secure transportation for delivery of the discovered bodies to Ivdel. They could take a careful look at the site of the accident when there would be free hands and more favorable weather.

CHAPTER 21. DYATLOV SIX AND ELEVEN.

The recovered corpses were finally delivered to Ivdel and laid down for autopsy in the N-240 infirmary morgue. The Mansi Bahtiyarovs from the Northern Toshemka were involved in the transportation. The bodies were delivered by sleds from the area of height 1079 to the base of the anomaly ground check and from there the bodies were flown to Ivdel by helicopter. To avoid undue rumors, the bodies were transported in boxes, disguised as specimen rocks or geological equipment. Those in the know were requested to sign pledges of secrecy.

Pelageya Solter, a nurse at the surgery in the N-240 Central hospital, recalled that the bodies were brought in several groups: *"First they brought three: two girls and one guy. One of the girls had her hair burned on one side, a sleeve, on one hand, was a little bit burned, with one sole lightly suffered in a fire. Two had ordinary clothes, but dirty. Next, they brought three more... One had his head wounded – it was a head fissure... The next bodies were brought much later... they had discovered three, but I do not remember on which date... in total, there were eleven corpses."*

> **Pelageya (Mariya) Ivanovna Solter (39)** was born in 1920. In 1950 she was arrested and sentenced to five years by the court martial of the Ministry of Internal Affairs of the Lvov region. She had served her sentence at the Ivdellag. After she was released in the 1953 general amnesty, Solter worked at the surgery in the N-240 Central hospital.

A good many people have no trust in the recollections of Solter, but there are a few details, which confirm her account. For instance, Anna Petrovna Taranova, the Central hospital gynecology doctor, recalled the forensic examinations undertaken at the Central hospital morgue: *"There was a rumor that some Sverdlovsk students have been missing... Then someone said that they were brought to the morgue. There were a few of them, not the whole group... They brought the students. Who does the autopsy... there were some people, some were coming out wearing white coats... We were told that it was a forensic examination... I know that no strange people should be there. But if we were not to pay any attention, we would not..."*

It might be all right, however, Taranova was telling about the forensic examination of the second party of the bodies delivered to Ivdel, which took place on Sunday, during voluntary works for cleaning up the Central hospital territory: *"I am talking about the second time."* According to the materials of the criminal case, forensic examination at the Central hospital morgue was performed only on the first five of the delivered corpses. For instance, the dissection of Slobodin's body was performed on Sunday, March 8. The forensic examination of the last four bodies discovered in May was conducted at the N-240 infirmary morgue i.e. inside the prison camp zone.

Solter was referring to the arrival of the first bodies and particularly to the morgue of the prison camp zone:

"– At the morgue in the territory of the zone or in the territory of the hospital?

– In the territory of the zone."

According to her, the one who dealt with the examination of the bodies was Iosif Prudkov, the chief of surgery in the N-240 Central hospital which served the administration's civilian personnel.

> **Iosif Davydovich Prudkov (30)** was born in 1929. Following graduation from the Sverdlovsk Medical Institute in 1952, he was sent to work at Ivdel. He had chosen surgery as his field as a third-year student. In 1953 he served as a physician at the infirmary of the 9th division, later became the chief of surgery in the N-240 Central hospital, where he worked simultaneously as the Ivdellag's consulting surgeon and forensic expert. One of Prudkov's early interests had become foreign objects in the stomachs and bodies of the inmates. His other interests were injuries, of which there was no shortage in the prison camp zone. These included gun and knife wounds, which had long been studied, but as well as specific wounds, such as inflicted on deteriorated plank roads ('lezhnevki'), made of logs lined transversely with planks nailed on top to serve as a track. Often one of the planks' ends disengaged from the logs and pricked up like a spear. If a car bumped up against it at night or in poor visibility, the plank would thrust through the car, piercing through the people who happened on its way. The wounded had to be sawed out; and later in surgery, it would take an effort to extract the huge debris to save the patient's life.

It is possible that Iosif Prudkov was invited in view of some specific injuries in the bodies. Solter was not present during the examinations of the bodies: *"Some military serviceman pointed at me and said to doc-*

tor Prudkov, 'What is her use to you?' Prudkov was a very polite man, but at that time he said immediately, 'Mariya Ivanovna, you may be free!' At the time I still had to sign under a pledge of secrecy and non-discussion of the incident. Such pledges were taken from everyone, including drivers and pilots, who were transporting the bodies..."

Prudkov is not mentioned in the forensic examination reports, which appear in the criminal case, no matter that Valentina Prudkova, his widow, who in 1959 served as the head of the children's ward of the Ivdel city hospital, confirmed his participation in the examination and in the autopsies: "My husband did not tell me anything about what was going on during the autopsy. But more generally, at the time there were rumors and conversations to the effect that when they [the bodies] were delivered, they did not have any serious injuries. There were broken ribs, certain minor face injuries. The arms and legs had many injuries." Does she know when the first bodies were discovered? – "No, absolutely not. There was a conversation that the military was taking part in the search."

According to the available information, Mariya Retiunskaya, a Central hospital surgeon, and Boris Bryuzgin, a forensic expert from Serov, might take part in the examination. Their names are not mentioned in the materials of the case, although in the 1960s and 1970s Bryuzgin was invited for forensic examinations at the Ivdel corrective labor colony.

In summary, the first six bodies were already in Ivdel. Three more had not yet been discovered. Examination of the corpses was being completed at the N-240 infirmary morgue. Execution of the formal papers (Acts) on the death of the hikers, certificates for their burial, or similar papers had begun. Korotaev might as well have taken part in these undertakings. He recalled that the examination of the first party was superficial: "With this first group – it was a perfunctory examination, because of the version that they had frozen to death. I no longer remember if they had stripped down any of the bodies or not." The corpses were sent to the refrigerator until the time when the remaining bodies were discovered and the final decision on the place of burial was taken.

Such sequence of the events is circumstantially confirmed by a radio cable, which was sent from the search camp on May 7, following the discovery of the last bodies in the stream:

"Ivan Stepanovich [Prodanov]... for your eyes only: the corpses are frozen, in the same condition as you have seen them. This applies to the open parts of the body..." Formally, the radiogram was sent by Ortyukov to Prodanov. Technically, the radiogram was sent by Nevolin, who could make corrections and additions to the text. The radiogram was received by Temnikov at the Northern expedition; it was definitely read by Sulman.

When could Prodanov or Sulman see the corpses? Recall that this radiogram was sent after the pilots had refused to take the bodies on board for transportation to Ivdel. There is documentary evidence that following the discovery of the bodies in May, Tempalov, Ivanov, and Vozrozhdenniy arrived at the pass. There are no recollections or documents about Prodanov or Sulman to have gone there. It appears that they might have seen the frozen bodies only earlier, at the morgue. There is no corroborative evidence of their presence during the forensic examinations in March. There is only one option left – that they saw the bodies in February, at the time when they were examined by Prudkov. We should not as well rule out that the text of the radiogram might have a typo, for instance, "you" written instead of "we". Otherwise, we should take into account that for some reason there is no evidence left of the visit to the pass by Prodanov or Sulman following the discovery of the bodies.

In all appearances, the rumors of the delivery of the first group of corpses to Ivdel were not widespread. Only a few people could know about the February examination of the bodies at the morgue in the territory of the prison camp zone. Moreover, those rumors had not caused any commotion among the residents, since the death in the winter taiga was not uncommon. The death of the hikers became a subject of frequent discussions only after the arrival of the search groups from Sverdlovsk, followed by the arrival in March of the representatives of the regional committee and the forensic examinations at the Central hospital morgue with the participation of Vozrozhdenniy and Churkina.

"The people were law abiding and did not ask too many questions. My husband did not share any details with me, but I know that he was performing the autopsy, and that physicians from Sverdlovsk were in attendance: a man and a woman… Here is what the people were saying: that after everybody was discovered, there were airplanes and helicopters, which were removing something from the site of the accident."

The recollection of Prudkova is a reflection of the situation when with the discovery of the body of Slobodin in March and the departure of regional officials from Ivdel, for the residents the search for the students was completed. However, the search continued until May. The flights that were servicing the search were as well underway. Very few residents had any idea of the final discovery of the bodies in May. Moreover, the forensic examination of the final four was undertaken within the prison camp zone. Even if the Ivdel residents got any wind of anything, they no longer had any interest in the perished hikers. There was nothing surprising about it: life was going on. For instance, Boris Martyushev, the chairman of the UPI hiking club, would not even mention the death of the Dyatlov group in his summary report from October 1959.

For Solter as well, the search for the missing students would be over in March, when five more bodies would be brought to Ivdel. However, she knew about the first six corpses, which were brought to the N-240 infirmary morgue in February. Six plus five makes eleven in total.

CHAPTER 22. OUTSIDERS IN THE AREA OF HEIGHT 1079.

Late at night on February 16, a phone call from Sverdlovsk came to Vizhay. Zakiy Hakimov, the chief of the camp division, said to the representatives of the UPI sports club that the student group had not returned to Vizhay and promised to report no earlier than February 15. Only a short time ago an inquiry regarding hiking groups that were passing through Vizhay, arrived from the Polunochnoe militia division. Under questioning, the residents recalled the return of Yudin, as well as his accounts about the probable time for the return of the rest. The findings in the course of the questioning were submitted to Hakimov. There was a little difficulty for Hakimov to find the necessary information.

Hakimov reported to Vitaliy Ivanov on the phone call. It was clear to everyone that the UPI was concerned with the fate of the hikers, and that the search could begin before long. The simplest way out would be to report to Sverdlovsk within the next couple of days on the discovered bodies of the hikers, who had died in the taiga from freezing.

But so far only six bodies have been found. Those not yet found may have specific wounds and injuries. It was decided to urgently find the bodies remaining in the area of height 1079, draw up all the necessary documents, notify the UPI and, if possible, organize the funeral of the hikers in Ivdel. A group of cadets of the regimental school of military unit 6602 was raised by alarm and dropped off at the height of 1079.

Hamza Syunikaev, a cadet of the Noncommissioned Officer school of the military unit 6602, recalled: *"At night in the regiment, all cadets received a warning order. Afterward, they selected all the best ski sportsmen. Right in the morning, we were taken to the Ivdel airport... We boarded a helicopter and landed at the headstream of the Lozva River... That was around February 15-16. It was bitter cold... Throughout the first weeks, some explosions could be heard on the left side northward, behind the headstream. We reported it to the commanding officer, who gave an assignment to the radio operator... After that incident, there were no more explosions... Our assignment was as follows: to find whichever documents there could be and to discover the corpses, wherever they were."*

The Mansi men, who took part in the search along with the cadets, said that two bodies, of a young man and a girl, had been found earlier: *"A robust reddish-haired guy. They say she was lying on top of him. She had her legs and arms broken. The guy was dragging her to the tent. He was about 200 meters from the tent... We stayed there until late February, searching. Found nothing, except for a flashlight. We also found pens for writing."*

Ivan Uvarov said in his testimony: *"I know that if anyone from the Mansi people were guilty in the death of the nine hikers, then not a single Mansi man would take part in the search for the hikers. I have learned that three Mansi men took part in the search."*

Ivan Evlampievich Uvarov (75) was born in 1884 in the "Bogoslovskiy factory" settlement in the Verkhoturskiy district of the Perm governorate in a family of a clergyman. In 1891 he enrolled at the Bogoslovsky rural school, from which he graduated in 1894, after which he enrolled at the Perm real school. However, with the death of his father, he could not continue education for lack of funds. In 1900, Uvarov passed exams for the qualification of a teacher, after which the Verkhoturskiy self-government authority (zemstvo) appointed him as headmaster of a two-year Verkhoturskiy boys school. In 1906 he was drafted into the Army and was detailed to Moscow, where he served as senior regimental record clerk in the 3rd Grenadiers Pernovsky regiment. In 1909 Uvarov was released from active duty and transferred to the reserve. In 1910, the Verkhoturskiy self-government authority appointed him as a teacher at the Nikito-Ivdel village two-year school, and in the summer of 1914 he enrolled at the St. Petersburg Polytechnic Institute; however, the study was interrupted by WWI. Uvarov was mobilized into the field army and assigned as senior record clerk at the 123rd reserve battalion in the city of Perm. Due to illness, in 1916 he was retired into the reserve and sent back home on a six-month leave. After the revolution, in 1917, he was appointed as the headmaster of the Ivdel school. In late 1920, Uvarov started collecting antique articles and in 1929 he initiated the opening of a museum on a voluntary basis, housed in a room at the Ivdel Lenin club. In 1944, the Ivdel museum received the status of a state local history museum, with Uvarov becoming its first director. At the same time, he continued teaching.

Uvarov knew the local Mansi very well. Back in 1935, the Sverdlovsk regional department of education ordered his detailing to the

Poma settlement to organize a school for the Mansi, in which he simultaneously taught singing and drawing. According to his information,
three Mansi men took part in the search for the Dyatlov group. Who
were they? There were four Mansi men among the Kurikov's group.
Most likely, it was in mid-February that Uvarov got the wind of the
Mansi participation in the search.

According to Maslennikov's notes on the search, from March 4,
Sinyukaev took part in the search as part of the Potapov group. However, his recollections are at odds with the chain of events in that
period, since Slobodin's body was discovered on March 5. No members
in the search had any recollections of the explosions. Quite possibly,
Sinyukaev had either been at the search site a few times, or he was retelling the words of other cadets, who were dropped at height 1079 in
mid-February.

There is an opinion that the trunk of the cedar might be partially
cleared of branches to hang the antenna of the radio station. On the
bank of the stream, they hastily laid flooring to facilitate access to the
water.

On February 20, the first representatives of the UPI arrived at Ivdel.
From the telegram sent by Vasiliy Pavlov, the deputy chairman of the
Sverdlovsk regional soviet executive committee, it follows that the
regional soviet executive committee had assumed the general supervision of the search. Yet another communiqué from Sverdlovsk had
only added into the panic. The arrival of Major-General Shishkarev, the
chief of the regional Department of Internal Affairs, was expected on
February 21. He had a scheduled meeting at the Polunochnoe settlement with the voters, who had nominated him as deputy candidate
for the Sverdlovsk regional soviet. The only hope was that the general
would not stay long. The situation was becoming critical. It was impossible to realize the plan, which had been elaborated earlier. Some of
the bodies were not yet discovered. They were also late with the execution of the documents and notification of the UPI on the discovery of
the perished hikers.

Still, they would not give up: too much was at stake. The fates of
the Ivdel leadership and as well their families depended on taking the
correct decision. Tempalov had a daughter named Svetlana and Sulman had two sons, Boris and Leonard; the Prodanovs had as many as
eight children. The only way out was to take the bodies from the N-240
infirmary morgue back to height 1079 and stage the scene suggestive
of the death of the group from unfavorable weather conditions. Fortunately, no autopsy of the bodies had been performed. Could this be

done?

The 1924 Corrective Labor Code of the RSFSR said: *"Any death of an inmate and its causes must be certified with an act of a medical examination of the deceased."* From the 1930 Resolution of the Council of People's Commissars of the USSR "On the approval of the resolution on corrective labor camps": *"An appropriate protocol to be drawn up by the camp infirmary on the death of an inmate and its cause."* The 1933 Resolution of the Central Executive Committee of the Soviet Union and the Council of People's Commissars (NKVD) of the USSR on the approval of the Corrective Labor Code of the RSFSR "On the procedure for the registration of the death of inmates": *"Any death of an incarcerated and its causes must be certified and attested by an act of the medical examination of the deceased."* From the 1939 Temporary Instruction on the regime of keeping prisoners in the forced labor camps of the NKVD USSR: *"The death of prisoners and its causes must be certified by an act of medical examination of the deceased."* In that same year of 1939, the Order of the NKVD USSR №00674 "On the procedure for the registration of the death of inmates" specified: *"...The Act of autopsy or medical examination of a convicted inmate who died in a prison, and whose case was investigated by an NKVD agency, is to be executed in 3 copies.... The Act of medical examination of a convicted inmate, who died at a camp or at a corrective labor colony, whose case was investigated by an NKVD agency, is to be executed in 2 copies."*

This means that in the pre-WWII time, an autopsy was prescribed only for those who died in prison. For those who died at the forced labor camps, there was a simple medical examination. After the war, the situation had somewhat changed. The analysis of the archival documents of the Polyanskiy forced labor camp, which in 1950-64 was located in the territory of the town of Zheleznogorsk, indicates that the autopsy report on each case of death was executed only in the first two years of the camp's existence. In the following years, it was executed only in cases of violent death. This being said, the certificates of death and burial were executed for each and every deceased, notwithstanding the cause of death.

It is not impossible that in the late 1950s at the Ivdel forced labor camp they were not conducting any post-mortem examinations of the bodies if the cause of death was apparent. The idea that an autopsy may not be required in case of an apparent cause of death has some currency even nowadays. Sergey Samischenko, a prominent criminalist, coroner, and forensic examiner, pointed out: *"Forensic examination of corpses is performed on the initiative of law-enforcement agencies, hence the decision of which corpse should be examined and which should not, rests with those agencies, as well as the responsibility for this decision. In most cases, the question of sending a corpse to forensic examination is resolved with reasonable facility, since the circumstances of the death predetermine the need for the forensic examination of the corpse. In particular, the corpses of the people, whose death was externally influenced, were to be sent for forensic examination, that is in cases of violent death, whether or not it was a murder, suicide, or an accident. Indeed, an idea that there is no need to perform an autopsy at the morgue if the cause of death were apparent has some currency among law-enforcement officials."*

During the exhumation of Zolotaryov in 2018, a saw mark on his skull was interpreted as an indication that in most cases at Ivdel, they preferred execution of an Act of medical examination without an autopsy and autopsy report. Someone had begun to saw off the cranial roof along a very low line. The mistake was pointed out to him and a new cut was made along the correct line. Most likely, it was Vozrozhdenniy who pointed to the mistake, with the sawing performed by a local attendant with no sufficient experience of sawing off skulls for autopsies. In other words, an autopsy at Ivdel was a rare occasion, although deaths at Ivdel were pretty frequent. The cause of death was determined by external examination.

Gennadiy Panin, a Vizhay resident, said: *"...I remember an occasion when in winter of the late 1970s a corpse of a settler was sent from Ushma to Ivdel for autopsy, and it had disappeared. It was not returned to Ushma, and at Ivdel they were saying with a persuasion that they had sent it as intended. For a long time, it had been looked for and finally discovered at a barn attached to that laboratory... After the accidental discovery, they had to bury him..."*

If such incidents took place in the 1970s, then what is to be said about the late 1950s. Back in 1957, Vasiliy Pavlovich Tsipkovskiy, the head of the sub-department of forensic medicine of the Vinnitsa Medical Institute, pointed out: *"Sometimes the abuse of regulation on the forensic examinations of the corpses originate with the investigative officials, who use their authority, give permission to bury corpses...with no forensic examination, limiting themselves to external examination. Although under the law both prosecutors and investigators have such authority ... the prosecution officials should use it only in extraordinary circumstances."* The situation had not changed as of the early 1960s. The 1962 Order of the Ministry of Healthcare of the USSR "On the measures for improving the forensic medical examination in the USSR", said: *"...certain shortcomings may still be observed in the work of the forensic medical examination. In some cases external examination is performed instead of a comprehensive examination of the corpses; ... on some occasions laboratory examinations are not performed in due time... With a view to the continuous improvement of the organization of the forensic medical examination in the USSR, I am hereby ordering: to ban any substitution of a comprehensive examination of the corpse with an external examination and on each occasion of the determination of the cause of death to conduct a comprehensive forensic medical examination of the corpses with an examination of at least three cavities (skull, thoracic, abdominal)..."*

The idea for the setup was prompted by Grigoriy Anisimovich Fedoseev – a geodetic engineer, who from the 1930s had taken part in the field of geodesic explorations in Trans-Baikal and Eastern Sayans. In 1938, he became a team head, later head of the expedition. In 1949, the "Sibirskie ogni" ("Siberian Lights") magazine published the story, "We are walking through the Eastern Sayan", that inspired the writer for a number of books which had earned national acclaim – all based on the pioneer's diaries, which Fedoseev was writing by the campfires during his travels.

Sedov and Bartolomey recalled that Fedoseev's books were popular among UPI hikers. His new book, "On the Road of Trial", was published in 1958. It is not impossible that it was that book that the hikers gave as a gift to Evgeniy Venediktov, the foreman at District 41.

"...A muddy curtain of bad weather appears on the horizon... We corral into the tent, huddled around the stove, where a faint light flickers a little, casting a pale glow on the gloomy, alert faces of people... from the north a snowstorm approached. And soon everything was whistling around, spinning in a mad whirlwind. Streaks of snowy dust flowed through the frozen slant; snow drifting ominously.

The tent is arched from the pressure of the wind. The stove has gone out. Firewood is over, the cold finds a gap, seeps inside. We are wrapped in warm clothes. It is impossible to fall asleep, but no one feels like talking... what will happen if the wind destroys our tent and we find ourselves face to face with a snowstorm on bare rocks, far from the forest?...

A snowdrift piled up heavily on the tent on the windward side, the wall bent dangerously, and soon the rope in the middle broke, unable to withstand the weight... The hanging snowdrift had already compromised a third of the tent and continued to press down, bending the crossbar. It was at that moment that a new ferocious squall hit, and the canvas wall broke in half. A mountain of snow fell on us.

– Get dressed and come out! – Lebedev is ordering. – It is all fuss in the dusk, nobody can find their stuff, the people are scolding. The wind is flop-

ping the torn sides of the tent, throwing handfuls of snow into our faces.

– *I'm saying, get out! – Lebedev's voice is heard through the wail of the snowstorm. – Presnikov, you are holding us all back.*

– *I've lost my cap, – he responds.*

– *Wrap a bag on your head and come out! – Lebedev orders, girding himself with a rope and passing its end to his friends.*

The snowstorm is pouncing upon us with all its rage. The bitter cold is blinding, burning the nostrils. Lebedev is walking ahead, with the rest following him, holding onto the rope.

Moving along almost blindly, we are reaching the slope with great difficulty. Walking is getting easier because we are going down and it is quieter here. We are walking wilder among small riffs, along ravines with steep slopes. We are likely going down into the gorge, where there should be a forest, hence we will make fire. We are not dreaming of anything else... Only after an hour, the downhill gradient has diminished drastically, with the stream gravel and the cliffs left behind. Now we are walking on smooth swelled snow, which is slippery like ice...

We are going still lower down the gorge, and here we notice freshly felled stubs and then the tents. Kirill Rodionovich is a great guy – masterfully taking us down to the camp! And here we are at a huge merry bonfire, which has recovered our energy and high spirits. The straps are unfastened, there is laughter heard around...”

There was precious little time left. The challenge was exacerbated with the need to discover the hiker's tent, besides searching for the remaining bodies. Along with part of the personal effects of the deceased, the tent had remained at the site of the tragic accident. At the time, everything was cloaked in snow, with nobody remembering its precise location. Everything around looked alike. The only good thing was that the four bodies from among the six ones delivered to Ivdel were discovered right in the snowed up tent. With their suspected fractures, they should be concealed so well that it would take as long as possible to discover them – until the snow melted with the animals gnawing round the bones. It was likely that the remaining hikers were able to leave the tent and got frozen. Most likely, they had no serious injuries – impact injuries at most. There would be no need to hide them.

Under the pretext of transporting the bodies from the N-240 infirmary morgue to Sverdlovsk, new clothes were purchased to replace the damaged ones. Solter recalled that the clothes for the funeral were bought in Ivdel. The bodies were washed, dressed, and taken by car to the airport in coffins. Most likely, the corpses were packed in plywood boxes and flown by helicopters to the anomaly ground inspection base disguised as equipment. From there the Bahtiyarovs transported the cargo on sleds to height 1079.

Moving corpses from the place of the accident was not unheard of for these places. In March 1959, a car drove over a drunken man, who was lying on the road at the Glukharnyi settlement. The perpetrators of the crime moved the victim's corpse to the forest at a distance of 250 meters (820 feet).

The bodies of Dubinina, Zolotaryov, Kolevatov, Thibeaux-Brignolle, Kolmogorova, and Krivonischenko were transported back to the pass. Doroshenko, Dyatlov, and Slobodin had not yet been discovered. Why these three in particular? In February the bodies were washed at the infirmary morgue, however, in March Vozrozhdenniy would discover traces of blood on these three bodies. *"...The mouth is closed. There is a trail of caked blood coming from the opening of the nose."* in Slobodin's; *"...the hair is stained with particles of moss and needles of conifer trees... There are traces of congealed blood in the nasal arch area, nose tip, and upper lip... In the right cheek area, the soft tissues are covered with a layer of grey-colored foamy liquid, there are traces of discharges of grey-colored liquid from the mouth opening"* in Doroshenko's; *"...The lips of bluish-purple coloration are covered with congealed blood"* in Dyatlov's autopsy reports. This is how Churkina explained in the late 1990s the absence of any traces of blood on the rest of the bodies: *"...the corpses had been washed, that was why they had no traces of blood, although there was no shortage of lacerations on the bodies..."*

Additionally, at the morgue, while clothing a large number of corpses, it was easy to mix up certain items. Lev Ivanov recalled: *"Their friend, his name was, likely, Yudin, who had fallen behind due to illness, was of great assistance. He knew how each of them was dressed and helped to ascertain who happened to be wearing what. All clothing items were mixed up."* It was particularly on the bodies of Kolevatov, Zolotaryov, Kolmogorova, Dubinina, and Thibeaux-Brignolle that many items of other hiker's clothes were found.

On February 23, the group of Slobtsov was dropped upstream of the Lozva River. The situation was getting dangerous. The students could arrive in the vicinity of height 1079 before the job of staging the scene would be over. Grigoriev said that they were to be landed at the mouth of the Auspiya, 15 km from Mt. Otorten. However, by the end of the day, they would be dropped off much further north.

It was the Slobtsov group – the only one among the search groups – which had local guides attached to it. Vladimir Androsov, who had known Pashin in person, said: *"He was very well familiar with the surrounding, which was the reason for involving him in the search. He was an excellent hunter and very well familiar with our surroundings, particularly with Matveevcкaya Parma. This is the territory from the source of the Lozva River up till Auspiya River. He was hunting in that territory."* The guides were given the assignment to prevent an untimely arrival of the UPI group at height 1079.

At the same time, the evacuation of the search group of military unit 6602 was underway. The cadets were unable to find anything and have not witnessed the process of staging the scene. All they knew was that they had taken part in the search for the hikers. Karpushin and Lebedev recalled: *"On that day, search groups from among the students, Ivdellag personnel and local hunters, were landed in a few locations"*; *"In-between the two flights to deliver the Slobtsov group, the crew spotted people, who were waving their hands to attract attention. The pilots thought they found the missing group; however, they turned out to be escaped prisoners. The unarmed crew picked up and brought them to Ivdel."* Doubtful that the crew was so careless – particularly that the only known group of the runaways was held up by a task team as early as February 21.

In the vicinity of height 1079, there were only a few people left from the anomaly ground check-up search team. Their bosses believed them to be the immediate culprits in the tragedy – The consequences in case they failed the assignment had already been explained to them –with those efforts already having some effect.

Vladimir Lyubimov, the former radio operator of the geological prospecting expedition, recalled that while surfing through the airwaves in February 1959, he came across radio communications of his colleagues Nevolin and Temnikov regarding some search. They said that two had not yet been discovered. The search was going on in the grid he was familiar with, code named "Posadka" ("Landing"), which was located in the mountains. The Northern expedition did not work in that grid.

Vladimir Alekseevich Lyubimov graduated from a special purpose Naval signals school in 1947 with a qualification of a radio engineer and international radio operator; he had access to documents classified as 'Top Secret.' That was the reason why he was commonly instructed by his chief signals officer to surf through the airwaves while working in the field. From October 1958 to May 1959, Lyubimov was servicing the winter camp of the geological base at Mt. Yaruta, where he heard the communications regarding the search works.

The bodies of Dubinina, Zolotaryov, Thibeaux-Brignolle, and Kolevatov, which were the first to be discovered right in the snowed-up tent, suspect of injuries, had already been buried in the stream. They were laid to rest in a thaw hole, covered with a jacket and snowed in. The bodies of Doroshenko and Slobodin were finally discovered – as well as the snowed-in tent at the site of the accident.

An instruction to immediately complete staging the scene and to leave arrived from Ivdel. At the search staff headquarters, it was decided to send search groups to the upstream of the Auspiya River. They could appear in that area the next day.

They were short of time. Krivonischenko was burnt when the stove fell down. His clothes were sooty, burned, and cut. The clothes of Doroshenko were as well sooty. It was for them that the new clothes were bought at Ivdel. It was originally planned to change the clothes of Doroshenko and Krivonischenko, possibly, to cover them with snow on the slope, however, there was no time left, and they were simply left under the cedar. Part of the unused clothes was burned with another part buried in the stream together with the four bodies, with still another part dumped on the flooring and snowed in. Some items of the clothes were lost on the way to the stream. Hence in May, the members of the search party would find one half of a sweater on the leg of Dubinina and a jumper, sweater, and pants on the flooring. A cut off ski pants' leg was discovered in the same place. The second halves of the sweater and pants would turn up about 15 meters from the stream. Some clothes articles, for instance, Thibeaux-Brignolle's white fur vest, would not be discovered at all.

Late at night on February 24, four men were pulling loaded sleds up the slope of height 1079. The bodies of Kolmogorova and Slobodin were snowed in on the slope. Small items were falling off the sled. Those were a small flashlight and a fragment of a ski. The man in charge set aside the sled, backed off, trying to find the place for setting up the tent.

The controversy is still going on about why the tent was set up at that very location. Many of those who were involved in the search are sure that the hikers were wrong in choosing the location. For instance, in 1959 and later on, Sahnin could not understand and explain why the Dyatlov group set up their tent on the slope. Others, on the contrary, believe that tactically the decision was correct – so that not to lose height in the subsequent movement towards the Otorten. The expert findings of the microclimatic examination, which was conducted in 2019 within the framework of the inspection by the Sverdlovsk regional prosecutor's office into the fact of the death of the Dyatlov group, observed that *"...the hikers set up their tent in the wind shadow, with a relative 10-15% less wind in that location in relation to the surroundings. Given the north-western wind on February 1-2, the only wind shadow zone was in the location of the tent..."* At the site of the tent's set up the depth of snow cover was determined to be 150 cm (5 feet).

And what if that was the location of Dyatlov's cache and not of his tent, with the purpose of not losing height on the return from the Otorten? Let us recall his plans to set up the cache above the forest zone, as well as his plans, on return from the Otorten, to go over from the upstream of the Auspiya River on the eastern slope of the Ural Range to the upstream of the Unya River on the western slope. Let us also recall Pashin's accounts that the tent was discovered by the pennon. Can it be possible that in early February it was the cache that was discovered at that place by the pennon, and not the tent? The hikers had left the cache in the wind shadow zone, with the depth of the snow sufficient to dig a hole. But how can we explain the presence of small objects, which were overlooked in early February during the discovery of the cache, but which might be discovered at the time when the search was underway? The only thing it would take was to set up the tent at that place.

But problems were arising. In the absence of any lateral ridgepoles, it was impossible to anchor the stove, which broke away during the fall and had remained in the tent since the time of the accident. The piping had suffered as well. So it was decided to set up the tent without the stove, which was slip-covered together with the pipes.

The controversy of whether there was firewood in the stove, is still on to this day. Sharavin recalled that the stove was stuffed with firewood. Lebedev recalled that the stove was slip-covered, with the pipes sitting inside the stove. Inside the tent, including at its rear end, there were about a dozen splinters 25 to 30 cm long, possibly, similar to the small log Lebedev found in 1959 behind the tent. Lebedev told about the log in his testimony from April, however, for some reason he had forgotten about the splinters inside the stove, and recalled it only decades later. That was what helped to find an explanation. Back in 2013, Bartolomey and Yakimenko were describing the stove of the Dyatlov group: *"The stove had the shape of a parallelepiped, with a chimney mounted in the rear. The chimney was folding, and to protect the walls of the tent had rings made of asbestos and an additional ring of wooden bars, fastened with a wire or cord. These raw bars were usually gathered and fastened on location."* Most likely that the splinters and the log, which Lebedev found in 1959, fell out of that additional protective ring when the conspirators were carelessly pulling the chimney out from the hole in the tent. Unfortunately, all those who saw the stove on February 28, had no idea of this detail, and the examination of the tent raised no suspicion. This detail might have been noticed by Maslennikov, as the most experienced hiker, had he stayed longer by the tent. Unfortunately, he went down too soon after its discovery. The searchers that stayed longer didn't notice anything suspicious. Moreover, the students mistakenly believed that the method of setting up the tent on skis was Dyatlov's 'signature' method, although among the military it had been known at least from the time of the Great Patriotic War (1941-45).

There was no time left. Instead of tearing the tent's ramp as if it was torn by the wind, they had simply cut it from the inside. Without completing the tent's set up, forgetting a small flashlight on top of it, they cut up the tent and covered it with snow. Sharavin recalled that when the tent was discovered, there was a depression in the snow on the side of the entrance and below along the slope with the size of around eight meters. Three men with their sleds went down to the camp. The man in charge moved aside a little, examined the tent, and hurried to join the rest.

Soon the tracks would be covered by snow. But a few days later, they would reappear, extruded like pillars. *"Six pairs of footprints [were going] from the tent to the ravine; to the left from them, in about 20 meters, there were two more pairs of footprints."* In fact, those were not the eight pairs of footprints going down the slope, but the tracks of an ascent and descent of four people. In his ruling on closing the proceedings in the case, Lev Ivanov specified that *"the investigation has not determined any presence on February 1 or 2, 1959 in the vicinity of height 1079, of other people besides the hikers from Dyatlov group."* Indeed, in the days specified by Ivanov, there were no other people there except for the hikers. The outsiders would appear later. Ivanov had not made any determination regarding the absence or presence of outsiders in the vicinity of height 1079 after February 2, and he left no comment in that respect.

As soon as the night of February 25, a report on the termination of the operation was forwarded to Ivdel.

In Yuri Yarovoy's book, The Highest Rank of Complexity, which had a documentary base, there is a confusion in the dates of the discovery of the hikers' tent: *"A tent was discovered under the snow on the eastern slope of the peak... The tent was torn down... It would take no less than four days to cover 70 kilometers through the mountains, which means that they were under the summit on February 4 or 5, and today it was already February 15...*" The dating in the novel is other than the actual one, but the sequence of dates is strictly observed. Let us make a note of the 15th.

A little below Yarovoy wrote: "*In the morning of February 15 we were going to fly... to the height, where the tent was discovered yesterday.*" Yesterday means the 14th. Yarovoy might have heard about the radiogram regarding the tent, which was received in Ivdel on the night of February 25. And he must have known about the radiogram from February 26, which as well dealt with the tent. This confusion found its way into the novel.

Among the materials of the criminal case, there are no radiograms on the discovery of the tent and the first bodies. Yarovoy said that at the search headquarters three radio stations were working on three different frequencies. In the notes of Grigoriev, there is information that the radiogram on the discovery of the tent was received at the geological party at the Tolya River and then transmitted to Ivdel.

The acceptance and transfer of radiograms via Tolya is circumstantially corroborated by the following radiogram available in the criminal case: "*March 1, 1959, To Sulman. No one is sick, but there are very few people up to the task, and some of them are tired. Melnikov.*" Indeed, a certain Melnikov served as a technical manager of a drilling party at the Tolya River. Grigoriev met him on one of his tours of duty. Such a complicated system of transmitting radiograms at the time of the search might be necessary only in case of the need to hide part of the information from prying eyes.

The traces of human activity in the vicinity of the cedar would be discovered a little later by the search groups, but they would ascribe it to the activities of the hikers.

The conspirators moved to the upstream of the Auspiya River and would soon join the integrated search team. Most probably, they had joined the Slobtsov group even earlier. The student participants in the search, who were assembled from among various groups and programs of studies, were poorly familiar even with each other. In their early recollections, they acknowledged that they did not know the exact number of participants in their group. For instance, Koptelov was not aware of the fact that local guides were part of the group. Sharavin recalled that in the course of the search they were finding ski traces, which, in all appearances, did not belong to the Dyatlov group. They did not arise any suspicions, since there were several search groups, which were simultaneously looking for the old traces of missing hikers.

The conspirators would leave the integrated search camp at the Auspiya River only on March 3, after the discovery of the cache. It is exactly in the period from February 26 to March 3, when we see the disparity in the calculations of the number of people in the search camp.

On February 25, Timofey Prokopyevich Bahtiyarov and Pavel Vasilyevich Bahtiyarov returned to the Bahtiyarov settlement at the Northern Toshemka River. Their whereabouts in the period from February 17 to February 24 are unknown. According to the Mansi men themselves, they were first hunting and then went to Ivdel on their own business. This information had never been verified. There is a high probability that throughout all that time the Bahtiyarovs were involved in the search in the vicinity of height 1079. On their way back they delivered the radio operator and the radio station to Ivdel.

On March 16, Tempalov interrogated Pavel Bahtiyarov, however, he had chosen not to ask any questions regarding his whereabouts in the later part of February. On March 7 and 9, Tempalov interrogated Valentina Spiridonova Mayorova and Elizaveta Pavlovna Lopatina, both of them Ivdel residents. Here is their account:

"...I was born in Ivdel in 1915, and have been living here ever since. At present, I have three brothers and three sisters. All my brothers and sisters are alive. One of the brothers works as a stoker at the Ivdel settlement, his name is Gorbunov Dmitriy. The second brother, Gorbunov Pyotr, from 1956 is serving his sentence for rape at the Ivdellag. The third brother, Gorbunov Evgeniy Spiridonovich, resides in Sverdlovsk and works at a local section. All the sisters are as well alive.

In 1941, our brother, Gorbunov Yakov Spiridonovich, died in combat. One more brother, Gorbunov Georgiy, before the war, then 19, worked as a charge hand at a mill at the Red October settlement. He died when a bagful of flour fell upon him. He was buried at Ivdel. The Mansi had not killed a single one from among my relatives and acquaintances; had there been any such occasion, I would have known about it. I have heard that the Mansi people have a mountain, where they pray, that they go there to pray once a year. I do not know where that mountain is located. I have no idea that the Russians are forbidden from going there."

"...in late April, my brother Lopatin Dmitriy Pavlovich, went duck shooting by boat on the Lozva River. My father, Lopatin Pavel Vasilyevich, went along with him, as well as one Mansi man with his son Nikolay. Both of those Mansi men are no longer alive – that was in 1934. My father was

on the back seat of the boat with the elder Mansi, my brother was on the back seat of the boat with son of the Mansi. In the morning, around the Sobyanino settlement, we did not find my brother in the boat. My father started asking the Mansi where was his son Dmitriy. The Mansi answered that the boat had overturned and he had drowned in the river. The boat had indeed overturned, as my father told me. At the time, my father filed a complaint with the militia, and they started searching for him in the Lozva River. The place where my brother had drowned was only 40 km from Ivdel. But they couldn't find my brother at the time. His body was discovered in the river only after six years when they blasted a plug. My other brother, Lopatin Venedict, went to identify the body, and buried Dmitriy at the Sobyanino settlement. My brother's corpse was examined by a doctor, whose name I do not know, and he remarked that my brother was not killed, that there were no signs of violent death. Nobody knows if the Mansi had sunk my brother. Indeed, my father had approached [the boat] immediately. Those Mansi men, who went hunting with my father and brother, are no longer alive. My father and brother had known those two Mansi well and were on friendly terms with them. As my father said, there were no quarrels. When my brother was discovered in the river, his legs and arms were not tied up."

Officially, these interrogations were carried out within the frame of implementation of the instruction, which Bizyaev received on behalf of Ahmin. But what could the accounts of the fate of the Gorbunov brothers or the death of Dmitriy Lopatin a quarter century ago have to do with the investigation into the causes of death of the Dyatlov group? Nothing.. Within the framework of checking the version of a probable Mansi attack at the hikers, they interrogated many residents, who had a far greater experience of communication with the Mansi. Still, there is a single very important detail. Both Mayorova and Lopatina worked as telegraph operators at the Ivdel communication office. What if they were already interrogated in early February regarding the fate of the missing hikers – as well as Popov, who was the chief of communications at the Vizhay logging division? What if they might occasionally have spilled the beans? Now, after the second interrogation, it would be always possible to present its protocol and to show that the telegraph operators were simply in confusion as of the dates of the interrogations. But it looks likely that they had forgotten to interrogate Popov for the second time.

CHAPTER 23. DYATLOV EIGHT OR NINE.

On February 26, at 6:00 pm, the radio station of the Northern Expedition received a radiogram from the Slobtsov group. A tent had been found, but it hadn't been inspected yet because a violent blizzard had broken out. The inspection eventually took place on February 28, establishing some extremely interesting facts.

A quote from the report drawn up on the spot where the camp of Igor Dyatlov's group was discovered: *"The place to sleep is a snow-leveled area, with 8 pairs of skis at the bottom."* According to the search party that found it, *"the only thing discovered outside the tent beside the ice ax was a Chinese lantern on top of it."* Maslennikov recorded this in a radiogram dated March 2. But on February 28, things looked different: *"An ice ax and a pair of skis were found near the tent. 10-15 meters away were Dyatlov's slippers, socks and anorak. A windbreaker was also found nearby..."*

According to the reports on the discovery and identification of items, eight pairs of skis were found originally. Later, a ninth pair appeared next to the tent. Another pair, a spare one, would be found in the storage. Yudin recalled: *"All of us took the same kind of skis from the UPI sports club, however, one pair looked different. But they might have been Krivonischenko's personal skis."*

Atmanaki's testimony was that *"Everything turned out to be untouched, except for one backpack that contained some small things, which were scattered around the tent and collected during the inspection."* The other eight backpacks were found laid at the bottom of the tent.

Nine blankets were shown to Yudin for identification in Ivdel, but only eight to the victims' relatives in Sverdlovsk. Also, Sharavin kept talking about the ninth blanket being found near the cedar.

There was confusion concerning the ski boots, too. Only eight pairs found in the tent were presented for identification in Ivdel and Sverdlovsk. A ninth pair was later discovered in the storage, but somehow never made it to Sverdlovsk.

All in all, many other things such as skis, ski boots, warm and bivouac shoes, gaiters, a windbreaker, a checked shirt, a ski cap, a ski mask, and an anorak were found outside the tent during the first days of the search. Considering the extra backpack and blanket, we get a complete set of equipment for one more participant. The ninth one.

This can only be explained by one scenario. On February 24, a tent with some items was left on the slope at the height of 1079 m, and the group of perished hikers was eight in number. By that time, despite enormous efforts, the ninth body still couldn't be found. The search continued even after re-enactors joined the Slobtsov group.

Dyatlov's body would not be found until the morning of February 27. The radiogram about the discovery of a ninth body made Tempalov fly to the pass. Meanwhile, a pair of slippers, a windbreaker, a checked shirt, and some small items from the ninth set of equipment would be planted in the area of the tent and the cedar.

The cache site (storage) was found on March 2, containing a spare pair of skis, a ninth pair of ski boots, and a ninth pair of warm shoes. Blinov would identify Dyatlov's warm boots, which might have been removed from his body on February 27, just upon discovery, to make hyperthermia the most credible cause of death.

In April 1959 Slobtsov gave evidence that the storage had been discovered by a group consisting of himself, Brusnitsyn, Lebedev, and two Mansi people. Later neither Brusnitsyn nor Lebedev could remember their participation in this discovery. Moreover, they could not even remember seeing the storage at all. No one could tell what kind of sketch maps or records were used to find it.

According to Yarovoy's records, the storage was located in the forest quite close to the ski track from the search camp to the pass, just ten meters away. When a storage is set up in a forest, products are usually hung in bags on trees to keep them away from animals. However, in this particular case, it was a pit in the snow lined with cardboard, which is the way to store things in a treeless area. There were skis nearby, with a torn gaiter slipped onto them looking like a flag. It seemed as if some unknown people made a storage similar to another one left by Dyatlov on the slope of height 1079, which had been found thanks to a flag. Some missing items of clothing, food, and other things that belonged to the group were put in it.

The food products, nineteen in total, were given over to the search party. But none of them ever mentioned that while searching, they were also eating from the products left by the perished group. Likely, these products were not much different from the ones sent to them on March 1. And it is impossible to confirm this, as the page listing the food supplies had been removed from Dyatlov's trek plan, while all other pages remained intact. Who could have done it? On February 28,

Tempalov flew away from the pass, taking with him all the group's documents, except for the sketch maps and personal diaries. Note that the names of products from the storage, except for several positions, are present in the daily allowance for various categories of prisoners held in corrective labor camps of the USSR Ministry of Internal Affairs, announced by Order of the USSR Ministry of Internal Affairs №550 of August 16, 1958.

It was very easy for the locals to convince people from Sverdlovsk that the footprints discovered that day on the slope of height 1079 belonged to the nine hikers going down from the tent to the forest. Captain Chernyshev noted confidently that: *"30-40 meters away from the tent, clearly visible human footprints were discovered. They trailed down in parallel tracks close to each other as if people were walking holding each other. It looked like the tracks trailed in two directions: 6 or 7 pairs of footprints headed from the tent to the ravine, and to the left, about 20 meters away, there were another two pairs of footprints. Then 30-40 meters away, these footprints (2 and 7 pairs) joined and never separated. On the stone ridges, the footprints disappeared, and below the stones, they reappeared and were then lost again. The footprints were very clear and visible. Some of them made it obvious that a person had walked barefoot or just wearing cotton socks, as there were even imprints of toes."* However, Tempalov was not so sure: *"I discovered eight pairs of footprints, which I examined carefully. But due to winds and temperature fluctuations, they had been deformed. I couldn't find a ninth pair, there was no such."*

Tempalov's caution is understandable. Assoc. Prof. Dr. Lyudmil Georgiev, forensic expert, a specialist in traceology, was asked to examine these three photos from the case files with the questions:

1. Were these prints left by people who were barefoot or shod?
2. How many people were the footprints left by?
3. In what direction did the people who left the traces move?

He conducted all experiments necessary and the bottom line of his 20-page expert opinion is that the footprints in all three photos from the Dyatlov case files were left by people wearing shoes (Dyatlov-pass.com/1079#chapter23).

Nevertheless, Tempalov was certain about something else: *"...In the right corner, near the entrance, there was some food: cans of condensed milk, 100 grams of sliced bacon, ship biscuits, some sugar, and an empty flask smelling of vodka or some other alcohol. There was also a jug of hot cocoa ready for consumption. Naturally, as it had been mixed with water, it had frozen. I found a big knife near the sliced bacon and I identified it as the one that belonged to the students. Apparently, they were drinking vodka and having a snack..."*

Is that a hint that alcohol consumption may have aggravated the situation up to a conflict in the group when trying to decide on the most reasonable way to save themselves? Could be. But the representatives of the UPI managed to convince the investigation experts that alcohol consumption by hikers was out of the question. On March 4, even before the chemical test was done, Vozrozhdenniy noted that no alcohol was found during the examination of the bodies.

There is also another explanation. In 2013, Sharavin recalled: *"We took the flask with alcohol we had discovered in the bucket to the basecamp and drank it at the table shared by all, commemorating the perished guys.*

Then, on the 27th we took the empty flask back to the tent." It is confirmed by the fact that the flask was not mentioned in the list of items taken by the search party from the Dyatlov group tent and later presented to Tempalov on February 27.

It could not have affected the conclusion in any way, though. On February 27, everyone agreed that it was the hurricane that had caused the hikers' death: *"To Sulman... The victims were thrown out of a tent by a hurricane. They didn't have any footwear. Some of them were without pants and jackets. The direction of the hurricane was north-east - east, so they are all lying in a line from the discovered tent ... Maslennikov."* Tempalov himself also supported this version: *"After reading all the documents and diaries, there is no doubt that the students died on February 1st or 2nd, 1959. According to witnesses, there was a very strong wind in the mountains and the area, and it was freezing..."*

The quick discovery of the tent and the widely accepted opinion regarding the cause of death of the hikers gave hope that the Sverdlovsk search party would not have to stay long in Ivdel.

On February 27, by order of Tempalov, Korotaev called in Y.I. Laptev from Severouralsk. In 1959, there was no medical examiner in Ivdel working for the Bureau of Forensic Medical Examination in the Sverdlovsk region. When necessary, his functions were performed by Prudkov or a volunteer specialist from the nearest settlement. Prudkov was not invited as he knew nothing about the reenactment. Most recently, he had already examined the bodies and could not help but notice that they had been brought back again.

Okishev recalled that Korotaev also phoned the investigation department of the Sverdlovsk regional prosecutor's office. He said that a group of skiers had gone missing in the mountains of the Northern Urals, that a search party had been organized and the first bodies had been found.

All the formalities had been completed, and there was no doubt about the cause of death. The investigation should not take too much time. Still, on February 28, L. Ivanov arrived at Ivdel and a special regional committee was set up in Sverdlovsk to control the search. To maintain control of the situation, Tempalov initiated a criminal case on the death of the hikers, but with an earlier date – the resolution was dated 'February 26'.

Urgent inquiries were coming from Sverdlovsk regarding the progress of the investigation. While preparing their responses, the Ivdel Prosecutor's Office used materials gathered in early February by the police station in Polunochnoe settlement. For example, the special message of the Ministry of Internal Affairs of the Russian Federation sent to the Central Committee of the CPSU on February 28, included information not about the route of the Dyatlov group, but about that of the Shumkov group: *"On January 28 this current year, the group in question left the Burmantovo settlement, which is 70 km north of Ivdel Mountain, carrying food supplies to last them until February 14."* Spitsyn and Karpushin received the same information on February 20 while preparing the air search routes at the Ivdel airport.

All these inconsistencies went unnoticed because everyone, without exception, was sure that the hikers had frozen to death. Only after March 5, when Slobodin's body was found on the slope of height 1079 with a closed craniocerebral injury, did Ivanov begin to suspect that the death of the group may have been caused by something different. An alternative version of a Mansi attack on the hikers has not been confirmed. None of the interrogated residents believed that Mansi had anything to do with the tragedy. Soon the special regional committee officially agreed with the hurricane version, and Ivanov himself began collecting materials on observations of anomalous celestial phenomena.

CHAPTER 24. ONLY THE SILENT SURVIVE.

The investigation was over, and the case was to be closed soon. The ongoing search for the remaining bodies was under control, and everyone in Ivdel felt relieved. Yet a lot of things could not be staged, and there were times when it seemed that the risky plan was about to fail. But eventually, everything worked out, and their lives and careers were not in danger. On March 1, 1959, Vitaliy Ivanov, Ivan Prodanov, Abram Sulman, and Vasiliy Tempalov were elected to the Ivdel city council of Working People's Deputies. Along with them, many other Ivdel residents whom we met on the pages of this book became members of the city council: Konstantin Bizyaev, Aleksander Gubin, Aleksander Deryagin, Grigoriy Kurikov, Mihail Mokrushin, Georgiy Novokreschenov, Ivan Uvarov, and Anna Taranova.

But, unwillingly, our thoughts keep returning to the moment when, on March 1, a radiogram arrived from the search camp: *"1/3 1025 Moscow time. To Sulman... It is well established: the disaster took place on the night of February 2... Maslennikov"*

On the night of February 2... It is well established...

Ground inspection of the anomaly began later. Neither on February 1, nor on February 2, were there any people near the camp of the Dyatlov group, or had any work been carried out. Neither the guards from the Ivdellag, the geologists from the Northern Expedition, nor the sappers of the railway troops, had anything to do with the death of the hikers. Apparently, natural forces, such as hurricane force wind, and severe frost, had been the cause.

The idiocy of it all. To convince yourself of an imaginary cause of the tragedy. To make others believe this, too. To have to decide whether to take part in the staging or to be sentenced and face career ruin. To leave behind families without breadwinners, or children without fathers. Hakimov had four children, Pashin seven, and Cheglakov three.

And to fear, for the rest of your life, that one of those who participated in the reenactment may someday, while drinking, blurt out the truth about the events of February 1959. Hopefully, those few who knew the truth would realize that if they wanted to stay alive, you had to keep quiet. This is precisely what Ivan Prodanov would tell his son, again and again, when someone started talking about the dead hikers.

Potyazhenko recalled that *"... during the search, rumor had it that geologists never carried out any survey and never blew up anything."* Grigoriev's diaries describe a whole scenario, most likely based on such discussions: *"...They might have been mountain climbers and geo-scientists. They might have decided to examine mountains in winter, to check for magnetic disturbances. There is a record about the geophysi-cists. ...To start with an airplane search, describing the beauty of the peace-ful Ural Mountains. ...It was grey and overcast when they began setting up the tent. Then came the night, it was dark, there was a rockslide. ...The tent was down at the foothill. But magnetic variometers began to detect iron ore. They saw the rockslide. But the variometer was on the top, so they went up in turns to observe. It was hard. A strong wind was blowing. And they decided to carry the tent over to the slope."* Apparently, theories about the incident involving geologists and geoscientists were often dis-cussed among the searchers. Different versions might have been dis-cussed later, too. Casual encounters in the city streets may have evoked memories of recent events. Normally, such talks would be harmless. But some memories could become dangerous...

During the next few years, many people who were in some way related to the search in 1959 left or were transferred to other cities in the country.

Vitaliy Ivanov would soon be transferred to the Arkhangelsk region and made Head of Department P 233, the former Kargapollag. He would later retire with the rank of colonel. At the end of December 1959, all the N-240 documents were already signed by Lieutenant Col-onel Karasev, the Acting Head of the Ivdel Correctional Labor Depart-ment.

Mihail Shestopalov would be dismissed from the railway troops with the rank of lieutenant colonel, too, in December 1959. Until his death in the 2000s, he never said anything to his family and friends about the death of the Dyatlov group or his participation in its search.

Vasiliy Vasilets was dismissed, in 1962, from the post of deputy head of the N-240 enterprise, which he had held since 1958.

Yakov Busygin retired in 1961 and left Ivdel. At the end of De-cember 1959, documents on the 32nd division of the detained escort (DDE) were already signed by Kotyurgin, the acting head of the 32nd DDE, Lieutenant Colonel.

Aleksey Chernyshev was promoted and transferred to the city of Tolyatti in the mid-60s.

Zakiy Hakimov retired in 1968 with the rank of Major of Internal Troops and returned to his homeland in the Chelyabinsk Region.

Abram Sulman retired in 1962. He left for Moscow, where he worked at the All-Union Geological Fund for several years before moving to Sverdlovsk.

Egor Nevolin moved to Sverdlovsk in the mid-60s. That was also when he burned the log he had been keeping of radiograms from the search work.

Vasiliy Tempalov remained in the position of the prosecutor of Ivdel until 1963. Later he moved to the city of Verkhnyaya Salda, and then to the Krasnodar Territory.

Aleksander Kuzminyh, Tempalov's assistant, was transferred in 1960 to the Sverdlovsk regional prosecutor's office to the post of deputy prosecutor of the Ivdel corrective labor camp (Ivdellag).

Vladimir Korotaev moved to Sverdlovsk in 1962.

Ivan Fyodorov, the head of the Ivdel airport, who gave permission for the departure of the aircraft which took part in the air searches for the Dyatlov group, was fired in 1960 after being involved in a case of alcohol poisoning of an electric welder from the Energy-Mechanical Department of the Polunochnoe Mining Administration in February 1960.

Rahimov, head of the aviation meteorological station of the Ivdel airport, was transferred to the city of Yanaul in Bashkiria in the early 1960s.

Still, many people continued to live and work in Ivdel.

Ivan Prodanov remained at the post of 1st secretary of the Ivdel city committee of the CPSU until 1963. He died in 1964 and was buried in Ivdel.

Pyotr Gladyrev, a member of the Dyatlov group air search, died in an accident with a Mi 4 helicopter 22 km (13 miles) away from Ivdel airport in 1960. The same fate awaited other participants in the 1959 air search. Vladimir Pustobaev died in a helicopter crash in the Ivdel region in the early 1970s. Gennadiy Patrushev died in the 1961 sowing season while flying Yak-12 aircraft 65 km (40 miles) north of Ivdel. Soon after that, in the summer of 1961, his friend Sergey Misharin, the captain of the KGB in the Sverdlovsk region, who had been looking for witnesses in the case of the death of the Dyatlov group, shot himself.

Aleksander Temnikov, the head of the communications service of the Northern Geological Expedition, received a severe head injury in the 1960s.

Aleksander Kuznetsov, a forester in the Vizhay forestry, who together with Dryahlyh had questioned the Mansi people in February 1959, died in a car accident in 1962. The culprit was never found.

Andrey Alekseevich Anyamov, a member of the Kurikov search party, was killed shortly after 1959.

Prokopiy Vasiliyevich Anyamov, brother of Nikolay Vasiliyevich Anyamov, who took part in the search together with the Kurikov group, was accidentally killed while hunting in 1961.

Timofey Prokopyevich Bahtiyarov, a potential participant in the search work in mid-February, died under unclear circumstances. His brother, Aleksander Prokopyevich Bahtiyarov, hanged himself in 1961.

A relative of the Kurikov brothers who took part in the search for the Dyatlov group committed suicide in the summer of 1959. The Prosecutor refused to initiate a criminal case, and members of the Ivdel prosecutor's office did not even go to the scene due to the remoteness and inaccessibility of the location.

Ivan Pashin lived in Vizhay until 1972, then returned to his native village in the Perm region, where he died in 1974.

Are these events in any way related to the death of the Dyatlov group? We leave it to you, the reader, to decide.

CHAPTER 25. FEBRUARY 1-2, 1959.

On the morning of February 1, the Dyatlov group was slightly behind schedule. The day before, a strong wind on the pass had forced them to return to the valley of Auspiya, though according to the initial plan they were to go over to the valley of Lozva and have a good rest before the radial ascent to Otorten.

After breakfast, several people went up to the pass to check the weather. A photograph taken on February 1 in the Auspiya valley shows that the majority of the group was busy removing the camp and gathering things. These were Kolmogorova, Kolevatov, Dubinina, Krivonischenko, and Doroshenko. If it was Slobodin who took the photo, then presumably Dyatlov went out on reconnaissance with Zolotaryov and Thibeaux-Brignolle.

Compared to the previous day, the weather on the pass had changed for the better and the wind had gone down. Aware that it could change again soon, the group headed upwards. Being in a hurry, they had no time to fold the tent properly and, judging by the photo, carried it crumpled up, obviously hoping it would not take long to reach the Lozva valley.

As a leader, Dyatlov stood out for being quite determined, even obstinate, when making decisions. There were no good reasons to reject the initial plan to make the storage in the area above the forest level. Igor may have expected to move further north, closer to Otorten, and into the valley of the 3rd Lozva tributary, and to go over the northeastern spur of height 1079 just in one passage. But again, like on the day before, the intensified wind interfered with his plans. With the north-western wind direction observed in the 2019 microclimatic examination in the area of Mt. Kholat Syakhl, on February 2, 1959, there was no protection from the wind north of the spur in those days. The wind shadow zone was right on the site of the tent, which would be discovered on February 26 – in the exact location where the group must have laid a storage before going down into the valley of the 4th Lozva tributary for a rest. The plan was that, on their return from Otorten, they would find the storage by means of a flag. The flag might have been tied to the circular cuts on the ski pole, which UPI searchers would later find in the tent discovered on the slope of height 1079.

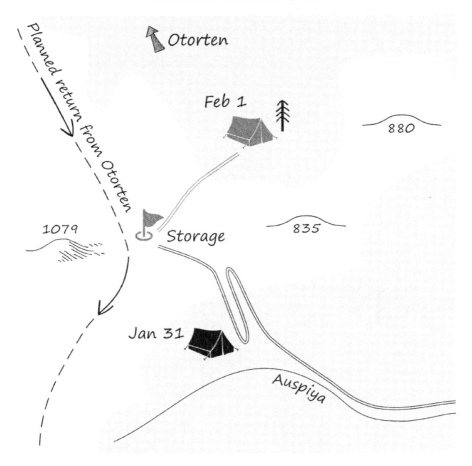

In the upper reaches of the 4th Lozva tributary, the Dyatlov group set up camp. Here are some tips on difficult hiking routes from the literature of that time: *"Usually, when setting up a bivouac, responsibilities are distributed as follows: four people set up a tent, two others prepare spruce branches and make a bed, and two people gather firewood for cooking dinner and heating the tent at night. Meanwhile, an appointed cook and his assistant should be making dinner. If all the duties are shared properly in the group and all participants are well trained, setting up a bivouac and preparing food can be completed in an hour and a half. In case of an emergency such as a blizzard approaching, the excavation of a pit in the snow and setting up a tent should be finished in 20-25 minutes. In that case, the whole group should focus on one task only."* These guidelines were usually observed, as suggested by the following quote from a hiker's report on a winter trek in 1956: *"...one person using a bucket clears a campfire site to the ground, while two other people prepare spruce*

branches for the tent. Another two people prepare firewood and make a
fire. The food is ready in 1.5-2 hours after setting up the bivouac."

Judging by photos taken during other mountain hikes by UPI groups, the preferred place to pitch a tent was between the trees, not far from a river or stream. Food was cooked on fire close to the water, often under the river bank, which provided protection from the wind. On February 1, the Dyatlov group was in no hurry – while setting up camp in the Lozva valley, Doroshenko and Kolmogorova could have assembled the camping stove within an hour.

Their recent record for assembling the stove was not forgotten when, after lunch, the hikers started writing the Evening Otorten. According to Yuri Yudin, the name was inspired by the Sverdlovsk newspaper Evening Sverdlovsk, which first came out on December 31, 1957, and quickly became very popular. The structure of the Evening Otorten resembled that of the last, 36th, issue for 1958 of "Crocodile" magazine. It is possible this particular issue was found in Zolotaryov's backpack.

The hikers were clearly so involved with their chores that they could not any make notes in their diaries, which is why there are no notes related to February 1. They had no time for that in the morning, either, and other things kept them busy in the afternoon. The sunset was at 5 pm and it got really dark after 7:40 pm so, after dinner, it was time to get a good night's sleep before the next day's passage and the Otorten ascent. Hikers climbed into the tent. Dyatlov and Kolmogorova scooted to the back of the tent. Doroshenko, Slobodin, Krivonischenko and Kolevatov settled in beside the stove. Thibeaux-Brignolle, Dubinina and Zolotaryov lay down close to the exit. Akselrod agrees with this disposition of the group: *"I think Lyuda Dubinina was lying next to Zolotaryov, then Kolya Thibeaux-Brignolle, Rustik Slobodin. Who was in the center and further, I do not know. At the far end of the tent from the entrance was a field bag with documents belonging to Dyatlov, and near it was Kolmogorova's diary. It seems like they slept there."*

"The diaries made it obvious that the weather was gradually changing for the worse: the wind was getting stronger and the temperature dropped as low as -25C. According to data from the Ivdel meteorological station, it was -30-35°C in the mountains on the night of February 1 to 2 and the wind speed reached 25-35 m/sec." These data from the report of Bardin and Shuleshko in 1959 were confirmed by the microclimatic examination of 2019: *"Analysis of weather conditions showed that at 8-9 pm on February 1, a cold front passed over this area, causing a sharp drop in air*

temperature and increase of wind, accompanied by snowfall and blizzards. The wind speed reached 10-15 m/s with gusts of up to 30 m/s."

Then came the split second when life ended and the nightmare began. A tree came down crashing on top of the tent and the group fell victim to a freak forest accident which, however, is neither impossible nor improbable in stormy and snowy weather.

It is now impossible to identify the exact location of the tent, but it was most probably put up not far from the cedar tree, where the reenactment party later settled and where there were signs of a camp present.

From the testimony of Chernyshev, Atmanaki, Brusnitsyn, and Sogrin: *"...In about one and a half kilometers from the tent down on the slope, there is a cedar. Not far from it, about twenty meters away, some cuts on fir trees were discovered. About 6-7 fir trees had been cut, probably to make a fire or for flooring... No knives were found near the corpses, and the trees near the fire were cut with a knife..."*; *"...Twenty meters or so around the cedar there were traces of someone who'd been near the cedar and cut off the young spruce with the help of a knife, there were about twenty such cuts, but the trunks themselves, except for one, were not discovered..."*; *"...More than a dozen of small fir trees had been cut with a Finnish knife..."*; *"...After inspection of the place it became clear that there had been not two people, but more, because some titanic work has been done to prepare firewood and flooring. This is evident from a large number of cuts on tree trunks, broken branches, and young fir trees..."*

Remains of cut-down firewood could still be noticed in 1963, when a group led by Yakimenko visited the place and installed a memorial plate on the pass: *"There was a fire-pit at the foot of a mighty tree, their last fire burnt here... All thin birches nearby were cut off with a knife at the same level, broken off thick branches of cedar high above the ground."*

Maslennikov noticed something else: *"...Not far from the cedar there were two birch trees with deep cuts as if someone had tried to cut them off."* Could these cuts have been made to fix the tent ropes and not in an attempt to cut down the trees? Unfortunately, the exact location of these birches was not mentioned in the reports.

However, the Dyatlov camp might have been in some other place, for instance, to the west of the stream, where the last four bodies were discovered. The tent could have been closer to the bed of the 4th tributary, where remains of an old fire pit and tent eyelets were found in 2008-2009. Our theory is that an old fallen tree can be a reference point to track the location of the Dyatlov group tent. Fallen trees of this kind were found close to the famous cedar and in other places.

A small fallen cedar lies on the right side of the 4th Lozva tributary, approximately in the place where Dyatlov's body was found. Some old broken-off tree trunks were found on the left bank of the creek, 70 to 80 m above the "den".

Why have we arrived at this particular scenario of events? The clue is in the nature of the victims' injuries.

In 2015 in the Kirov region, a cut down tree fell and struck a man nearby.

"The death of the victim occurred as a result of an open traumatic brain injury including: a bruised head wound on the left, fractures of the frontal bone on the left with spread to the bones of the base of the skull, which form the anterior cranial fossa, hemorrhages: in the soft tissues of the head, above the dura mater, under the soft cerebral membranes, bruising and destruction of the brain tissue of a severe degree, complicated by edema and wedging of the brain substance."

A similar case took place in 2013 in the Kurgan region.

"A tree trunk broke off and fell on a victim who was nearby, causing bodily harm including: a closed craniocerebral injury, bruising of the eyelids in both eyes (a spectacle haematoma), extensive hemorrhage in the soft tissues of the head, depressed fragmentary fracture of the vault and base of the skull with the formation of subdural (250 ml) and total subarachnoid hemorrhages, partial crushing of the brain substance of the left parietal and occipital lobes, multiple small-focal and focal hemorrhages in the brain substance and trunk, extensive bleeding in the soft tissues of the head; closed chest injury: extensive bruising of a pale bluish color of the anterior surface of the chest, with a transition to the anterior surface of the right shoulder joint, straight oblique-transverse fractures of 1, 2, 3, 4, 5, 6 ribs on the left along the scapular line, with damage to the parietal pleura and tissue of the left lung with extensive hemorrhages in the surrounding soft tissues; direct oblique fractures of the 6th, 7th rib of the paravertebral line without damage to the parietal pleura with extensive hemorrhages into the surrounding soft tissue; scomminuted fractures of 3, 4, 5, 6 thoracic vertebrae with extensive hemorrhages in the surrounding soft tissues; extensive bruising of the upper third of the left shoulder, direct comminuted fracture of the right humerus with the formation of extensive hemorrhage into the surrounding soft tissues; extensive bruising of the lower third of both thighs. Direct, oblique fractures of the lower third of the diaphysis of both femurs with the formation of extensive hemorrhages in the surrounding soft tis-

sues ... which resulted in death."

In 2015, in the Republic of Mariy El, a cut down tree fell on the head of a victim who was close by and caused the following injuries:

"...hemorrhage in the scalp, multi-splintered depressed fracture of the bones of the cranial vault, comminuted fracture of the basal skull, rupture of the dura mater of the left hemisphere of the brain with hemorrhages along the edges of the rupture, crushing of the substance of the outer surface of the temporal lobe of the left hemisphere of the brain, into the ventricles of the brain, crushing of the substance of the outer surface of the temporal lobe of the left hemisphere of the brain, hemorrhages in the substance of the medulla oblongata and the left hemisphere of the cerebellum, complete rupture of the brainstem at the level of the Varolian bridge with crush and hemorrhage in the area of rupture, fractures of the lower jaw with hemorrhages at the edges of the fractures... From these injuries... the victim died on the scene of the accident..."

In 2013 another man was also found under a fallen tree in the Udmurt Republic.

"According to the medical report stating the nature of the injuries received, the diagnosis was made: open craniocerebral injury, brain contusion, open depressed fracture of the right parietal bone... According to the forensic medical examination report, the death was caused by a basilar skull fracture"

In all these cases, trees fell on standing people. First, the head and the upper part of the body were struck. The traumatizing continued while the victim was falling, which resulted in polytrauma. Some of these traumas are similar to those found on the bodies of some members of the Dyatlov group, such as rib fractures, craniocerebral injuries, bruises. But the injuries of the dead hikers were localized.

In 2018, after Zolotaryov's exhumation, a forensic medical examination report was drawn up.

"The examination of the bones revealed fractures of the right 2nd - 6th ribs along the parasternal and posterior axillary lines. The nature of the fractures along the parasternal line is extensor, along the posterior axillary line it is flexion. On the peri-sternal line, extensor fractures of the 3rd - 5th ribs are complete, there are no fragments; the extensor fracture of the 2nd - 6th ribs is incomplete. There are three linear fractures of the right scapula: in the supraspinatus fossa it is horizontal, in the infraspinatus fossa it is vertical, and it is hori-

zontal above the lower angle. All the fractures are extension ones. The detected fractures of the 2nd - 6th right ribs and fractures of the right scapula were formed simultaneously as a result of excessive compression of the right half of the chest in the direction from the sternum to the spine and somewhat from right to left. The area of traumatic impact is the front and, partially, the lateral surface of the right half of the chest. It is most likely that S.A. Zolotaryov was lying on his back at the time of the traumatic impact..."

In 2020, a big tree fell on a tent in Bulgaria. People were lying inside, and a woman died.

"On the skin of the left cheek, in its upper part, a superficial, irregularly shaped round abrasion with a diameter of about 1.5-2 cm is visible. On the skin behind the left auricle, two more small superficial abrasions of a rounded shape with a diameter of about 2-3 mm and a linear abrasion of about 1 cm long are visible. Along the anterior surface of the right auricle in the middle upper part, there is a spotted bluish bruise about 2.5 to 3 cm in diameter. Two superficial linear abrasions about 3x0.5 cm in size are visible on the skin of the upper front of the neck. A similar abrasion about 4x0.3-0.8 cm is also present on the skin of the lower jaw. In the upper part of the neck, on the right side, there is a bruise about 1 cm in diameter. On the skin of the chest, in the upper right part, above and below the collarbone, several oval-shaped bruises about 8x5 cm are visible. Two superficial reddish abrasions with a diameter of about 0.5 cm and a size of about 1x0.5 cm are visible on the skin of the abdomen in its upper half on the left in front. Along the anterior surface of the right lower leg in the upper two-thirds to the lower part of the knee, there is a large longitudinal wound of a linear shape about 35 cm long. On the skin in the rest of the upper and lower limbs, mainly on the front and outer parts, there are several linear abrasions ranging in size from 1x0.5 cm to 15x2 cm in different directions and several bruises with a diameter of 1-3 cm... No injuries of the sternum, both collarbones, and all ribs... The pelvic bones are broken, there are vertical fractures in the front and back to the right in the sacrum... The rest of the pelvic and spine bones are not injured..."

All the injuries are localized. The man who was lying in the tent next to the deceased woman survived and his only injury was a fractured collarbone. The head of the forensic medicine department where the body was taken noted that there was gray foam coming out of her mouth. The cause of death was mechanical asphyxia. This is very similar to Doroshenko. The woman lived under the rubble for 15-20 minutes. This sounds familiar too. Dubinina could have lived for 10-20 minutes, Zolotaryov even longer (Dyatlovpass.com/case-files-381-383#sheet382).

The experts assumed that, at the time of the traumatic impact, Zolotaryov was lying on his back. Dubinina received similar fractures. The rest of the hikers were most likely also lying at the time of the injury. The incident in Bulgaria shows that a tree falling onto lying people causes local injuries of varying severity, from bruises to severe fractures. Similar injuries were observed in 1959.

When given the autopsy reports and asked to comment on the possible causes of injuries of Zolotaryov, Dubinina, and Thibeaux-Brignolle, Plamen Dimitrov Doctor of Medical Sciences, Head of the Department of Forensic Medicine at the Kaneff University Hospital (Ruse, Bulgaria), said: *"If you are asking me whether these injuries could have been caused by a tree falling on the three of them while they were lying down, I cannot exclude such a version, it is consistent - it sounds plausible!"*

In which case, in winter conditions, can a blow take nine lying hikers unawares? Only if they are sleeping in the tent.

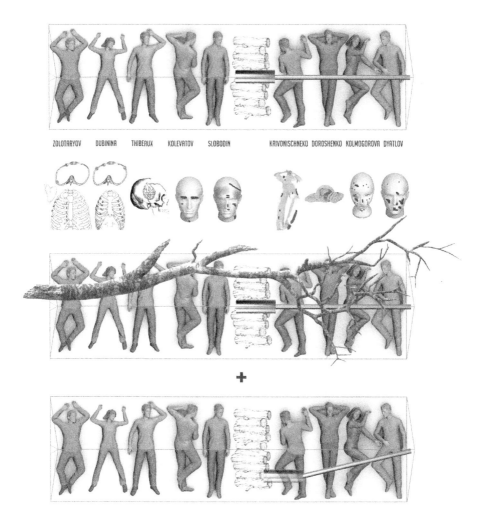

A massive tree trunk fell on the front part of the tent, crushing the pots that were there and breaking Dubinina and Zolotaryov's ribs. There are some signs that Zolotaryov was struck on his forehead, most likely, by a tree branch. Only thick twigs and branches hit Thibeaux-Brignolle, Slobodin, Krivonischenko, and Kolevatov, who were further away from the entrance. Thibeaux-Brignolle received a severe cranio-cerebral injury by a blow to the right temporoparietal junction, and his shoulder was injured. Slobodin was sleeping near the stove; his head was thrown onto the firewood by a violent blow, which is why he bore certain signs of a counterblow. The stove and pipe system were ripped off the ridge poles. This is how Krivonischenko got burnt. Kolevatov received a blow in the mastoid region, behind the right auricle. Such a blow to the sternocleidomastoid muscle area can result in an instant loss of consciousness and even death.

The tree fell right on top of the tent, bringing the whole of it down, from the front entrance to the far back end. Dyatlov, Kolmogorova, and Doroshenko were caught under the tree crown. The canvas of the tent softened the blows of the relatively thin branches, but the hikers could have received craniocerebral injuries of varying severity. Doroshenko, Dyatlov, Krivonischenko, and Slobodin had mydriatic pupils, which might have been caused by traumatic brain injury resulting in dysfunction of the midbrain nuclei. This means that even those who did not have anything broken could have received head injuries.

The tent was caught under the rubble. The backstretch was ripped off. The front one, which was fixed to a fallen tree, remained intact. You could get out of the tent only through the gaps in the back. This is where the least injured members of the group ended up.

Dyatlov and Doroshenko crawled out of the tent with great difficulty. They had to drag Kolmogorova out. She had abrasions from branches on her lower back and stomach, but she did not care – she had to help the others. The tools had not been brought into the tent the day before as there was not enough room inside to sleep. It was risky to make cuts in the tent from the outer side as that could hurt those remaining under the rubble. Having broken off or cut off some of the branches, they got to the slope. Putting a hand holding a knife into a small cut, they made several cuts and managed to drag Slobodin and Krivonischenko out, but four unconscious people still remained inside the tent under a massive tree trunk. The trunk was too heavy to move and there was no way to cut it.

At 4 am the moon rose. They managed to take some clothes out of the tent through ruptures and cuts. It is possible that those who survived even managed to make a fire and warm up a little bit. They were not even worried about deadly risks, all they could think about was how to rescue their friends who were still under the tree. No one was aware that, as the expert opinion states, Zolotaryov, Thibeaux-Brignolle, Dubinina, and Kolevatov were dead within half an hour after the accident.

No chance to rescue friends without any help. But who could help them? Then they remembered that the day before they had noticed planes and helicopters appearing in the sky quite frequently. Kolevatov even suggested that some kind of aerial photography was being carried out. Dawn would come at 7 am, and soon after that the planes might appear over the pass again. They needed to have climbed the slope by that time so that they could try to draw the pilots' attention. It was the only possible way of rescue.

Possibly, Bardin meant something along those lines when he wrote to Maslennikov in the spring of 1959: *"If the search is still on and if you are something like a prime consultant there, then instruct them to search on tops but not in the hollow. If Kolevatov was such an erudite, as Yuri Yudin said, then from some moment of retreat he had to go straight up-ward, gaining height. Probably, right from the campfire. But then not along the hollow, but a bit to the side onwards the slope. It is also possible that he and those who were with him kept going round the tops for quite a long time..."*

The survivors went onto the slope. But the adrenaline rush was already over. Exhaustion, lethargy, and a feeling of emptiness over-whelmed them. Slobodin, who had received a severe craniocerebral injury, did not notice the gully in the 4th tributary of the Lozva and ended up in the water, where he would later be found in the reenact-ment. When interrogated, Akselrod noted that *"there was a layer of half ice and half snow, about 70-80 mm thick, under the knees and chest, i.e. under those parts of the body on which the weight of the prone per-son was distributed. That allowed me to conclude that Slobodin did not die instantly, but lived after the fall for some time."* Eight centimeters (3 inches) of icing is too much to be caused by a cooling dead body. It is more likely that Slobodin's clothe s were wet, i.e. that before reaching the slope, he had been in the water.

The temperature reached -30°C (-22°F), the value of the wind-cold index exceeded -40°C (-40°F), which meant a high risk of hypothermia and frostbite of open skin areas within 5-10 minutes. One by one the rest of the group stopped struggling and lay freezing on the slope.

At half past nine in the morning the sun rose over the pass and soon some planes appeared in the sky. Flying over height 1079, the pilots noticed something strange on the slope. It looked like human bodies...

Printed in Great Britain
by Amazon

70808647R00169